Praise for
Out of the Question...into the Mystery

"Len Sweet has really done it this time! In true midrash form, Len exposes the beauty of a relationship with our Creator. He asks all the hard questions and leads us to a place of grace beyond the formulaic answers. Throw all your self-help books in the trash and immerse yourself in a book that will help you see your faith journey in a whole new way."

—CHRIS SEAY, author of *The Gospel According to Tony Soprano*

"No charts, no boxes, no to-do lists. Just everything we thought we knew about faith but didn't. This is the book we should be reading in our small groups."

—SALLY MORGENTHALER, author of *Worship Evangelism,* founder
of Sacramentis.com and Digital Glass Videos

"Way back in the 1970s, some thoughtful Christian leaders began talking about a *relational theology.* The term held intrigue and promise. Now, Leonard Sweet has given us a great gift. Here is a panoramic view of what a relational theology can mean for Christians today. Whether you're a spiritual seeker trying to get the lay of the land, or a seasoned traveler trying to make sense of what you've experienced, or even a disillusioned leader who feels it's all gone stale—this book will help you see in a fresh, inspiring, profound, and invigorating way."

—BRIAN MCLAREN, author of *A New Kind of Christian*
and *The Church on the Other Side*

OUT OF THE QUESTION . . .

GETTING LOST IN

INTO THE MYSTERY

THE GODLIFE RELATIONSHIP

LEONARD SWEET

WATERBROOK
PRESS

OUT OF THE QUESTION...INTO THE MYSTERY
PUBLISHED BY WATERBROOK PRESS
2375 Telstar Drive, Suite 160
Colorado Springs, Colorado 80920
A division of Random House, Inc.

All Scripture quotations, unless otherwise indicated, are taken from the *Holy Bible, New International Version®*. NIV®. Copyright © 1973, 1978, 1984 by International Bible Society. Used by permission of Zondervan Publishing House. All rights reserved. Scripture quotations marked (NRSV) are from the *New Revised Standard Version of the Bible,* copyright © 1989 by the Division of Christian Education of the National Council of the Churches of Christ in the USA. Used by permission. All rights reserved. Scripture quotations marked (RSV) are taken from the *Revised Standard Version of the Bible,* copyright © 1946, 1952, and 1971 by the Division of Christian Education of the National Council of the Churches of Christ in the USA. Used by permission. Scripture quotations marked (MSG) are taken from *The Message.* Copyright © 1993, 1994, 1995, 1996, 2000, 2001, 2002. Used by permission of NavPress Publishing Group. Scripture quotations marked (NASB) are taken from the *New American Standard Bible®.* © Copyright The Lockman Foundation 1960, 1962, 1963, 1968, 1971, 1972, 1973, 1975, 1977, 1995. Used by permission. (www.Lockman.org.) Scripture quotations marked (NEB) are taken from *The New English Bible.* Copyright © 1961, 1970 by the Delegates of the Oxford University Press and the Syndics of the Cambridge University Press. Scripture quotations marked (REB) are taken from *The Revised English Bible* © 1989 by Oxford University Press and Cambridge University Press. Scripture quotations marked (KJV) are taken from the *King James Version.*

Italics in Scripture quotations represent the author's added emphasis.

ISBN 1-57856-647-9

Library of Congress Cataloging-in-Publication Data
Sweet, Leonard I.
    Out of the question—into the mystery : getting lost in the GodLife relationship / Leonard Sweet.— 1st ed.
      p. cm.
    Includes bibliographical references.
    ISBN 1-57856-647-9
  1. Christian life. I. Title.
    BV4501.3.S943 2004
    248.4—dc22

                                                                                    2004012086

Printed in the United States of America
2004—First Edition

10 9 8 7 6 5 4 3 2 1

To Lyn and "Picasso"

———

with lasting gratitude for your
loyalty, laughter, and love.

CONTENTS

ACKNOWLEDGMENTS

I write this book with one foot on a banana peel. I'm one of the least qualified persons to publish anything on the subject of relationship. I confess to
Cro-Magnon capacities for canalizing and cannibalizing the emotions. I
can't tell the difference between a makeover and a makeup. I trudge through
the boggy world of relationships like a troglodyte. In the words of the old
African American adage, I'm trying to "hit a straight lick with a crooked stick."

There are many who are more qualified than I to speak on these matters.
But often those who are most qualified are least likely to work on the subject
for fear of misleading or being misled. In other words, they're too smart. I'm
too dumb and weak, which makes me unafraid to be wrong and hopeful for
the healing that comes from immersing oneself in hot water. Besides, I have
no choice. I am compelled to do this. Relationships are more than recreation.
They are the very work of being human…and divine.

The title for this book is a high-seas act of piracy. Folk singer David
Wilcox wrote "Out of the Question," one line of which forms the title of his
fantastic 2002 CD *Into the Mystery.* For those of you who don't want to read a
couple hundred pages on the subject, go right to his CD. It's all there in less
than one hundred words. I'm grateful to Tom Morris, atmospheric architect
of Westside King's Church of Calgary, Alberta, for bringing David and me
together on the same stage.

It seems that I'm either spending my life writing about Jesus or spending
my life struggling *not* to write about Jesus. No one knows this better than my
doctoral students, who heard this book as lectures and whose contributions are
reflected in both text and endnotes. From George Fox University, I thank
(Cohort 1) Peter Balaban, Greg Boulton, Eric Brown, Dwight Friesen, Craig
Henningfield, Chad Johnson, Donna King, Raymond Leach, Terry O'Casey,
Ray Peacock, Earl Pierce, Shane Roberson, Rob Robinson, Warren Schatz,
Marty Williams. From Cohort 2, I thank Rick Bartlett, Tony Blair, Doug Bryan,
Jason Clark, Winn Griffin, Rick Hans, George Hemingway, Nick Howard,
Todd Hunter, Randy Jumper, Eric Keck, Mike McNichols, Ken Niles, Craig

Oldenburg, Kevin Rains, Rob Seewald, Rick Shrout, Dwight Spotts, David Wollenburg. From Drew University, I thank Thomas Biatek, William Brown, Kenneth Harrington, Todd Harrington, Alan Lyke, Daniel Meister, and Rachel Shoemaker.

While I was writing this book, my major mentor, Winthrop S. Hudson, died. I have continued to be mentored by certain people, however, some of whom have read the manuscript; others have not. Philosopher Stan Grenz has shown us all that *classic orthodoxy* and *postmodern* are not oxymoronic. Brian McLaren's superconductive brain and vanguard spirit inspire me to explore the hidden depths and heights of faith. Judge Jesse Caldwell III, who is everything I am not—a master at the art of friendship—continually inspires me with his undentable spirit and inexhaustible creativity. Biblical scholar Loy Witherspoon should not be held accountable for my antique but unique musings on certain passages. But I'm grateful for his heads-up that some of this is about as welcome as a piano at a Church of Christ convention. Joe Myers makes support a sport. My WaterBrook editor, Ron Lee, gave me encouragement when I needed it the most and did his best to minimize Job's (wonderfully mistranslated) warning: "Oh…that mine adversary had written a book" (31:35, KJV). He is every author's dream-come-true editor. The diligence and devotion to the project of WaterBrook publisher Don Pape kept me at the computer screen even when life drained the color from the purple.

There are as many kinds of teachers as there are kinds of love. My family is perhaps my greatest living mentor. Elizabeth, Thane, Soren, and Egil are like the sidebar quotes in this book. Sometimes they agree with my narrative. Sometimes they don't. But their teacherly treachery blesses me with the magic of high-definition-colors wisdom and everyday affection. My research assistant, Betty O'Brien, endured multiple surgeries on her eyes while I was writing this book. Even though her vision is now severely impaired, she still insisted on bringing this project to its conclusion. Our friendship is one of my life's richest treasures.

My ministry is approaching a ten-year anniversary: The nightmare job of handling my schedule and coordinating my calendar has been done by one person. It is my deep appreciation for her friendship and partnership in my ministry this past decade that I dedicate this book to Lyn Stuntebeck and her sidekick companion, "Picasso."

This book has been a long time coming, partly because I have censored my thinking about the Abraham-and-Isaac story for the past two decades. My worst nightmare is for my faith to depart from classic Christian orthodoxy. When I began struggling with this text, which for me is the most difficult passage in the Bible, I adopted the strategy of desert father Antony (251-312) when he was troubled by the meaning of a demanding text in Leviticus. He withdrew into prayer and silence, begging God to send Moses to teach him the meaning of this sacred text before he said anything.[1] Before Antony, the theologian Origen (185-254) did the same, and during his self-imposed moratorium, begged his students to pray with him for "spiritual edification" as he struggled with a hard text.[2]

Not until I discovered that my approach to this story was not original but was part of a living and lively tradition of Jewish exegesis did I venture to speak my mind. If my exegesis is misguided, I ask for your forgiveness and forbearance. As with everyone who tries to make an initial case, or challenges received opinion, I may have overegged my pudding. But if you stay at the table with me, see if you don't find yourself singing with deeper meaning than ever before this Isaac Watts classic:

> Not all the blood of beasts
> On Jewish altars slain,
> Could give the guilty conscience peace,
> Or wash away the stain.
>
> But Christ, the heavenly Lamb,
> Takes all our sins away;
> A sacrifice of nobler name
> And richer blood than they....
>
> Believing, we rejoice
> To see the curse remove;
> We bless the Lamb with cheerful voice,
> And sing His bleeding love.[3]

—LEONARD SWEET
Drew University
18 April 2004

WHERE DID WE MISS THE PERSON AND GET THE POINT INSTEAD?

We know how to save the world. We just don't realize that we know what we know.

The way to save the world is not through more rules to live by, but through right relationships to live for. People are fast losing the art of being with one another. So it's not surprising that the number one problem in the world is people's living disconnected lives. They are detached from God, from others, and from creation. People are losing the art of living with one another.

Relationship is the soul of the universe. And the soul is sick.

How sick? So sick that the worlds of business and finance are proclaiming a biblical truth that the church has lost: "The Right Relationship *Is* Everything."[1] We have entered a relationship economy where high-quality customer relationships are the key competitive advantage. When you purchase a cell phone, the cell-phone company takes a loss. Why? Because they aren't selling cell phones, they're seducing you into a long-term relationship. (Ever try to get *out* of one of these "committed relationships"?)

Real estate developers no longer sell houses, they sell relationships.[2] In more and more cities and suburbs, new houses are designed with a retro look—the most prominent feature being a large front porch. And in more and more new subdivisions, houses are grouped together in a friendly arrangement that caters to neighbors getting to know one another. Walking trails and community greenbelts, neighborhood playgrounds and even community garden plots, all underscore the importance of spending time with other people. You might need a house, but you want a relationship.

When I consider that I'm more intimately involved with two of my credit cards—American Express and Starbucks—than I am with the family that lives three doors down the street, then it's time to rethink relationship. Did you know that American Express keeps a detailed transcript of every conversation they have with their customers? I found this out when the check I used to pay my bill bounced. As soon as I received the overdraft notice from my bank, I called American Express, explained what had happened, and asked what I should do. They told me not to worry; they would simply resubmit the check.

I asked if they would freeze my American Express account until the check cleared the bank. Not at all, they said. As long as I was talking to them, my credit card would work just fine.

A week later my checking account still showed no payment made to my credit card company. So I again called American Express and, once again, they weren't worried about it. They had a record of every call I had made to them, and just to relieve my anxiety, they said they would update my account as if the bill were paid. What mattered, the American Express representative said, was that "we're talking, and as long as that relationship is still strong, we'll work with you and make it as easy as we can."

At the same time I was talking to American Express about my bounced check, I was also dealing with an unpaid monthly bill to the Christian school two of my kids attend. The school provides my children with as good an education as I can imagine anyone's receiving. We have been part of this school from its inception, and to help get it off the ground, we had been making significant donations above and beyond the tuition fees. Since money was tight at home just then due to a two-times-the-estimate construction project, I called the school and alerted them that I'd be late making the current tuition payment, but that I'd get back on track the following month.

They were not happy. If my bill was not paid in full, they informed me, they would not release my kids' report cards. I apologized for adding to their cash-flow problems but reminded them that they knew I was good for the money. I even offered to pay interest on the overdue fees. Penalize me, I said, but not my kids.

Their response was polite but principled: Rules are rules. No payment in full, no report cards.

I have to agree with Chase Bank: "The right relationship *is* everything." But it's not with a bank. Or even with Starbucks or American Express, as much as I rely on them in my everyday life. It's time for individual Christians and the church to become as relationship driven as some of the leading multinational corporations.

THE TAIL THAT WAGS THE WORLD

To save the world we need something more biblical than higher standards. We need higher relationships. We need less to be "true to our principles" and much more to be true to our relationships. To save the world we don't need the courage of our convictions. We need the courage of our relationships... especially the courage of a right relationship with the Creator, the creation, and our fellow creatures. Our problem in reaching the world is that we've made rules more important than relationship.

The inherent tension that exists between rules and relationship is not of interest only when we're talking about Christian witness. This same tension lies at the heart of the church's struggle for identity in an increasingly hostile culture. And a misguided allegiance to rules over relationship also has impoverished the pursuit of the life of faith for every one of us. This book is a first attempt at a corrective. We need to rediscover Christianity's "trimtab factor"—the small but crucial element that orients the course of the entire church, as well as the lives of individual Christians. In fact, it's not an exaggeration to say that this trimtab factor orients all of life. The trimtab we're seeking is the truth of relationship and its power to save.

> If you would speak to others with authority, you must first speak to God with intimacy.
>
> —PASTOR AND THEOLOGIAN
> JOHN BAKER-BATSEL

Philosopher/inventor Buckminster Fuller asked his students to imagine they are on the deck of an ocean liner with one thousand people. Rocks are looming ahead and the passengers must find a way to steer the ship to safety. One person stands on the bow, pointing out the rocks, and the crowd of passengers tries to guide the ship by shifting their weight. They run from one side of the deck to the other in response to the guide's instructions.

But Fuller, a fulcrum figure in science and philosophy, suggested that there's a much better way to guide the ship to safety. In the steering mechanism of an ocean liner is a piece of metal six inches square, called a trimtab.[3] One person moving the trimtab can steer a great ship more effectively than even ten thousand people running back and forth on the deck. The trimtab is the place to position yourself to take action that will maximize your impact on the course of human history.

The more complex our world becomes, the more important it is to find that small trimtab simplicity—to concentrate on the one strategic thing that will steer the world to safety. When things aren't going well, every coach will tell you it's time to return to the basics.

When a history of Christianity can be written in which Jesus is largely absent,[4] any coach with his eyes open will tell you, "It's time to work on blocking and tackling."

When studies of the gospels can be written without the name of Jesus appearing even once in the index, it's dribbling, passing, and screening time.[5]

Vice versa, when one reviewer can criticize a textbook on philosophy because "space is given to people whom one might not expect to see considered in any detail," and he lists as his first complaint the inclusion of Jesus,[6] it's keep-your-head-down and follow-through-with-the-swing time.

When an average of twelve to fifteen churches in the United States are closing their doors every day, it's time to find the trimtab.

When atheist Michael Martin can evangelize people into atheism by asking, "Who wants to be like them?" (meaning Christians) and claiming that following Christ involves being "punitive, unforgiving, violent, mean-spirited, hypocritical and inconsistent; and [if we followed Christ] we would tacitly approve of slavery, forsake reason, and have no opinions on the central issues of the day,"[7] it's definitely trimtab time.

When half of all high school kids are sexually active, and there's only a 7 percent difference (43 percent) between the sexual habits of non-Christians and conservative Christian teenagers who are involved in a church youth group, it's time for the trimtab.[8]

When the special millennium edition of *The Economist* begins its treatment of the last thousand years by observing: "Already Christianity, the faith once almost synonymous with Europe, is decaying in its homelands—as its rival, Islam, is not,"[9] it may be trimtab time.

When a Baptist Internet entrepreneur can advise from experience: "Never do business with someone with a fish on his business card," and when the loudest horns and meanest swerves come from cars with fish on their bumpers, it's time for the trimtab.

How Did We Get Here?

How did we arrive at the place where Christians are providing some of the best arguments *against* knowing Christ? In the words of one Christian leader, "because Christians are largely irrelevant...if there's a life-changing message to present, we'll make it boring and put it in a context you're not involved in."[10]

Over a two-thousand-year period, but especially in the last two hundred years, we have jerked and tugged the Christian faith out of its original soil, its life-giving source, which is an honest relationship with God through Jesus the Christ. After uprooting the faith, we have entombed it in a declaration of adherence to a set of beliefs. The shift has left us with casual doctrinal assent that exists independent of a changed life. We have made the Cross into a crossword puzzle, spending our time diagramming byzantine theories of atonement. How did the beauty of Jesus's atoning work get isolated from the wonder of restoring an authentic relationship between God and humanity?

It's time to replant the Christian faith back into the ground from whence it first grew. Henry David Thoreau once warned that words, when derived properly, come with the earth still clinging to their roots. In the case of Christian faith, the soil has been scrubbed off the roots until much of the fruit of the Christian life has lost its juice—leaving it dry and sour and distasteful.

What else would explain why the broader culture now understands Christianity to be tacky and tactless? How else to explain the Christian faith becoming so graceless, artless, joyless, intellectually impoverished, and fearful of the future? Why are Christians the ones who like to hover around the Tree of Knowledge, as pastor and theologian John Baker-Batsel puts it, baiting the serpent and battling each other, rather than being the people who like to play in the garden?[11]

The church may clutch Jesus to its side, but it no longer clutches Jesus to its insides. For the Jews, the unique place where God encountered humans was the temple and (before that) the tent or tabernacle. For Jesus, the unique place where God encounters humans is the human heart. But the church has embalmed Jesus in rules, codes, canonicities, and traditions that have everything to do with the church's saving itself and nothing to do with the church's saving the world. Sometimes it seems as if the Buddha has

> We want more from religion now than rules. We want something to help us find meaning in life when all the rules cease to make sense, when all the old systems break down or fade away. We want a glimpse of God here and now.
>
> —THEOLOGIAN JOAN CHITTISTER[12]

more authority for Buddhists than Jesus has for Christians. In fact, Jesus has been so far removed from Christianity that non-Christians are starting to co-opt Jesus as a guide for life. Even some members of the Jesus Seminar are now starting to realize that "Jesus is missing and we miss Jesus."[13]

When much of the church has devolved into an arrogant, clubby institution that looms so large it obscures a person's view of Christ, it may be time to return to the Jesus trimtab. No, it *is* time to return.

When, and Where, Did We Lose Jesus?

Given the universal hunger for relationship, and the church's habit of pushing relationship to the back of the bus, we must answer this question: How did we lose the Jesus trimtab? The simple—but precise—answer is that it got lost in the shift of focus from relationship to object.

The first Christians didn't proclaim a creed or a statement of faith; they didn't demand assent to a list of facts; they proclaimed the Cross; they proclaimed the Resurrection; they proclaimed the coming kingdom of Christ.[14] They proclaimed Jesus. Faith is not vested in creeds, or invested in institutions, but vetted in relationships.

> What is almost unbelievably remarkable is that God chooses friendship, available to everyone, as the means of changing the world, its people, and societies.
>
> —Michael E. Williams, "The Midwives' Story"[15]

Western Christianity is largely belief based and church focused. It is concerned with landing on the right theology and doctrine and making sure everyone else toes the line. The Jesus trimtab, in contrast, is relationship based and world focused. It is concerned not so much with what you believe as with whom you are following. It is less invested in maintaining and growing an institution and more invested in Jesus's passion for saving the world.

We have yanked ourselves from the soil of relationship with God so we can do the work of tidying things up. We are now sanitized and correct, factual and precise, but tragically bereft of relationship. We are disconnected from our source so that we have become sterile. We may be doctrinally correct, but we have become spiritual cadavers.

We don't need more time off to meditate and conference and "reimagine."

We don't need to search out a new solution or a reengineered vision for the church. We have the answer already, but we're working hard to silence it. Thankfully, Jesus won't be silenced. So we might as well shut up and learn something.

We need to replant the faith in the rich biblical soil from which it has been uprooted.[16] To that end, this book explores the two most famous father-son stories in the Bible: Abraham and Isaac, the *locus classicus* for what it means to live "by faith"; and the God-the-Father, God-the-Son story that we read throughout the Scriptures. You will also find sideways glances at other father-son stories, including that of the prodigal son.

Getting our roots back into the soil involves asking and answering the trimtab questions: Why did God create us? What does God require of us? What is the essence of "faith in God"?

The bottom-line benchmark from the ancient Hebrews? Again a simple—yet precise—answer: "To do justice, and to love kindness, and to walk humbly with your God."[17]

The answer of a Palestinian Jew named Jesus? "For God so loved the world…"[18]

In other words, whether you're reading the Old Testament or the New, the answer is "relationship."

AT DAWN WE SLEPT?

For the past decade a variety of voices have claimed that we are living in a "new reformation." Some have called this the Postmodern Reformation or the Second Reformation or even the Third Reformation.[19]

God does seem to be up to something big, and I confess to having used reformation terminology myself. But I am increasingly bothered by the language of "reformation" and would suggest another way of viewing what the church is going through. Here is why we need new words to describe what God is doing.

First, talk of the Protestant Reformation must be turned into a plural: There were many reformations in the sixteenth century: Karlstadt of Basel; Menno Simons in the Netherlands; Zwingli of Zurich; Calvin in Geneva; Luther and Melancthon in Germany; and many others. If we are to use reformation language to describe what is happening today, we must at least talk about new reformations, plural, for God is at work on many global fronts and through diverse (and even bickering) ministries today, just like before.

Second, use of reformation language delivers more questions than answers. A reformational paradigm implies reform, but of what? For five hundred years we've struggled with reformational questions: What are the marks of a true church? How do we make a pure church, or a restructured church? A reformational paradigm is inward looking, revolving around the word *come.* Such a paradigm suggests that outsiders should be concerned about the family feuds within the household of faith.

Besides, if we can't get the reformational "issues" right after half a millennium of trying, then having another go at coining new reformational terms and lists and requirements won't help things now.

Watching what God is up to today suggests less a reformational paradigm than a missional paradigm. In other words, rather than a call to take care of family business, yet again, after five hundred years of trying, God seems to be calling us to take care of the world. This raises outward-focused questions such as: How do we communicate with a post-Christendom, anti-Christian culture? How do we let go of the word *come* and instead obey the command of Jesus to *go?* Just as the reformational paradigm made every disciple a minister (the "priesthood of all believers"), the missional paradigm is making every disciple a missionary as well as a minister.

Since mission is not reformation, I would suggest calling this new movement of God a re-Orientation, partly due to the meaning of the word *Orient. Orient* means "east." When Christians started building churches, the first thing they did was get the community of faith "oriented." This tradition of getting oneself oriented has been largely lost to Christianity while being maintained by other faiths, such as Islam. Hotels are increasingly placing little arrows in windowsills to help Muslim guests orient themselves in prayer toward Mecca. So important was such orienting that King Khalid of Saudi Arabia owned a Boeing 747 with a gyroscopically rotating prayer room perpetually oriented toward Mecca.[20]

Our Christian ancestors oriented their churches eastward for theological reasons. First, toward Jerusalem.[21] Second, toward the direction of the returning Christ. But most importantly, toward the person of Christ, a Christ who comes to us in three tenses: the One who is, who was, and who is to come. The eastward orientation was an Eastering orientation toward a living Christ who is active and at work in our world today. The *go* of the Great Commission calls us to connect not only to a memorialized Christ or a coming Christ but also to a living Christ. We are to join what Jesus is doing in the world right now.

An Easter faith is not a Resurrection belief, it is a Resurrection reality: "Christ is alive and among us." An Eastering people are in a relationship with Christ himself, not just his message or his memory. The relationship is with a Person, not with history. It may take the speaking of our name, as it did for Mary, for us to recognize Jesus; or it may take a meal together, as it did for the Emmaus disciples, for us to recognize Jesus. But Easter is about recognizing the risen Christ among us and walking the same way with him.

The center of gravity of global Christianity is shifting from the North and West to the South and East. Western Christianity was tutored by Greece and Rome. It will now learn from Asia. What Christianity learned from Greco-Roman culture (Stoicism, neo-Platonism) was how to express itself in rhetoric and reason. When we start learning from Asia, and the cultures of India, Tibet, and China, we will move beyond the rational to the mystical. As we will see in the chapters that follow, God is a mystery, not a master's thesis. We have much to learn about the truth of God that is revealed only through relationship.

God is re-Orienting the church to the context of its Founder. Jesus was not a Greek, nor was he a classical thinker. He was a Hebrew, Eastern in thought and culture, relational in

> Our Easter faith is that we really do encounter Jesus himself; not a message from him, or a doctrine inspired by him, or an ethics of love, or a new idea of human destiny, or a picture of him, but Jesus himself.
>
> —DOMINICAN
> HERBERT MCCABE[22]

practice, and mystical in spirituality. We do not follow a Savior whose life was shaped by Western thought. Perhaps God is now addressing the church's Western presuppositions, which it took to extremes (rationality, individual freedom, the privileging of "high" over "popular" culture). In this re-Orientation, we see God guiding the church back to its originating but forgotten modes of experiential, participatory, image-rich, and connective spiritualities.[23] What Western Christianity received initially as revelation from God-in-the-flesh has been turned into rationality, a form of divine idea or holy argument—rhetoric not relationship. Could this "re-Orientation" of Christianity be a rediscovering of our very own Christianness?

The Reformation paradigm, which tempts us to replace relationship with reason, is captured in the word *belief.* It is concerned with right thinking and adherence to a particular way of articulating biblical teaching. It involves systematizing and assenting—and excluding those who don't fully subscribe to the current fashion in creedal statements. Belief is inert. It is intellectual, defensible, and typically irrelevant.

In contrast, the missional paradigm is a way of life—the life of *faith.* It is a quest for discovery. It is nothing less than the pursuit of the GodLife relationship. Faith is kinetic and transformational. It is described in Scripture as following, forgiving, seeking, rejoicing, sharing. It is the life of relating to God, to others, and to God's creation. To the Western mind it can appear sloppy and unpredictable and meandering. Yes, it is all of those things, and much more!

Belief is Plato; faith is Jesus.

As we consider God's re-Orientation of Christianity, bear in mind that it is movement, not statement. It is more about exploring than about ensconcing.

Jesus asked his closest followers: "Who do you say I am?"[24] Each of us, if we are to follow him today, must answer this same question. And as we seek the answer, we find that it is less a question than a quest.

The yoking of relationship and quest is deliberate. In the Bible, it is more that God seeks us out for relationship than that we seek God out. In fact, the more we insulate, the more God insinuates. The more we hide, the more God hounds.

We have been losing the battle in finding attributes that distinguish humans from the rest of creation: Crows use utensils, orangutans spell, parrots tally, dolphins and chimps fake and feint, songbirds experience REM sleep just like humans, bird brains can outsmart human brains at finding things. But there is one thing that clearly sets *Homo sapiens* apart. Part of the uniqueness of humanity, beings created in the image of God, is our instinct to seek and to enjoy the pleasures of seeking. It is born in us to dare, to desire, and to delight in the Quest. Questing-made-possible is who we are. Some say it's our sole advantage as a species.

But the Quest is not a set of questions. The Quest is the mystery of getting lost in the GodLife relationship.

PART I

FAITH IS A RELATIONSHIP

A Life That's Beyond Belief

Is It Better to Believe, or to Follow?

Io sono la Via, la Verita, la Vita
I am the way and the truth and the life....
Follow me.

—Jesus[1]

M uch of history has been determined by personal relationships, especially the "personal" in relationships. Why did USAmerica drop the atom bomb on Hiroshima and not Kyoto? Because Secretary of War Henry L. Stimson had a personal relationship with the city of Kyoto. He spent his honeymoon there in 1926 and loved the Japanese art and culture. Although Kyoto was at first designated as the target for the atomic blast, Stimson intervened with President Truman, and Kyoto was spared.[2]

If you give it some thought, you'll see how your own life has been spared from destruction by personal relationships. One of the most important phrases a leader can hear is this one: "I've got your back covered." Think about who your protectors are. Who are the people covering your rear? Every leader in church history who moved Christianity forward had protectors whose gift was the words "I've got your back."

At the most basic level, of course, your life can be considered "life" and not simply existence because of a relationship with God. And what would become of faith if there were no relationship? The Christian faith is built on the multiplicity and complexity of relationships: God to God, God to human, human to human, human to creation, God to creation. Why would Jesus sacrifice his body and his life for a people that he knew nothing about and cared nothing for? If Jesus's heart did not beat in rhythm with the human condition, why would he bother?

Amazingly, the segment of the church that's rooted in the Reformation has lost touch with the key doctrine of that movement: justification by grace *through faith*. Evangelists still preach faith, and pastors continue to urge parishioners struggling with life's setbacks to "have faith." But in the daily life of faith we have lost sight of faith. Or more accurately, we've developed more of a faith "perspective" than a faith "posture." We're there in theory but not in practice.

The Bible does not cast faith as a spiritual footpath to heaven or an inner stirring that we try to rev up when the chips are down. Neither does Scripture describe faith as a cognitive capacity that God activates to effect our justification. Rather, faith is consistently defined in Scripture, at base, as a set of trust relationships—with God, with neighbor, with the world, with creation.

One of the greatest thinkers on faith in the Hebrew tradition was the medieval philosopher Maimonides. For Maimonides, the knowledge of God was more than *amor Dei intellectualis*—ideas about loving God. Far from a mere idea, faith was a living encounter with the living God. And this encounter with the divine was the summit of any person's existence, life's highest good and goal.

But we don't have to hearken back to a Jewish thinker from the Middle Ages. For Martin Luther, one of the greatest theologians of faith in the history of Christianity, faith was a new kind of relationship that Jesus makes possible. This doesn't mean there are no cognitive components to faith, of course. But for Luther, it was faith's "relational capacity—uniting the believing sinner with Christ—that faith justifies."[3] The gospel is more than our salvation from sin.

The good news is our incorporation into the life of God. We have been raised with Christ so that we "might walk in newness of life"[4] and be raised to new levels of relationship.

> Faith is the distinctive word of the New Testament, as much as love and far more so than hope. Faith occurs once or twice in the Old Testament, perhaps two hundred times in the New. So if you think there is nothing new in the New Testament you are mistaken.
>
> —SOCIOLOGIST DAVID MARTIN[5]

In the ancient world, faith did not mean subscribing to the convictions of theology; it meant living in the confidence of relationships. Whether it is Abraham, Isaac, and Jacob; or Sarah, Elizabeth, and Mary; or Father, Son, and Holy Spirit; the Bible defines faith in more than cognitive terms. Faith in God is a relationship involving all of who you are and all that is around you. Faith is a lived encounter, a relationship of truth with the divine.

Jesus came to make possible new kinds of relationships with God, with people, and with the world. When Jesus used the intimate Aramaic word *Abba* in his prayers, never before had God been addressed in such a way. Only Jesus broaches this intimacy with God. Only Jesus opens the door to this approach to God.

And this new understanding of faith goes beyond the example set by Jesus. It is seen first in the nature of God. Is not relationship the essence of the Trinity? We do not sing "God in three thesis points, blessed Trinity" but "God in three Persons, blessed Trinity." The Trinity does not deal with time, space, matter, doctrine, or reason, but relationships. God is "Communion" and invites us into that same communion.[6] At the core of who we are as humans is an inner drive for relationship with God and with one another. Our greatest need is "not communication," Eugene Peterson has written, "but communion."[7]

Christianity tells a "killing the Messenger" story because the messenger was the message. The good news of the gospel is not an announcement or a proclamation, it's a Person: Jesus the Christ. Jesus is the gospel. God-made-flesh is the gospel. God-became-one-of-us is the gospel. The good news is that "in Christ God was reconciling the world to himself."[8] This is relationship at its best, relationship as God defines it.

FAITH IN THE FLESH

The soil of our faith, the gospel, is the mystery of how in Jesus "the Word became flesh."[9]

The conceptual became perceptual.

The abstract became mystery.

Statement became story.

Principle became person.

Michael Rie, a Jewish surgeon at the University of Kentucky Medical Center, is active in the bioethics discussion. He tells about one session of dialogue, when a Christian theologian expounded on bioethics from a perspective of God as Reason rather than God as Person. Rie blurted out defensively: "You are blaspheming the name of Jesus Christ." His defensiveness surprised even himself. But the realization that many theologians were "bent on reducing substantive moral content of their religion to what they took to be the general requirements of moral rationality" alarmed him.[10]

Rie was concerned that these theologians had chosen to construe God as a source of philosophical rational principles, rather than experiencing God as the Person Who confronted Abraham and Moses with very particular moral obligations.[11]

When moral theology is demoted to the level of "what should be embraced by rational persons," then moral theology is no different from moral philosophy. God is factored out of the equation, and theologians have no reason for being.

Why did God create us? There is only one answer: for relationships. God decided not to have a life of God's own but to share the divine life with us. God gets lonely when God has no one to walk with in the dew of the day. This is one of the greatest self-disclosures in all of history. Amazing, vulnerable, divine self-disclosure. God created us for companionship.

Ultimate reality can be experienced only in relationships. Hence the Hebrew concept of "covenant." Hence the Jesus concept of "salvation." Relationship is one of the things that distinguishes Judaism and its radical Christian revision from other religions: God calls us into a relationship. Christianity is much more than a wisdom tradition or a moral system or a path leading to higher states of existence.

The essence of the Christian faith is as simple and complex as this: God loves us and desires a relationship with us through Jesus, God's only begotten Son. Our identity is found in Christ—in a relationship, not in an organization or a system or a philosophy. The essence of the physics of faith is reflected in the simplicity and complexity of quantum physics: The universe is not comprised of objects but of relationships between objects. Identity is found not in things themselves, but in their relationships. Superstring physics is based on the inescapable science of the interconnectedness of all things. There is no isolated or disconnected matter.

THE NONLOCALISM OF THE LOCAL CHURCH

Relationships and interrelatedness are as primary in the spiritual realm as they are in the physical world. In theology, what's important is not things themselves, but relationships between things. In fact, nothing is ever one thing or another, but rather a relationship between things.

God loves you, desires a relationship with you, and hugs all things to himself. Faith goes far beyond the articulation of general principles to live by or universal laws that govern social morality. Biblical thinking is less about principles and places than about patterns and relationships. When Christians become more intent on learning the principles than knowing God, biblical Christianity is abandoned.

What makes us human is the same thing that makes us created in the image of God. We are not isolated entities, self-contained, existing apart from God or from one another or even from God's creation. We are made for "community" and "communion" and "ecology," in the words

> Few were so careless of orthodox formulas as Jesus, and there is something more than a little precious in affecting a greater concern for orthodoxy than his.
>
> —BIBLICAL SCHOLAR C. K. BARRETT[12]

of Roman Catholic theologian Joseph Sittler. Being created in the image of God, he says, "specifies a relation."[13]

The robot COG at the Massachusetts Institute of Technology agrees with Sittler. COG is the name of the first robot that emerged from Embodied AI (Artificial Intelligence). Embodied AI differs from Pure AI in that the former says that giving a machine intelligence means giving it a body as well, so that it can enter into relationships. Anne Foerst, the theological advisor of the COG project and the first director of the God and Computers Project at MIT, argues that "our humanity does not come from our brains or our body but from our complex interactions with the community. We are human because we must deal with other humans and the rest of creation."[14]

CHRISTIANITY IS NOT WHAT YOU THINK

If science and technology are coming around to agreeing with Jesus and the prophet Micah that the basis of life and humanity is in connections and relationships, where does that leave the life of faith for ordinary Christians in the twenty-first century? For starters, it demands a new focus on "life" and "faith" and a willingness to demote "objects" and "propositions" from their current preeminence. The Jesus trimtab is more than packets of theological information filled with objective rules or objectified rituals. The Jesus trimtab is a life-or-death relationship with God through faith practices, stories, songs, beliefs, ongoing traditions, upcoming technologies, and the connectedness of a social brain. It is a life posture, not a life principle.

The difference between an object-based church and a relation-based church is the difference between a church that sells itself versus a church that brings people into a living, lifelong relationship with Christ and one another. A relation-based church is less a place where creeds are dispensed and adherents conscripted than a place where people can connect with God and with one another, and where their faith journeys can be encouraged and enabled.

> Truth, like love and sleep, resents approaches which are too direct.
>
> —ATTRIBUTED TO W. H. AUDEN

SOCIAL MALNUTRITION

How often have you moved your place of residence? How many different careers have you had? In how many different states do your children and your siblings live? Demographic shifts and economic trends are moving us away from relationships, from the core reality that God built into each one of us. Heightened mobility and disintegrating communities—from dissolving marriages to disappearing places of employment—join together to create our current state of social malnutrition. Yet the more the culture moves us away from relationships, the more the human heart is moved to reach for relationships.

On average, USAmericans move to a different residence once every five years. In an average year, 2.5 million of us move away from our spouses and 3.5 million experience homelessness. In 1930, only 2 percent of the USAmerican population lived alone. By 2000, 10 percent of the 105 million households were individual adults without children, roommates, or other people in the residence.[15] This figure does not include the burgeoning phenomenon of commuter marriages, where spouses in dual careers maintain separate households. Nor can figures convey the psychological consequences to a culture that is always "moving on" and leaving behind relationships with friends, neighbors, coworkers, and employers as if we were kids waving good-bye and going home at the end of summer camp.

In a culture overdosed on empty entertainment, a culture that conditions people to being treated without dignity (in airports, banks, or the DMV), people are searching for a more intimate, more spiritual world. Digital technology makes interaction easier but intimacy harder. People seem to be heavy into relationships, just not with those who are physically present. People are constantly talking with others on cell phones and the Internet, but most people are treating those around them as objects to get past, not as subjects to pass through.[16] The people reached through technology are now more real than the people who are present in physical form.

The more blurred the dividing line between the real and the virtual, the more difficult and troublesome relationships with other human beings become. In the marriage market, a man who is divorced actually has a higher stature among women than someone who has never been married. Divorced means "once married," which indicates the man at least has demonstrated he can make a commitment.

We live in a smart world where machines are talking to machines (your car is talking to your insurance company through those hidden little black boxes), some toilets are already talking to doctors and laboratories, and biofriendly interfaces are giving us learning agents that know more about us than anyone else in our lives. These technologies are changing our sense of ourselves and our relationships with ourselves and others.

Think about sending and receiving messages. It used to be that the greater burden lay with the person initiating the contact. You had to remember the date of your mother's birthday, find an appropriate card, locate a stamp, and allow time for the card to travel through the mail. With the advent of e-mail, however, the sequence has reversed itself. The personal, emotional, and financial costs involved in receiving and responding to messages are now much greater than in sending and delivering messages.[17] As anyone knows who sits down each night to a hundred e-mails, some of which are one sentence long but "require" a two-page response, it's far better today to be at the sending end.

Or consider how potential marriage partners are finding each other. We don't know how to choose a long-term partner, and we don't trust our own judgment. We lack relationship readiness, and we lament the lack of psychological intimacy in the marriages of our parents. Hence, television shows like

Married by America and *Meet My Folks.* People are open again to the idea of arranged marriages. And in a twenty-first century form of arranged relationship, online dating services function as virtual matchmakers, attracting the participation of one-fifth of all singles in USAmerica.

University of Chicago researcher Amy Kass argues that old-style courtship provided a "distanced nearness" that offered intimacy and protection at the same time. Today, she says, cyberspace provides this service: It "encourages self-revelation while maintaining personal boundaries."[19] Even "one-night stands" hearken back to the "contract" marriages arranged long ago in a world where strangers climbed into bed together without emotional protocols or entanglements.

> I have reached an age where my main purpose is not to receive messages.
>
> —UMBERTO ECO[18]

Our offspring, these cyber-suckled generations mainlining the Internet, are changing how we create and conserve personal relationships.[20] The mechanics of relationship have shifted from "what are we doing today" to "*how* are we doing today?" And complex, new, irregular relationships are emerging, including virtual relationships that have their own satisfactions and limitations. Why do I turn on the *Today* show and not *Good Morning, America*? Because I'm in a "relationship" with Katie, Matt, and Al. I have never met them, but still I'm in a relationship with them. And I feel a lot closer to them than I do to Charles Gibson and Diane Sawyer.

ANYONE BEEN PROPOSITIONED?

Mother Teresa once was asked about the worst disease she had ever seen. Was it leprosy or smallpox? Was it AIDS or Alzheimer's? "No," she said, "the worst disease I've ever seen is loneliness."

In spite of, or perhaps due to, the digital revolution, relationships have become the most valuable, most important form of cultural capital in our globalized world. That's one reason the rediscovery of a relation-based spirituality is crucial to ministry in the twenty-first century. With Christians now largely indistinguishable from non-Christians in how they live and think, there is no longer a startling freshness to the proclamation of biblical truth when it is presented as principles and propositions. How a person lives speaks much more loudly than what he or she asserts, now as always. And with Christians nearly identical to all others in the culture, what they say loses its impact. George Barna has argued for building relationships as the only effective foundation for evangelizing teenagers.[21] We can and should apply this truth more broadly: Relationship is foundational to *all* evangelization, not just the challenge of reaching teenagers. People find and experience biblical truth in relationship.

The worst thing you can do to Christianity is to turn it into a philosophical endeavor. Faith is more than beliefs to be learned; it is bonds to be lived. Faith is more than holding the "right" beliefs; it is holding the "right" (that is, the "least of these") hands. We are judged by the world not on the basis of how "right" we've gotten what we believe but on how well we're living it—on how we love God and people. Elie Wiesel has said, "Christianity did not 'come true' during Auschwitz."[22] More than 20 percent of the German SS officers, the expert killers, were professing Christians. This is a disturbing nightmare, a religion that is so impotent and so removed from relationship that it could not "come true" when millions of Jews were being incinerated. Jesus gave us a relationship test whereby we can know whether faith "comes true." The test, according to Jesus, is that his disciples are known not by how well they defend orthodox propositions, but by how well they "love one another."[23]

Abraham Lincoln claimed that America was founded on a proposition and that Thomas Jefferson wrote it: "We hold these truths to be self-evident..." Unlike USAmerica, Christianity wasn't founded on a statement or even a rational argument. God didn't send Jesus to deliver a proposition. God sent Jesus to deliver a proposal: "Will you love me? Will you let me love you?" In fact, Jesus not only got on his knees to deliver this proposal, Jesus was nailed to a cross to deliver God's proposal.

THE TRUTH ABOUT COMMITTING

Belief and Faith Are Two Very Different Things

You did not choose me, but I chose you.

—JESUS[1]

CHAPTER TWO

Most Christians use the words *belief* and *faith* interchangeably. But to admit (believe) falls far short of to commit (faith). To become a Christian is not to adopt a different belief system. To become a Christian is to experience a transformation into the image of Christ by the power of the Holy Spirit. Admitting is useless without committing.

The psalmist's chief delight was in "the law of the LORD"[2]; our delight is in the "new law" of the Lord, which is the love of the Lord. Christianity is more than an intellectual assent to certain propositions about God, Jesus, and the Bible. Indeed, Jesus demonstrated this in his own ministry. He was crucified because he insisted on relationship over adherence to a set of laws or a moral system of behavior. Jesus died an outlaw, showing with his body the supremacy of love. The greatest "law," Jesus said, was the law of love, a law that wasn't a law at all but a relationship. One of the problems of the church is its forceful insistence on intellectual adherence to certain beliefs, in the relative absence of a holy passion for the incarnational practice of those same beliefs.

The purpose of Christianity is to help people come to faith, which means to establish a relationship with God. Faith is not salvation per se, or liberation per se, or correct belief about the Godhead per se. Faith is the willing acceptance of Jesus's invitation, "Follow me." As a result, it is kinetic and interpersonal. It is transformational, not status quo. It is not satisfied with simply trading one set of convictions for a different, more orthodox set.

The world at large views love as life's prime virtue. Humorist Dave Barry attempts to capture just how big and important love is, calling it "the only truly important topic, the Super Bowl of Topics, the King Kong of Topics, the Big Bang of Topics, the Young Mozart of Topics, the 32-ounce Prime Rib with Your Choice of Scalloped or Baked Potato of Topics, the Michael Jordan in his Physical Prime Taking Off with the Basketball from the Foul Line and Coming Down Several Minutes Later from the Rafters to JAM that Baby Home over Three or Four Larger Defenders of Topics."[3] But for the Christian, love may be primary—"the greatest of these"—but faith is the primal Christian virtue. Why faith and not love? Because agape love—the love of God—is formed in us by grace through faith. Christian love is a form of plagiarism: We repeat and copy God's love. In fact, our loving is based on faith in God's first loving us. Faith is what the Christian life is made of.

ABSOLUTE REVELATION

Lest you suspect that I am detouring you into ambiguous, touchy-feely spirituality, let me clarify. Christian revelation is not a subjective experience. God defines us; we don't define God or a relationship with the divine. But Christian revelation is a Person named Jesus who calls us into a graced relationship through faith.[4] Christianity was built not on doctrine, but on the person of Jesus. The Christian church was created, not to preach doctrine, but to preach Jesus. As Paul stated: "We preach Christ crucified."[5] The purpose of doctrine is to keep us focused on the Christ who is, who was, and who is to come. Thus, truth about Christ is a means to an end. It helps us arrive at Christ himself. Doctrine, dogma, and theology all serve Christ, not the other way around. Are we called to defend doctrine or to love God and love what God loves?

Each person receives a call from God through Christ, and the nature of that call is simply, "Follow me." When Jesus reminded his disciples, "You did not choose me, but I chose you,"[6] he meant those words to be taken literally. In the ancient world, a person became a disciple by seeking out a rabbi. In rabbinic Judaism, and in the Hellenistic philosophical world, the initiative lay with the student to select a teacher. But with Jesus, the teacher chose his students, not the students, the teacher.

Jesus turned ancient tradition on its head by selecting his disciples. And he chose them with two words: "Follow me." This demonstration of the Ultimate Authority, God-in-the-Flesh, pursuing his own followers, is absolutely unique in the ancient world.

The power of these two words—"Follow me"—will not be nuclear until they are no longer unclear. Jesus did not say "Follow this teaching" or "Follow this idea" or "Follow this commandment" or "Follow this ritual life." He said, "Follow me"![7] We don't follow Jesus because we understand him or because we know the truth about him. We follow Jesus because he *is* the Truth, and he leads us into truth through our relationship with him. Our basis for confidence in Jesus's Truth-fullness is the call and claim on our lives of the Bible story, the beautiful creeds of the church, and the rituals and relationships of Christian community wherein we find the faith to keep following him and thus come to know him more deeply. For disciples of Jesus, knowledge is interactive relationships. True knowledge is moral knowledge.

Of course, we must enter into a learner relationship with Jesus. In traditional arrangements, the teacher offers teaching. But Jesus rejected tradition and offered *himself.* The Jesus call to discipleship is an invitation to enter a relationship with the person doing the teaching, not simply an intellectual encounter with the principles he taught.

As Jesus showed what "Follow me" means, it consisted less in knowing this or believing that, but most in losing oneself, bearing one's cross, denying oneself, embracing the other, and following after Jesus. The call to follow Jesus is an invitation to enter into the same relationship that exists between Jesus and the Father.

Jesus privileged his disciples by giving them "the secret of the kingdom of God."[9] And the secret is not a formula, a map, or a principle. The secret is Jesus's suffering, death, and resurrection. And those who are to follow him must be prepared for the same. The secret is not some gnosis (secret knowledge) but a noetics (experience) of the revelation of God. Theology is not discursive rationality. Theology is a relationship with God that issues in reflections on revelation. For Evagrius of Pontus, prayer is what qualifies anyone to be a theologian: "If you pray truly, you are a theologian."[10] To be a theologian is to "know" God.

> The Christian faith is the faith of Christ; not only the faith which believes in Christ, but the faith which Christ believes.
>
> —AUSTIN FARRER[8]

The mysteries of God's kingdom are not in some pot of gold that brings you self-fulfillment but a relationship with Jesus that costs you everything. We may not know where our next meal is coming from; we may face people who come to drag us away in chains; we may even take a premature route to eternity.

Of such is the "way of the cross." It costs us everything because faith in Jesus is a lived relationship. Biblical truth is not a possession you wield, but a life you yield.[11] The ultimate content of Christianity is not propositions, but Jesus. Or in Saint Paul's phrase, "In him we live and move and have our being."[12]

There's a musical expression: "He's inward with it." It means you have so merged with the piece of music that the sound is not just something being performed but something coming from the inside out. Getting "inward with it" is the essence of Christianity. The postmodern quest has been misunderstood as an abandonment of the quest for truth. It is far from an abandonment, but is rather a rerouting of the quest for truth along more relational and less rational paths. The question at the heart of Christianity is not a philosophical one or a political one or a liturgical one. The question at the heart of Christianity is a relational one: "Who do you say that I am?"

> It is better to have a heart that makes love than a mind that makes sense.
>
> —L. ROBERT KECK[13]

Who we say that Jesus is says who we are.

BELIEF AND THE KINGDOM OF GOD

The phrase "kingdom of God" is completely original with Jesus. It was Jesus's trademark phrase, his personal signature. And what is the kingdom of God?

The kingdom is not a set of ideals; it's a life of relatedness and faithfulness to what the kingdom is. Jesus is both the kingdom's form and content. The kingdom starts with Jesus and with his cross and grave. The kingdom proclaims God's reign over nature and history with His crown and glory. Jesus is the kingdom. Jesus is the reign of God.

The definition and destination of faith is not *what* but *who*.[14] Our confessions and beliefs center on a Person: "If you confess me before others, I will confess you before the Father;"[15] "He who believes in me believes in the Father."[16]

To believe is not to adopt certain principles.

To believe is not to assent to certain creeds.

To believe is not to keep certain laws.

To believe is to trust your whole being to God.

To believe is to "get inward with it."

It is one thing to conceptualize the encounter with the divine. It is another thing to make conceptual the encounter with the divine. James Wood, critic-turned-novelist, has written *The Book Against God*, in which he argues the case for doubt and disbelief. "To find or lose a faith is to find or lose belief in a series of propositions or guarantees, laid out by Jesus and the Gospel writers."[17]

Wood begins from a place of misunderstanding. His definition of "belief" is off. Ironically, his confusion on this point is shared just as widely among "believers" as among "nonbelievers." Rodney Needham tried some years ago to persuade scholars to drop the word *belief* because of its multifarious meanings, but predictably, his brilliant argument went unappreciated.[18]

The word *believe* is an ancient compounding of the verb *be* and the noun *life*. To "believe" is to "be live"—to live your being, to trust your "being" to "life."[19] The root meaning of *believe* as "credo" did not originally mean nodding in intellectual assent; it meant "to give my heart to" or "to hold dear" or "to love."

Philosopher of religion Wilfred Cantwell Smith suggests that the German word for belief *(belieben)* comes the closest to conveying the word's true meaning. The adjective *lieb* means "dear" or "beloved." *Die Liebe* is the noun "love," and *lieben* is the verb "to love." *Belieben* then is to treat as "lieb" or to consider lovely, "to love." In modern German, *sich verlieben* means "to fall in love with," and *sich verloben* means "to betroth, to engage."[20]

Smith's definition of *belief* as "beloved" comes the closest to bringing us to the deeply relational context of the Hebrew idea of "believer." In almost every place where the Torah talks about someone "believing" God you can insert the word *trusting* or *be living*. In Genesis 15:6, the Hebrew word *he'emin* means that Abraham trusted God as a beloved more than that Abraham intellectually assented to ideas about God.[21] The real question of a true believer is, "Who are you going to 'belove'? Who are you going to give your whole self to?" The English phrase "right relationship" captures more accurately the biblical meaning of the phrase "right belief." Until we can rehabilitate the original and true meaning of *belief*, it would be better to use some other expression. That's why I refuse to call disciples of Jesus "believers." It sets the bar so low that even Lucifer would qualify. If one understands "belief" as intellectual assent, even the devil is a "believer." If the demons "believe and tremble," they're actually doing better than some of us. At least they're trembling.

We are more in love with our principles of peace than we are with the Prince of Peace. We are more in love with our words about life than we are with the Living Word. We are more in love with our propositions about truth than we are with the One who is the Truth. We are more in love with our gilded-lily Golden Rules and star-studded Seven Habits than we are with the Lily of the Valley, the Bright and Morning Star.

Faith and Witness

Our daughter, Soren, is terrified of dentists. She had this fear before she ever set foot in a dentist's office. It was a major achievement to arrange her first visit, and we chose the dentist who had the best reputation in town. Others spoke glowingly about his skill.

Soren nervously climbed in the medieval-looking contraption called a "chair," which she called a "torture chamber." To make her feel more at ease, the dentist started showing off his new equipment, which was designed to hurt less and take less time. The tour of his cutting-edge equipment was followed by immediate drilling. She screamed, she cried, she twisted and turned, she had to be held down.

The dentist asked us never to return. The fillings he put in lasted two weeks.

It took almost a year to talk Soren into trying another dentist. This time we chose Dr. Michael Triplett. Dr. Triplett spent the first fifteen minutes doing nothing but getting to know Soren. He talked to her about her likes and dislikes, reminding her of when he had seen her around town, of his twin daughters who sometimes played with Soren, of his admiration for her dalmatian coat.

After fifteen minutes of doing nothing but chatting, he introduced Soren to "strawberry air," and soon my daughter was relaxed. She leaned back into the chair (she had been sitting erect all this time), and she asked the dentist questions. She still wouldn't open her mouth until he explained what he was going to do and why.

Finally, after twenty-five minutes of conversation, she opened her mouth, and he was able to do in the next fifteen minutes what the first dentist was never able to do. Dr. Triplett's compassion led to Soren's trust.

If we shift our focus away from truth as right teaching and correct doctrine, and instead center our lives on truth as a Person and faith as a relationship with that Person, what does this do to evangelism? Evangelism shifts from an attempt to indoctrinate a skeptic into a new belief system and makes the gospel proclamation a process of inviting others into a relationship with God.

Evangelism is as much invitation as it is proclamation. It is inviting others into a relationship with God so that the Holy Spirit can make Christ come alive in them and live in them and they can live in God's fullness and providence. Evangelism is not leading people to right beliefs about Jesus. It is introducing people to a relationship with Jesus the Christ.

> If God held all truth in [the] right hand, and in [the] left hand held the lifelong pursuit of it, [God] would choose the left hand.
>
> —PHILOSOPHER GOTTHOLD LESSING[22]

When you ask Christ into your life, are you letting in Someone who's going to give you tests you have to pass? rules you have to learn? principles you need to master? Or are you entering into a relationship with God that lets the Spirit of God live in you and transform you into the likeness of Christ?

The essential destination of Christianity isn't *what* but *who*. Being in the household of faith means having a relationship with God through Jesus the Christ as revealed in the Scriptures. The furniture of faith is the creeds, the confessions, the doctrines, and the articles of religion that have been handed down to us by our ancestors.

MEASURING FAITH

Separating sheep from goats is a favorite preoccupation of the church. Who's in and who's out? And how do we distinguish between the two?

There's an old story about a notorious bandit in the Far East who had been badly injured and taken to a Christian mission hospital. After weeks of excellent care, the bandit recovered from his injuries. He was so grateful for the treatment he received that he resolved he would never again rob a Christian.

The word got around, and everyone he tried to rob would immediately say, "I'm a Christian." And so the robber was faced with a problem: *How can you tell whether a person who claims to be Christian really is?*

He returned to the hospital and asked the missionaries, who explained: "Well, every Christian should know the Lord's Prayer and the Ten Commandments." From that time on, the robber would ask potential victims to recite the Lord's Prayer and the Ten Commandments. If they couldn't do it, he would rob them.

If the bandit were doing business today, how many Christians would he encounter who could recite these two touchstone texts? And if they couldn't, what difference would it make—other than a lightening of their wallets? Does reciting anything, even holy writ, make a difference either in this life or in eternity? Some of the meanest people I know can quote astounding amounts of Scripture while they walk up and down your back. How can this be? They know the rules, they know the law, they know the facts. But they don't know the Master of Relationships. They have the information but not the transformation of the Way, the Truth, and the Life.

The true test of faith is not knowledge based. The true test of faith is a revelational, and relationship, test. Is Christ dead or alive in your life? Has the Jesus virus infected your life until your spirit is becoming his spirit? A relationship with God—loving God—is the ultimate fulfilling of the Law, according to Jesus.[23] The moral law was written on tablets of stone. But Jesus rolled away the stone. The Jesus trimtab is now grafted into the human heart until "as he is, so are we in this world," until "Christ is formed in you."[24]

Form Without Substance

How can "belief" in all the right things produce such a lifeless church? Shouldn't it produce just the opposite?

Paul put his finger on the connection between sterile orthodoxy and spiritual lifelessness: "He has made us competent as ministers of a new covenant—not of the letter but of the Spirit; for the letter kills, but the Spirit gives life."[25] To be sure, the modern church would deny any reliance on law or legalism for the life of faith.

But by their fruit we know them. Where is the fruit, and what kind of fruit is there for the picking? The modern church has a propositional attitude rather than a relational attitude. The letter has taken the upper hand, choking off the life of the Spirit in the life of faith. We have even managed to make Jesus into a principle, an answer to a question: "Christ is the answer."

What does God want from you and me? Does God want us to think the right thoughts or to do the right things? Of course. But above all God wants us to be involved in right relationships. When the Bible says, "God is love," it is saying that God is a relationship. Love has no value or meaning in a vacuum. Right relationships are not produced by right thoughts or right actions. Just the opposite. Right thoughts and right actions are produced by right relationships.

If right teaching supplied the complete answer to the life of faith, then why hasn't our society sold out to God? No other generation has had as much access to so much Christian teaching via radio, television, the Internet, and print sources. Our society is bombarded with Christian propositions like never before. We're practically buried in Christian "information." Yet, at the same time, our society is less enamored of Christian orthodoxy today than ever before.

What's missing is the right relationship, a deepening relationship with God. The modern world made asking questions the highest task. The lifelong quest for answers was the highest journey. Now it's time to acknowledge that faith is not a problem to be solved or a question to be answered, but a mystery to be lived—the mystery of a real, live relationship with God—the GodLife relationship.

> For Christian leadership to be truly fruitful in the future, a movement from the moral to the mystical is required.
>
> —HENRI NOUWEN[26]

Christianity is not for "professionals." Christianity is meant to be lived by amateurs. *Amateur* is based on the Latin word *amator,* which means "lover." Christianity is meant for lovers, not experts.

PRACTICING TRUTH

Is Christianity a proprietary doctrine of the church, or is it a continuation of Jesus's ministry on earth and an embodiment of his spirituality? Is Christianity a method and strategy, or is it a community with throbbing hearts, bleeding hearts, broken hearts, hearts bound together by and in God? Faith is not something you have, but something you live. Not something you believe, but something you practice, every day, in all of life—a lived relationship. To affirm Christianity is not to make a point. Instead, it's a decision to begin a journey of following.

The best way to understand Christianity is as a matrix of fresh relationships. Christianity is less a unique way of thinking than a unique way of linking. Christianity is not a system of laws and principles, but a pattern of relationships.

All spiritual practice leads to relationship. The "practice" of faith is like the "practicing" of any relationship. Instead of looking for underlying laws and unvarying principles, we need to explore the broader landscape of connections and relationships of faith. Instead of seven beliefs or principles, I am proposing a sevenfold repertoire and relationship matrix for faith.

TRUTH IN THE RELATIONSHIP MATRIX

As we learn about relationship in the Scriptures, we see seven webthreads in the relationship matrix. It is not wise to try to separate out one from the others, since they all interrelate. Indeed, the way they interact with one another is vivid testimony to the complex realities of relationships. The mark of a true disciple is the vibrancy of this relationship matrix.

The church of the future must build ministry not around fixed propositions but around this rather simple but complex relationship-matrix repertoire. The use of the word *repertoire* and "repertory" language here is deliberate. In the modern world, concepts of this magnitude were made part of a canon, not a repertoire. But a *canon* is a rule of thought. A *repertoire* is a program of action.[27]

The essence of personhood is not "I think" or "I believe," but "I do" and "I choose." In other words, the essence of personhood is a social universe of relationships. In the biblical repertoire of relationships we find these seven:

- our relationship with God
- our relationship with God's story, God's written revelation
- our relationship with other people of faith
- our relationship with those outside the faith
- our relationship with God's creation

- our relationship with symbols, arts, artifacts, and "things"
- our relationship with the spiritual realm

As we live in relationship with God and with the entire relationship repertoire, we shift our purpose from gaining more information that we are required to believe, to living in such a way that we become the body of Christ.

Truth is right relationships. The right relationship is everything. And for the Christian, truth is a Person.[28]

PART II

OUR RELATIONSHIP

WITH GOD

Abraham's Big Break with God

Doing It Right and Still Failing the Test

> I will make you into a great nation and I will bless you.
> —GOD'S PROMISE, SPOKEN TO ABRAM[1]

When you come to a turning point, what do you do? When your life turns over, when people turn against you, when your world turns upside down—where do you turn?

I turn to the story of Abraham and Isaac. But I go there now for a different reason than I used to. When I was a boy growing up in mountain culture, I found Abraham to be one of the most alive characters in the Bible. When my faith would falter over life's small challenges, a quick review of what Abraham dealt with encouraged me forward. My wimpy, questioning faith seemed so inadequate compared to this pioneer of faith who carried out a dynamic, complicated, lifelong pilgrimage.

Abraham was my patron saint of journeying into the future. Unlike the tower builders of Babel, who wanted to construct a centralized altar, Abraham was willing to be "kept moving" by God as a blessing to the world. With nothing but God's promises in hand, this man abandoned the familiar world of Haran, a place where he had built a comfortable life. He went at an advanced age into an uncertain future, leaving behind everything familiar for only the embrace of God's promise.

As much as I admired Abraham, I found the story of Abraham and Isaac—the child of God's promise—to be too painful for me. When I was forced to think about it, I drew the typical parallels between Isaac and the Messiah. It always struck me that just as Isaac had to carry his own wood for the sacrifice, so, too, did Jesus carry the "wood of his own passion."[2] (I latched on to these words from Tertullian and never forgot them.) How could a father slay his son? All I could come up with was the standard but unsatisfying explanation that Isaac was a prototype of messianic suffering, and that Abraham knew that God would provide a substitute sacrifice. And if not that, then God would bring Isaac back to life after the knife killed him, an early demonstration of resurrection.[3]

Abraham is still my patron saint of "going." No one else surpasses his willingness to leave home and follow God based on nothing but a promise. But as a patron saint of faith, his example is very different to me now from the traditional interpretation outlined above. What follows is the story of my own moving out as I made a pilgrimage of faith, traversing from one view of Abraham into a very different one. I've found that the Abraham-and-Isaac story teaches unexpected and even troubling lessons about the intersection of faith and obedience.

> We're here to go.
>
> —NOVELIST
> WILLIAM S. BURROUGHS[4]

A QUICK CAVEAT

Before we go, let me issue a quick word of warning. My mother once gave me a salt-and-pepper set that belonged to her mother. The food that showed up on Gramma Boggs's table was as good as it gets, and memories of those shakers sitting on my gramma's country table fill up my soul and spirit. When I brought the salt-and-pepper set home, my wife immediately cleaned them out, filled them with condiments, and began using them. She fattened our family's soul and body with their use. But I was horrified that she would take this treasured family heirloom and put it to daily use. (If my wife had her way, there would be no museums!) So I requisitioned the set and lovingly located a safe place where my grandmother's shakers could be preserved and honored.

My wife and I had two very different ways of looking at this treasure from my family's history. If you are like me and prefer the "look, don't touch" approach, you might want to skip this chapter and the next. If you do go ahead and read them, then please accept my apologies if you feel I have improperly honored a biblical treasure.

But perhaps you are more like my wife: You are enriched through the touch and feel of treasured heirlooms, and you believe that putting them to fresh use is a way of honoring and communing with your ancestors. If so, these next two chapters may be for you, with no apologies necessary.

The Dome of the Rock in Jerusalem is the most hotly contested shrine in the world. It is sacred to three of the world's monotheistic religions: Christianity, Judaism, and Islam.

For Christians, this is the rock from which Jesus told a parable. For Muslims, it's the holy ground where the prophet Muhammad made his famous "night flight" on the back of the winged barak. For Jews, the rock marks the spot where Abraham prepared to sacrifice his son Isaac[5] and, later, where Solomon built his magnificent temple.

But the fierce religious contention surrounding this piece of real estate is nothing compared to the controversy that arises over the story of Abraham's agreeing to kill his son in ritual sacrifice. Like the Dome of the Rock where that test took place, the Abraham-and-Isaac text is one of the most problematic in all three religious traditions.

In rabbinic Judaism, the preparations for the sacrifice of Isaac, known as the *Akedah,* are seen as the tenth and greatest test of Abraham.[6]

In Islam, the submission of Abraham is pivotal, although it is unclear whether the unnamed son who was taken to the "high place" before a ram appeared was Isaac or Ishmael (the legendary ancestor of the Arabs).[7]

In Christianity and its eucharistic worship, Abraham's sacred sacrifice was a foretaste of another Father-Son sacrifice. The hold that the Abraham-and-Isaac story has on the Christian imagination would be hard to exaggerate. Paul was deeply influenced by it as a central mystery of faith,[8] and the most common scene depicted in early Christian art was the sacrifice of Isaac by Abraham.[9]

So contentious are the feelings elicited by this story that the dispute about Abraham ("Are you sons of Abraham, or sons of God?") is what got Jesus condemned to death. "Before Abraham was," Jesus said to a hostile crowd, "I am" (thereby claiming for himself the divine name).[10] Jesus asserted that his work was superior to that of the epochal figure of Abraham: "me, a man who has told you the truth that I heard from God. Abraham did not do such things."[11] What's more, Jesus said Abraham himself was moved to jubilation at his coming to Earth: "Your father Abraham rejoiced at the thought of seeing my day; he saw it and was glad."[12]

This is when they first "picked up stones to stone him."[13]

All my life I have struggled to understand the Abraham-and-Isaac story. I have constantly knelt before the mystery of this text. I have tugged at its sleeve in an attempt to rid myself of its haunting presence. I've even tried singing it away with "We'll understand it better bye and bye." But I'd like to understand more of it now, thank you.[14]

THE BIG TEST

The evening was just passing into darkness, the first stars were becoming visible. Cristos Valenti took his youngest child, his most beloved child, with him in his truck. She loved to ride along with him to visit friends. They drove to the place he had been directed to—to the place in the park where all the trees are. He took the child's hand and together they walked into the quiet darkness. She held on to his hand more tightly.

"Don't be afraid," he said. "We are going to meet God."

"I don't know anyone named God."

"You will meet him soon" was the answer, and they walked on in silence. When they arrived at the appointed place, Valenti told his daughter to lie down on the grass. "Start praying the Our Father who art in heaven," he said as he took the knife and took her life.

He sat next to her body and prayed for several minutes. When he looked up, he saw her star shining brightly in the night sky; he saw two stars moving closer together. He knew then he had fulfilled her destiny. He picked her up and took her home. When his oldest daughter opened the door she saw her father holding the child, like a *pietà*.

"Call the police," he said. "I have given her to God."

This account is summarized from a report given to the police on the night of 6 January 1990 in a small California town. At a Christmas pageant in which his daughter played a star, Valenti said he had heard God speaking to him. When he was arrested, he told police, "God needed her, to put her in a star." "Cristos Valenti" is a pseudonym.[15]

If any father can read this story without crying, one wonders what kind of a father that person is. You explain it to me: What makes Valenti a murderer and Abraham a hero of faith? You say, "Easy. Because Abraham heard from

God and Valenti heard either from a demon or from his own insane psyche." I say, not so easy. How did Abraham know it was God and not a demon or madness? And why did Abraham eventually listen to a voice that wasn't God's—it was the angel's voice—canceling God's command to sacrifice Isaac?

In the traditional interpretation of this story, which was intensely debated by Jewish scholars in Jesus's day and is undergoing a renaissance of Jewish scholarship in our day, God gave Abraham a tenth and final test. Abraham had already passed nine tests of ascending difficulty, according to the midrash.[16] The Bible is no stranger to tests. Joseph tested his brothers.[17] The Queen of Sheba tested Solomon.[18] Even Jesus was tested, constantly tested in fact—by Satan, Pharisees, Sadducees, lawyers.[19]

Jesus periodically "tested" his disciples. In the Sea of Galilee test, Jesus went to sleep in the boat to see if they could still trust him even though he was asleep. They failed the test.[20] The disciple Philip flunked a test—failed it so badly, in fact, that Jesus had to supply the answers.[21] When Jesus's disciples failed their tests, Jesus didn't kick them out of the boat, or out of class; he worked with them and gave them a new test.

God still gives God's children tests. In fact, God launched the nation God would call "mine" by using a test. God decided to push this obscure nomad named Abram out of his homeland, demanding that he pull up stakes and wander with no known destination. Abram passed the test. Later, after he was renamed Abraham, God chose to push this man of faith to the limits. The words of Genesis 18 telegraph something big is coming: "I have chosen him, *so that he will direct his children and his household after him* to keep the way of the LORD by doing what is right and just, so that the LORD will bring about for Abraham what he has promised him."[22] When God told Abraham to sacrifice his son, the son of promise, was God testing whether Abraham would "direct his children…to keep the way of the LORD by doing what is right and just"? Was Abraham "directing" his children in the ways of righteousness and justice by killing one of them?

Just as God gave Abraham a series of tests, so did Abraham test God and God's covenant. What else would you call his laughter, his skepticism, his constant picking at the Almighty for more details? Isaac was named for laughter, but not the laughter of joy. It was the laughter of parents who greeted God's promise as a laughing matter and who always wanted more proof that God really did mean what God said. God honored Abraham's "tests" by repeating the promise eight times.[23] Abraham was not reluctant to demand that God make things perfectly clear before Abraham would move ahead with these seemingly outlandish demands.

But now, with the intended sacrifice on Mount Moriah, God turned the tables and tested Abraham. What was God trying to find out about this faithful servant? And what grade did Abraham receive?

We're all familiar with the view that this was a test of faith and that Abraham passed the test with flying colors. His name is recorded in the New Testament's Faith Hall of Fame, with specific reference to his willingness to sacrifice his "one and only son."[24] Who else but a man of incredible faith would follow such a seemingly flawed command? And while the traditional view satisfies us on one level, we can't help but ask a torrent of questions.[25] If Abraham got an A+ on this exam, then one wonders why there are so many not just loose ends, but *lost* ends, to the story. If Abraham merited great reward for his obedience, why did so much punishment follow his near-sacrifice of Isaac?

TWENTY QUESTIONS OF FAITH

For centuries, the rabbis have sought to find the core of truth about God, about faith, and about obedience in the convoluted logic of the Mount Moriah narrative. While the traditional interpretation might, in the end, prove to be the only faithful understanding of what happened—and why it happened—let's consider for a moment another interpretation that is supported by the biblical record.

> We will have peace with the Arabs when they love their children more than they hate us.
>
> —FORMER ISRAELI PRIME MINISTER GOLDA MEIR[26]

We'll narrow our investigation to just a handful of questions that immediately come to mind when we read Genesis 22. Through his persona Johannes de Silentio, Søren Kierkegaard posed his own questions throughout his classic *Fear and Trembling:* For example, why didn't Abraham travel alone to Mount Moriah and sacrifice himself in place of Isaac? But without a persona to ask questions for me, here are my Twenty Questions about this story:

1. Why didn't Abraham argue with God about the killing of his innocent son like he did when God told Abraham about God's intention to kill the Sodomites' sons and daughters?

2. Why did Abraham keep the planned sacrifice a secret from those closest to him? Why didn't he tell Sarah, Eliezer, or Isaac about what God had ordered him to do?[27]

3. Why did the very Son of God, the perfect God-man, wrestle with his Father on the cross about his own death more than Abraham wrestled with God about the death of his entirely human son?

4. If Abraham was so special to God, why didn't Abraham get translated into heaven like Enoch and Elijah?

5. Why did God no longer speak to Abraham after the outcome of this test was known? God delivered the Mount Moriah test in person, but as Abraham was about to carry out the command, an angel intervened and stayed his hand. Why didn't God show up to intervene? And after the conclusion of this episode, God never spoke to Abraham again. The intimacy of their relationship was over. Likewise, from that point on, Abraham "never speaks *to* God" but only speaks *about* God.[28]

6. How did Isaac deal with the fact that his father had to be forcibly restrained from cutting his throat? What went through Isaac's mind as he stared at his father with a blade descending? Abraham may not have wounded Isaac with a knife, but he wounded him nevertheless.

7. What did Abraham and Isaac talk about on their three-day journey home? In fact, it appears more likely that Abraham returned alone to Beersheba.[29] Abraham climbed Mount Moriah with his son, but he arrived alone when he returned from the mountain. And he never spoke to his son again. Isaac never saw his father alive again—only reuniting with his brother Ishmael to bury their dead father. Even though God gave Abraham back his son on the altar of sacrifice, Abraham never did get his son back.

8. How can it be a good thing that Isaac and Abraham no longer "walk together" after Abraham's triumph of faith? Abraham didn't pass on the blessing to Isaac in person. He didn't even pass on his marriage instructions to Isaac personally.[30]

9. Is it reading too much into the text to wonder why Isaac grieved for his mother when she died, but the Scriptures say nothing about his grief upon his father's death?[31]

10. What did Abraham say to Sarah when he got back from the high place? He never seemed to explain himself to those around him. Why?

11. Why did Sarah die at the end of this story? Remember that Abraham had not previously told her anything about the purpose of his trip with Isaac to the land of Moriah. So upon her husband's return, did she die from shock upon hearing that her son had been spared execution?[32] Was she devastated that her husband would do such a thing? It takes Rebekah to comfort Isaac after the death of his mother. There was no sign of Abraham's even being there to console his son.

12. Why did God choose to name the people of God after Jacob, or Israel—"one who wrestles"—and not Abraham?[33]

13. Why did Abraham call the place of the interrupted sacrifice "The LORD Will Provide"? Not Faithfulness. Not God-fearing. Only "The LORD Will Provide"? Isn't that a pretty wussy name to come up with after the severity of the test? Also, the name refers to the angel's act of intervention, which saved Isaac and substituted a ram. The name does not call to mind the radical obedience of a great man of faith.

14. How could it be good that in the end, Abraham was alone? He dwelled in Beersheba. Sarah was in Hebron. Ishmael and Hagar were in Egypt. Isaac was far from his father. God had withdrawn from Abraham's life. Abraham ended his life separated from all those he loved the most.

15. The angel applauded Abraham for his "fear" of God. But the "fear" of God is the *beginning* of wisdom—not the end of wisdom or even the middle of wisdom. Shouldn't Abraham have been further along this path?

16. Abraham told his servants to stay with the animals while "I and the boy" go to "worship."[34] I will echo here a question from W. Dow Edgerton: "Why 'worship' instead of 'sacrifice'? The word seems so

cruel in its choice. To obey is one thing. To obey through clenched teeth is one thing. To sacrifice your son is one thing. But worship, that is another thing. The word becomes horrible in a way 'sacrifice' does not."[35]

17. Isaac was of an age when he knew what was happening to him (he was strong enough to carry wood up a mountain). Why did Abraham make his son carry his own funeral pyre? Was this like Jesus's carrying his own cross?

18. How does Abraham's willingness to slaughter his son qualify him to be the founder of the faith? Why would such a thing as this be the litmus test?

19. Does God expect followers to commit immoral acts when commanded to do so by divine voices or holy prophets?

20. If God sometimes asks us to suspend moral judgments, how do we distinguish the true voice of God from counterfeit voices such as the one that spoke to Cristos Valenti, who took his trusting daughter to a park and killed her, or those that speak to Palestinian teenagers to convince them to strap bombs to their chests and blow up buses?

These questions and many more have struck blows on my soul my entire life. At times they have brought me to the brink of despair, and in my late teens they were partly responsible for my deconversion from Christianity. It's entirely possible for one question to cause a person to break down or bolt. The Abraham-and-Isaac story is the founding story of our faith, so why does it have to be so inscrutable? I can't answer that question. But I invite you to join me in an exploration—a journey that has delivered me to a place where I now claim something deceptively simple and blindingly obvious, but spiritually revolutionary. At the outset, the analysis that follows might seem unorthodox, but stay with it through to the end and see if it delivers grace into your life. In my life, it had the power to restore me to orthodox faith.

THE STARTING POINT

Any search for truth has a starting point, both a point in time and an identifiable assumption. In this instance, we'll begin with a premise about truth itself. That premise is that truth and God do not exist independently of each other. Closely following is a related premise: Truth is found in relationship. Since God is a personal God and since God and Truth are one and the same thing, it follows that truth exists in relationship. Conversely, there is no truth that is freestanding, existing in isolation and independent of relationship.

Said another way: The only good life is a GodLife relationship. The essence of our humanity is not our free will nor our rationality. The essence of our humanity is our capacity to be in a relationship with God. That is truth.

Such assertions seem commonsense, especially for Christians, who believe in absolutes when it comes to truth. Of course, there is an inseparable linkage between God and truth. However, the need to pursue truth in relationship is not as self-evident. It takes us much deeper.

As I wrestled with the Abraham-and-Isaac story until it brought me back to true faith, I saw that the test God gave to Abraham might have two parts. The first part, the Obedience Test, posed "objective" questions such as "Will you obey me no matter what?" and "Do you fear me?" Abraham passed the Obedience Test, the true-false portion of the exam, with the highest grade possible.

But what if this test had a second part, as I believe to be true? What if Abraham needed to excel also in the "essay section," which we'll call the Relationship Test. What grade did Abraham get on his essay, which is the more subjective portion of the test?

I propose this thesis about a two-part exam because the story of the people of Israel actually begins in Genesis 12, when God called Abraham to leave Haran. This was long before the story of God's asking Abraham to sacrifice his son.[36] And when you approach the Abraham-and-Isaac story from the start of God's dealings with Abraham, not at the climax, and attend to the context of the entire narrative through Genesis 25, this theme pops out: The story of Abraham is the story of the divine and the human engaging in so strong a relationship that it leads to a covenant. Read that again. This divine-human relationship leads to a covenant. It's startling in its simple force and in its jaw-dropping significance.

Abraham did not go through a process of growing stronger in his beliefs about God. Instead, he grew in a *relationship* with God. Between chapters 12 and 22, God and Abraham speak together as you or I would speak to each other and to our closest friends. God and Abraham watch the stars together, argue together, laugh together, rage together, mourn together. There was no precedent for this in the ancient world. Humans simply did not have a relationship with a god. In the world of ancient Israel, one lived in fear and terror of the gods.[37]

God enjoyed this relationship with Abraham so immensely, and there was such mutual trust between them, that God decided to establish an unprecedented covenant with ninety-year-old Abraham. And this was no small matter. In Genesis 17, Abraham engages in some fairly significant body modification to enter the covenant.

This was not the first covenant God made in human history.[38] In the earlier covenant with Noah, God revealed patterns for relationships, including a specific directive against the taking of another human's life.[39] But the covenant with Abraham was different. Within the relationship of this covenant, God revealed things about God's own character and being. God revealed God's own being as *tzedakah* (righteousness, justice).[40]

That revelation, along with the covenant itself, emboldened Abraham to get in a bidding war with God when God told Abraham straight out what God was planning to do to Sodom and Gomorrah. Abraham negotiated with God, talking God into withholding judgment if a mere fifty, or even forty-five, or even forty or thirty or twenty righteous men could be found. Abraham was such a savvy and bold negotiator, in fact, that he bargained God all the way down to just ten righteous men. If that handful of men could be found, God agreed to relent. One law professor calls this "the first instance in religious history of a human being challenging God to be just."[41]

It's amazing that the relationship was so important to God that the Maker of All That Is bothered to engage in such dialogue. It's even more astounding that God revised, and revised again, God's plan based on Abraham's appeals.

Adam and Eve were the first to experience God's desire for closeness with his creatures. "Where *are* you?" God the Seeker said to a hiding Adam and Eve. The very familiar pronouns Adam and Eve used to address God are startling, given the Jewish tradition's refusal to write or speak the name of God. Of course, the taste of forbidden fruit put distance between the Creator and the created. But God's original design was for intimacy of relationship, and the Abraham story reveals the lengths to which God goes to bridge the chasm created by humankind's preference for sin and death.

So as Abraham took the second part of the biggest test, what kind of essay should he have written to complete the exam? He had already passed the Obedience Test. But when God said, "Sacrifice your son," how should Abraham have answered to pass the Relationship Test? If we were as close to God as Abraham was and God gave us such an instruction, how should we answer?

The True Test of Relationship

God Settles for Nothing Less Than Full Engagement

CHAPTER FOUR

> Abraham is subject, Isaac is object; Abraham takes, Isaac is
> taken.... The wood is laid upon Isaac as Isaac will soon be
> laid upon the wood. The father takes in hand, not the son,
> but the fire and knife.... Here they are subjects together.
> The victim trusts his executioner, the sacrifice carries his
> pyre, the son obeys the father as the father obeys God. The
> dramatic ironies are vivid enough upon the page.
>
> —W. Dow Edgerton[1]

Both Nobel laureate Elie Wiesel and philosopher Immanuel Kant offered widely studied takes on the Abraham-and-Isaac story, and both ignored the intent of the text. Holocaust-as-*Akedah* theologian Wiesel argues that God was wrong for asking, and that Abraham was wrong for agreeing.[2] Meanwhile, Kant thought Abraham should have cried out in outrage to this "supposedly divine voice" that commanded the "butchering and burning" of his son: "That I ought not to kill my good son is quite certain. But that you, this apparition, are God—of that I am not certain, and never can be, not even if this voice rings down to me from (visible) heaven."[3]

For Kant, the Abraham-and-Isaac story proved the need to get beyond the Bible. Abraham failed his final trial by failing to discern the true voice of God. Kant wasn't suggesting that there is a misreading of the text. Rather, that the text is rightly read, Abraham is being lauded for his "faith," but this only proves to any sensible person that "biblical theology" needs to be replaced by a "rational theology" and a purely "moral religion." Ironically, the story from Scripture that is traditionally held up as the premier story of faith in God is thus cited as the foundational text for arguing *against* God and against biblical faith.

Søren Kierkegaard defended Abraham against Kant's critique in his classic *Fear and Trembling,* perhaps the most famous treatise ever written on the

Abraham-and-Isaac story.[4] Kierkegaard's confessional reading of the story led him to propose "faith" as a category of defense. Abraham's "faith" trusted in God's promise that through Isaac a great nation would emerge.[5] But it was this "faith" defense that led Kierkegaard to his radical relativization of ethics, in which the individual's faith transcends all ethical categories and actions.[6]

The concept of "the ethical" as a universal set of moral laws was not part of the intellectual world of ancient Israel, much less pre-Israel. At that time, moral decision making was relationship based more than rule based. Abraham could not "transcend" the "ethical" when all he knew were personal directives and relational imperatives from the divine.[7] To be in a relationship with God meant not subscription to universal principles or rules but living in a state of "commandedness" (the real meaning of *mitzvah*).[8]

So what does this say about the choices and actions of a man who, whether faith based or fear driven, is tested on his willingness to commit one of the most hideous, heinous crimes imaginable?[9]

A HIDDEN SCHOOL OF INTERPRETATION

Although not widely known in the Christian tradition, a long line of Jewish interpretation and rabbinic tradition argues for alternative readings of the story that are faithful to both text and tradition. Some explanations make a case for Abraham's never intending to kill Isaac. In others, Abraham is fiercely criticized on a variety of counts. But there is a third line of midrashic interpretation that argues that God never wanted Abraham to kill Isaac and was hoping that Abraham would argue with God and ultimately refuse to carry out the directive.[10]

It is this third strand of interpretation that rings most true to what we know of the relationship between God and Abraham. A plain reading of the text does not celebrate Abraham's willingness to sacrifice his son as being the ultimate test of faith.

Remember, this was a two-part test. Abraham passed the Obedience Test, the objective portion of the exam: He was clearly willing to obey God even though the command violated everything he knew about God. So the correct answer to "are you willing to obey me?" was a resounding "yes!"

But in the essay portion of the test, God expected Abraham to engage with the One giving the command, to grapple with what it really meant when God issued the command, and to plead the case for Isaac. This is the Relationship Test, and the biblical account provides at least three textual reasons for accepting the validity of such an essay component to the test. First, in Genesis 22 we see the first appearance in the Bible of the word *love*. "Take your son, your only son Isaac, whom you *love*, and go to the land of Moriah, and offer him there as a burnt offering."[11] The context and the word choice resonate with John 3:16: "God so loved the world, that [God] gave [God's] one and only Son."

The second textual reason for seeing this as a Relationship Test is the Hebrew word for "tried" or "tested." The word *nisayon* is less related to "tempt" or "prove" than it is to "to give experience" in the sense that "God gave Abraham experience through this trial."[12] In other words, the purpose of the test was less to ferret out information than to "exercise" and "train" Abraham in the ways of truth and goodness.[13] The word for "test" is more a relationship word than a juridical word.

God had bragged earlier about his friend Abraham's "keeping the ways of the Lord" and "doing righteousness and justice." Now it's time for a stress test of Abraham's heart muscles "in order that the LORD may bring upon Abraham what he has spoken about him."[14]

A third textual reason for considering an essay portion to the test is God's instruction to *"Lech-Lekha"* or "Get up and go." These were the divine words that began their relationship, when a childless Abram was told, "Go forth" *("Lech-Lekha")*—to leave Haran with his wife, Sarai, his orphaned nephew Lot, some family possessions, and others who felt the calling to "go" with him.[15]

These are now the same words that "test" their relationship in Genesis 22:2: *"Lech-Lekha* (Get going/Go forth)." Up until now the story has been about God's relationship with Abraham. We are now going to learn about Abraham's relationship with God. The double meaning of *Lekh-Lekha* implies that you go outward and inward simultaneously. Had Abraham's outward journey produced an inward maturation?[16] The Jewish-Christian tradition is an outward *and* an inward story.

A fourth reason for positing an objective-subjective exam is nontextual. Only in the light of a relationship essay test can we begin to understand the twenty questions posed in chapter 3. Such questions, which reach to the heart of Abraham's relationship with God, can be answered only with personal engagement, assessment, and grappling in the self-expression of an essay. True or false simply won't cover it.

To pass the Relationship Test, Abraham should have been what Jehoshaphat called him: God's friend.[17] He rightly should have trusted and honored God enough to take his son on that three-day, fifty-plus-mile hike to the mountain. But every step of the way, he also should have called on God to be faithful to God's own character. He should have wrestled with God. He should have looked up from the very start—not waiting until the third day—and hammered the door of heaven with his fists:

- *Lord, you've got to give me more than this…*
- *Lord, forget about all those descendants you talked about—I just want this one…*
- *Lord, this is what the Canaanite gods ask of their people. You're not like them; You're Yahweh!*
- *Lord, I'm not going to drive this knife into Isaac's neck until you talk to me; Lord…*
- *Lord, take my life as your sacrifice, not that of my beloved son…*
- *Lord, show me something that proves that the voice I heard telling me to do this wasn't Satan's voice…*
- *Lord, I know your voice; I know you. You and I are friends. This is not the same God of justice, righteousness, and compassion who covenanted with me…*

But that's not what happened. When God said to Abraham, "Kill your son," Abraham said dutifully, "Okay." His only question was, "Where?" Abraham had three days to think about it…and he still went ahead and prepared the sacrifice. No lifting up his eyes to engage God in sorely needed discourse. He simply lowered his eyes and remained silent.

The ancient Mediterranean world was awash in blood sacrifice. But Abraham should have known from his Enoch-like "walk with God" that God was unlike the other regional deities that required child sacrifice. By not wrestling with God over this directive, as he had done on other occasions, Abraham demonstrated a stubborn misunderstanding of God's nature. Indeed, Abraham, above all people, should have recognized immediately that this command was contrary to God's nature. So why didn't Abraham issue the challenge that God must explain why God was asking him to do this? To do so would have been bold, yes, but far less cheeky than his earlier negotiations with God over the nameless citizens of Sodom and Gomorrah.

These questions are important on a level much higher than technical matters of obedience to God's voice or philosophical questions of ethics versus morals. Abraham's silence in the face of an outrageous command from God signals a failure of relationship on his part. If you give up the struggle of discernment and hearing, you are not in a right relationship with God. If obedience does not take place in the context of a relationship, no matter how tumultuous the relationship, it is not true obedience. In fact, if obedience is rightly understood, it may be that Abraham didn't even do so well on the true-false part of the exam, the Obedience Test, either.

You can't truly obey until you first listen. True obedience emerges from relationship through "hearing." The etymological relatedness between *hear* (audio) and *obey* (action) reflects a deeper reality. *Hear* (Old English *heren,* akin to Greek *akouein* [acoustic]) means "to hear, to have the power of hearing." *Obey* (Latin *oboedio* [ob/audio]) means "to give ear to, to listen, to hearken."

In short, without "hearing" there is no "obeying." The first and last prayer of a pious Jew is "Hear, O Israel." The *Schema* reminds us that the struggle of hearing precedes the acts of obedience.[18] If we become what we hear, one wonders whether Abraham truly leaned his life into "hearing" God with the heart.

There is a world of difference between superficial obedience and substantive relationship, between obeying orders and doing the right thing. You can do the right thing in a strictly ethical or juridical sense and still be wrong. Following rules is not necessarily a moral act, just as breaking the rules is not necessarily an immoral act. Being obedient is not the same as being right or moral. Disobedience can be moral when the governing rules are immoral.[19] Sometimes obedience is an abdication of moral responsibility, as the German church discovered through the lessons of World War II. Without relationship there is no truth.

Here is the real point of the Abraham story: What God wants from

> Human history began with an act of disobedience, and it is not unlikely that it will be terminated by an act of obedience.
>
> —ERICH FROMM[20]

us, even more than our obedience, is our *relationship*. If obedience were all that mattered, God would not have created us in God's own image. God would have gone no further in creation than creating angels. God would not have bothered with us.

But when God created the universe, the only thing God said "no good" to was nonrelationship. It is for this one reason—dynamic relationship—that the human species was created. We were designed by God for God. God created us out of the love relationship of the divine, and Adam and Eve were the offspring of that love. God created Adam and Eve so that there could be a relationship on Earth between humans and God like that in the heavens among the Godhead itself. If heaven is defined as union with God, then eternity is a relationship Eden.

Sin is not primarily rebellion against God's laws or an assault on moral principles. Sin is an offense because it violates our relationship with God. Abraham carried out a very difficult assignment at God's request, so in a technical sense he was obedient. But God wants our obedience in the context of a relationship—which far exceeds unthinking obedience played out in a vacuum. God wants our hearts, our minds, our bodies, our souls. God wants fully engaged obedience, not reflexive obedience. God wants our love.

> In the beginning didn't God create Adam to love him?
>
> —CHARACTER
> IN THE MOVIE A.I.[21]

For the first year at West Point, it is tradition that you can only make four responses to an upperclassman: "Yes sir," "No sir," "I didn't understand the question, sir," and "No excuse, sir."

These kinds of exchanges may be good for military discipline, but they don't build a good relationship. Some people think these four responses make up the entire repertoire of our allowable exchanges with God.

Ever hear someone on a cell phone saying, "Uh-huh…uh-huh…uh-huh… uh-huh…"? One person is talking on the other end, and this guy is making unintelligible grunting noises in response. You wonder: *What kind of a conversation is that?* God created us for two-way conversations—for full-blown, no-holds-barred conversations. God wants us to be fully engaged in the exchange.

With our children, we want more than their "uh-huh" obedience. We conceived them for a reflective not just a reflexive relationship. Would you rather have a child who obeys everything you say but doesn't want a relationship with you? Or would you prefer a child who is rebellious and contentious but who has a deep and affectionate relationship with you? What makes your children *your* children? The fact that they obey you? Or the fact that you take pleasure in them, delight in being close to them, miss them when they aren't around?

THE ANSWER IN PARADOX

Christianity pivots on paradox. Truth is polyphonic. There are two sides to every story. Too much theology can be characterized as the lively shifting of weight from one foot to the other. It is time to land with both feet on the ground, with both sides of the paradox carrying equal weight.

God lives both apart from and in relationship with God's creation. The life of God exists apart from the world God created. But the creative energies of the Godhead created a world in which God chose companionship over control, offering us free will over foreknowledge and offering up the very being of God to restore darkened humanity to the right light.

There is no happy medium in orthodox Christianity. Truth plays both ends against the middle. The definitive contribution of orthodox Christianity to an understanding of reality is both the world's contingent existence upon a transcendent creative agent and the voluntary self-limitations of interactivity and immanence between the infinite with the finite. Only the way of the Cross, the cruciform life that brings together our loose ends—the vertical and the horizontal, otherness and openness—leads home.

Apart from me, you can do...*nothing*.

With me, you can do...*anything*.

God is a relational God not just starting with Jesus, but starting with Adam and Eve, Abraham and Sarah, even Jacob. There is nothing more face-to-face, body-to-body than wrestling. Jacob's wrestling match symbolized a relationship with the divine tough enough for hand-to-hand combat and tender enough for holding each person in God's loving arms. When Jacob wrestled with God and refused to let go, his name was turned to Israel, which means "one who wrestles with God." God honored Jacob's impertinence by using a word to name God's chosen people that identifies them as the ones who importuned, interacted with, or "wrestled with God."[22]

Indeed, the final test of a prophet seems to have been whether he had the courage to argue with God.[23] In the midrash traditions, Moses three times argued with God. All three times his objections not only altered God's plans but even elicited God's praise. On one occasion, when Yahweh pledged to "visit the iniquity of the fathers upon the children," in the midrash Moses rose to protest God's words and was rewarded with a reversal.[24] On another occasion, Moses changed God's mind about making war with Sihon.[25]

The most famous instance of Moses's interceding for Israel, however, was in the golden-calf episode. In fact, God was so angry with the dancing Israelites circling the golden idol that God fended off his friend Moses with these words, "Don't start on me." Or in the exact language of the Hebrew, "Let Me alone that My wrath may wax hot against them."[26]

In his wonderful book *Jesus Asked,* biblical scholar Conrad Gempf contends:

> The God of the Jews and Christians is unlike any other god. Dispute with Jupiter and you'll have one of those yellow-painted wooden lightning bolts shoved down your throat. Talking back to Allah is likely to get you into even more trouble than talking back to my sixth-grade teacher, Mr. Davidovitch. Try arguing with Buddha and he'll laugh at you derisively for treating any conversation as if it referred to something real. But when you start arguing with Yahweh, he smiles, rolls up his anthropocentric sleeves, and starts to look interested. The strangest thing is that he likes losing the arguments even more than he likes winning them. Jacob, the trickster, is beloved of God. And Abraham didn't just get away with asking, "What about if there are only twenty righteous men in the city?" The God of the Jews and Christians is the only God that allows his followers to hear him say, "Oh, all right, you win."[27]

What does this bring to mind if not good friends who get together for dinner and engage in a spirited and compelling discussion of their differences? One wins over the other, and they part better friends than before. In other words, a "relationship."

Abraham engaged in such a relationship with God when he argued for mercy on the children of strangers living in Sodom. In fact, in going toe-to-toe with God over judgment on the two cities, Abraham prophesied the naming of Israel as "one who wrestles" and muscled out of God a change of mind. But when it came to his own son, why the uncharacteristic silence?

WORKING THE PUZZLE

Here is the question we must answer to solve the puzzle: Why did Abraham not struggle with God about his beloved son? Why was he so willing to barter with God over strangers in Sodom and Gomorrah and yet was so willing to sacrifice his own son? Abraham had the courage and confidence to demand that God act like the God Abraham knew and loved rather than unleash the wholesale slaughter of innocent children.

"Hashofet kil ha'arez lo ya'asseh mishpat?" ("Will the Ruler of the universe not do justice?")[28]

Abraham was happy to go to the mat with God as he interceded for strangers, but he would lay down his son's life with nary a murmur of protest. Why the disparity? It has to do with human relationships—in particular, the relationships between parents and their children.

I received this uncomfortable answer from one of my own kids. When my only daughter Soren was six, she wrote me her first short story as a present for Father's Day. She entitled it: "The Frog That Had No Firends" (sic).

Ouns a pona tim thar wus a frog that had no firends So it ascd his
Mom and dad if tha cud play with Him But his parins had to work.
So he wint to find firends but he can't find frogs that wntid to be his
firend but he foud one... I wont to be his firend. The End.

And now, translated into English from "Sorenese":

Once upon a time there was a frog that had no friends. So it asked his
Mom and Dad if they could play with him. But his parents had to
work. So he went to find friends but he couldn't find frogs that wanted
to be his friend. But he found one: "I want to be his friend." The End.

Having received such a Father's Day present, who am I to condemn Abraham? Aren't we still practicing child sacrifice in the twenty-first century? And who are the first to sacrifice their kids? Religious leaders rank near the top of the list. An elementary school kid was caught throwing rocks at a church building. When the police summoned the boy's father, the church's pastor, to pick him up at the station, the sergeant read back the boy's confession. He was upset because "the church keeps taking his daddy away." The whole PK syndrome is basically another name for rebellion against a parent's neglect, as pastors give themselves to a congregation or to a cause at the expense of their children and their families. Like Abraham, clergy can get too attached to the calling God places on their lives and idolize their ministries.

We go out of our way to help those in need and forget about those at our feet. The Bible says we are to present *ourselves* as "living sacrifices," not that we are to offer our children and families as human sacrifices.[29] Who am I to condemn Abraham? How often did my own little frog need a friend just when I "had to work"?

Child sacrifice was a pattern in Abraham's life. He had already sent Ishmael and his mother, Hagar, into the desert with virtually no provisions, almost a certain death sentence.[30] Noting that even in his argument with God over the future of Sodom, Abraham said nothing about his nephew Lot, essayist Karen Armstrong wrote: "Abraham could act with exemplary charity toward total strangers, but he could be murderously cruel toward his own family, particularly his children."[31]

Abraham wasn't the only one. Aaron, Eli, and Samuel were great leaders who did great things for their people. But all three had kids who turned out rotten and whom God punished severely. Or how would you like to have been Hosea's daughter, who was named "Not Loved" (*Loruhamah*) by her father? Or what would it have been like to be Isaiah's son and be named by your father "Bad Times Are Coming" (*Mahershalalhashbaz*). But the treatment Isaac received from his father was of an entirely different order.

By the way, religious professionals are not the only ones who practice child sacrifice. Others of us sacrifice our families and loved ones, even our own lives, at various altars: material gain, social comfort, success, fame, crusades, intifada.

What are many *madrassas* (Islamic religious schools[32]) but training centers for child sacrifice, places where *jihadist* suicide is lifted up before five-, six-, and seven-year-olds as the highest and noblest aim in life? When the front lines of battle become suicide bombers or stone-throwing children used as shields by gunmen, the connections between child sacrifice, suicide, and mass murder are pretty explicit. Like everything else, the policy of child sacrifice has even achieved monetary value. "Martyrs" and their families are paid $300 for a mere injury, $2,500 for a coveted death, with a "bonus" $10,000 supplied initially by Saddam Hussein, now by a shadowy host of despots.[33]

MORALISM VERSUS RELATIONSHIP

Biblical faith is not about living a moral life. That's religion. Biblical faith is not about living the "good life." That's capitalism. Biblical faith is about living the GodLife. An abundant life with the living God is living in a GodLife relationship.

Obedience, in the biblical sense, is not "doing what you are told." Obedience is living relationally, even "indivisibly," with the Holy One so that we honor, uphold, receive, and follow all that God is and all that God is calling us to become.[34] Biblical obedience means living in the light of who God is as much as in submission to what God says. That's obedience in relationship.

To speak the truth about God, you must know God. And to know God you must love God. And to love God you must be in a relationship with God. Christians are relational fundamentalists: We put the primary relationship at the beginning, making it the foundation of all else we do and say. The primary relationship of life is a relationship with the one true and holy God. Everything else follows.

Faith in God is less "do I believe this or that about God?" than "can I accept that God loves me and chooses me?" Faith is not a discovery of something higher than I, but being discovered by a power higher than I and being caught up in that higher-power relationship. The truth of Christianity defies argument because it defines argument in nonphilosophical terms. The truth of Christianity is not a metaphysics of reason (which requires statements) but a metaphysics of relationship (which requires embodiment).

Many documentary films have been made about Mother Teresa of Calcutta. In one, an interviewer for the BBC went on a walkabout with Mother Teresa through homes for abandoned babies, children, orphans, and the dying.

At a certain point Mother Teresa stopped and became the interviewer: "Why are you asking me all about my work, and asking me nothing about my Employer?"

The history of the church in the twenty-first century will be an extended job search leading to employment by the divine Employer. The fullness of human identity is found only in relationship with God. It's not your happiness that matters. It's the fulfillment of your gift of life from God that matters.

> The path toward holiness is not revealed in rules but in God.
>
> —ORTHODOX LAY THEOLOGIAN PAUL EVDOKIMOV[35]

I was recently reminded of the story of a German bishop who stood up to Hitler and the Nazi regime. It's natural to ask, "What was the source of the great power in that bishop's life?" The answer comes out of the bishop's own book. "I sometimes told my confirmands that they must retain at least three words of the instructions. If they forgot everything else, those three words they must remember. At every opportunity I would say to them, over and over, 'God is present.'"[36]

The power of living is incarnational and relational. God is present with us, which means that holiness itself is relational. Holiness doesn't lead to the dogged mastery of rules, principles, or practices, but to a dynamic, life-giving communion with God. Seek holiness and you seek a relationship with the God who accomplishes holiness in you.

But be forewarned. Be careful about "wanting" a relationship with God. C. S. Lewis somewhere compared it to a child's playing hide-and-seek in the attic. You hide. It's dark. Then, suddenly, you hear or sense a movement, just inches from you. You scream and jump.

Similarly, it's like going fishing for the first time. You cast your line into the water, then wait. Suddenly, out of nowhere, you feel a tug on the line. It's alive! There is a sudden jolt revealing that what you had been playfully pursuing was seriously seeking you all the while.

Maybe it is less true that we find truths than that Truth finds us. Maybe we don't have to find God—especially if God is always making the first move. Maybe God is seeking us before we seek God.

God is present, and God is relational. This means that truth is relational, found in the give-and-take of honest engagement with God. Faith and obedience are not reflex actions, or blind and mindless conformity to rules and regulations. Faith and obedience are instead played out in a life in full pursuit of God, knowing that at the same time we are being fully pursued by God. Faith and obedience are found in listening to God, questioning God, being challenged by God, and challenging God.

That's the truth of relationship and the truth found only in relationship. It's the truth that Abraham missed when he chose not to challenge God in the matter of sacrificing Isaac. Abraham's relationship with the Holy One ruled out a God who required child sacrifice. Yet Abraham failed to "take God on" to clarify the confounding order. Abraham willingly took his life in his hands by standing up to God and negotiating over the judgment placed on Sodom and Gomorrah,[37] yet he was unwilling to ask even one question that might have spared his son's life. Abraham heard God's word and then turned away from his community to carry out the call to kill Isaac. Just as Abraham did not enter into relationship with God to discuss the nature of the calling, so too Abraham left his community to blindly march to the orders he had received. It was a double failure of relationship—Abraham to God and Abraham to community.[38]

Abraham's great gift was his willingness to obey no matter the cost. Abraham's great blind spot was his inability and unwillingness to engage with God when it mattered most. This great man, this father of a nation, this hero of the faith, missed the truth of God that is found only in relationship.

Lest we miss out on the same thing, we will explore the delicious, inviting, restorative relationship of truth in the chapters that follow. As God self-reveals in Scripture, God lays out a lavish banquet and invites us to pull up a chair. This is table fellowship, the most intimate of nonmarital relationships from biblical times.

So prepare to gorge on the feast of truth—the banquet of the GodLife relationship. Taste and see that the Lord is good, very good.

PART III

OUR RELATIONSHIP
WITH GOD'S STORY

The Truth in Text

Faith and God's Written Revelation

> The only two things that can satisfy the soul are a person
> and a story; and even a story must be about a person.
> —G. K. Chesterton[1]

T he gift of life is to know the truth, and not just intellectually, but to experience its power and impact. At least Jesus thought so.[2]

With life's GPS set on the knowledge of truth, it follows that how we define truth will direct the journey of our lives. Does the category of "truth" fit best in an intellectual classification, such as a proposition (if A, then B)? Or does the category of truth belong more appropriately to a perceptual entity, such as a judgment (knowing the difference between good and evil)? Or as we read Scripture's description of truth, does it rightly belong to a social entity, such as a relationship ("The Word became flesh and made his dwelling among us"[3])?

WHAT'S THE TRUTH?

Our reading of the Abraham-and-Isaac story suggests that God wanted Abraham to act both dutifully and truthfully. Abraham fulfilled half of this mission. He was dutiful to a fault, but he was not truthful. We know this because truthfulness in the biblical sense requires relationship. Abraham failed the test because he missed the relationship.

But even if we look at truth apart from the biblical drama of the Akedah, we see from a purely historical and philosophical perspective that truth means relationship. Saying to someone a millennium or two ago, "I believe in God," meant more than, "I intellectually concur with some widely accepted views on God's existence, character, and activities." The root meaning of the Greek word for truth is "the unforgotten." To become part of a story that is "unforgettable," a story so transcendent that it structures every aspect of your life, is to "believe in God." In Old English, words like *bilefe* and *bileve* designated investment, embrace, allegiance, love, putting your life on the line.[4] Not until the fourteenth century (at the earliest) was the idea of truth removed from relationship so that it could be embedded in propositions and doctrinal positions.[5]

Following propositional truth bears the same relationship to following Jesus as the recorded soundtrack to the movie *Amadeus* bears to a live performance of the best orchestra performing the music of Mozart and conducted by the composer himself.

> When one reads the Gospels rapidly, one after the other, again and again, one cannot but be struck by the towering figure of Jesus. Though they reflect the church's convictions, the Gospels are not about the church's convictions: They are about Jesus Christ. His excellence, his uniqueness, his authority, his compassion, his love, his wisdom, his holiness—all shine through passage after passage.
>
> —THEOLOGIAN D. A. CARSON[6]

The truth of God is closer to a marriage than it is to a wedding announcement. The announcement contains in clear words the facts surrounding the names of the couple, the date of their wedding, and their intentions to join their lives together. There is no disputing the facts. But that's not truth as God embodies truth. God's truth is a marriage, not a wedding announcement. When two people marry, they aren't saying yes to vows (objective statements of intention) so much as they are saying yes to each other (a relationship). Some of the wedding ceremonies I remember attending as a child still used the ancient language of the liturgy: "I plight thee my troth." This charming phrase means "I covenant with you my truth," although it has been reduced to the less strenuous and less poetic "I give you my love."

Truth, which once resided in relationships (covenants between people) has shifted to truth grounded in documents and scientific proof. With the spread of a literate print culture (following Gutenberg's invention of movable type) and changes in governmental authority, people began to think of truth much differently. By the time of the Renaissance, the new scientific sense of truth as something independently verifiable was well established. The effect this shift had on the earlier view of truth was profound. Now truth was thought of as doctrine, as a system of belief, and as propositions that exist apart from those who incarnate truth. This spelled a profound social and religious change, a clear departure from the initial practice of the Christian faith.

Until a few centuries ago, "truth" had no independent status outside of relationships with and obligations to God and to others. When read in this light, the following biblical admonitions have a very different ring to them.

"I am the way, and the truth, and the life."[7]

"You will know the truth, and the truth will make you free."[8]

The wedding liturgy's plight-thee-my-troth language beckons us back to a biblical drama where Absolute Truth was embodied not in an abstract but in a Person. For Christianity, the bracing realm of absolutes is an embrace by the very image and incarnation of God. God kept hidden a "mystery" for ages. When the time was ripe, God revealed the mystery to the world.[9]

That mystery of the ages is not a philosophy or a worldview. It's not a creed or confession or statement of faith. The mystery of the ages is that Truth is a Person, the Person of Jesus Christ, who seeks us out for such intimacy of relationship that it can be said of us—"Christ in you, the hope of glory."[10] God's "secret plan" is not some puzzle or treasure map but a Person.[11] We seek solutions in magic pills shaped like a host, or in principles or propositions that we can check off the list as we become aware of them and decide we agree with them. But Jesus is not a checklist; he is the Curriculum Vitae of Christianity. He is the object and the end of written creeds and confessions, cyboriums and axioms. They all exist to point us to the Person of Christ, not to themselves. When we "affirm" our faith, the words we say aren't what we are affirming. Our words are affirming Jesus the Christ, our crucified, risen, and ascended Lord. The wisdom of God is not truth explained but Truth embodied. Jesus can't be nailed down. Nail him to wooden dogmas and locked-tight, shrink-wrapped doctrines, and the Holy Spirit pulls a Harry Houdini: Jesus breaks free every time.

THE WHOLE TRUTH

One of the most quoted philosophers in North America, Richard Rorty, once dismissed the concept of "truth" with a curt kiss-off: "Truth is what your peers let you get away with."[12] In a world where the tissue of philosophical truth is so thin, where truth is a "drug" (the "truth drug"), Christianity offers the thick skin and warm flesh of incarnational truth. There is something truer than truth: *Jesus!*

Jesus is the Whole Truth. If Truth resides in GodLife relationships, not documents or principles, the Whole Truth resides in a Person. The gospels don't teach us about Jesus as principle, but Jesus as Person. Christianity is much more than a worldview. Christianity is a GodLife relationship. It is more than the fact that in Jesus I get the best and truest look at who God is. In Jesus I get the best and truest *experience* of God. It is not a distant, objective, delineated look. It's a bone-deep, blood-red experience.

> The son of God became the Son of man, that man…might become the son of God.
>
> —IRENAEUS[13]

The essence of salvation is not so much a saving faith in Jesus Christ as it is an embodied relationship with Jesus Christ. The words *the Word became flesh* remain at the centerpiece of Christian faith no matter how much our culture chooses to rely on technological and scientific precision. *Logos* literally means "that which enables you to be in relationship with another." We have translated *logos* using the English words *reason* or *word.* But the relationship word *logos* means so much more than what *reason* or *word* convey today.

The power of a logo is that it transmutes image into identity, creating in one's mind the very thing it symbolizes. In Jesus, the *Logos* and logo became one. In the Eastern Orthodox tradition, in which the Incarnation reigns as the core relationship of existence, the salvation of *theosis* (divinization) means that without becoming God, we do become participants in the divine life and communion of the Triune God. Our relationship with Christ enables us to participate in the exchange of love between the members of the Trinity.

A WHOLE NEW CATEGORY OF TRUTH

On 3 July 2002, Christianity lost one of its most unusual and unheralded voices. Michel Henry was widely celebrated among philosophers in Europe and Japan, but remained virtually unknown in North America. Henry was professor at the Paul-Valéry University at Montpellier, Canada, but taught as a guest professor at places including the École Normale Supérieure and the

Sorbonnes, the Catholic University of Louvain, and the University of Tokyo. His academic writings on phenomenology led him after 1992 to a view of Christianity that he summed up in the title of a posthumously published English translation: *I Am the Truth*.

The "extraordinary originality of Christianity," Henry insisted, lies in its very conception of truth. In fact, the Christian understanding of truth is of such "radical foreignness," differing from all other kinds of truth and violating "everything that common sense, philosophy, and science, call (and continue to call) 'truth,'"[14] that Henry proposed that Christianity invented a whole new category of truth.

What kind of truth does Christianity offer the world? A form of truth that Henry believed "has the power to reduce the two others [truth in language and philosophy] to insignificance."[15] In a word, the truth of Christianity is life, and the "whole life" is Jesus: "In Him was Life." Or in Jesus's own words, "I have come that you might have Whole Life."[16] Against scientism, against pragmatism, against positivism, against any and all other "isms," Christianity says this: Jesus is The Life. Thus, truth is a lived relationship, not a set of rules for living or a list of views about the divine. Truth is not certainty, nor is it doubt—both of which reject Christ. Instead, it is mystery. When we choose life, to look outside of ourselves, we are left with the mystery of choosing Christ. And in choosing Christ we choose that which is Real but unprovable, that which is Truth but far more than objective fact. Jesus doesn't offer us the key to living. Jesus *is* the key to living. "For to me, to live is Christ," Paul said.[17] This is an inclusive statement: To love is Christ; to pray is Christ; to obey is Christ; and to die is Christ.

The essential content of Christianity is Christ, who dares name himself the Way, the Truth, and the Life.[18] Jesus is the singularity that altered humanity's relationship with God. God's name, Yahweh, was no longer something that could not be spoken. God's name was now proclaimed to the ends of the earth, and the name was Jesus.[19] In the black church tradition, the question is not "Are you saved?" but "Do you know the Man?"

The nature of our relationship with Christ is the prime indicator and index of our Christianity. In fact, Christianity took this notion that truth is relationship to the max.[20] "God sent forth his Son," the Bible says. "Unto us a son is given."[21] It does not say: "Unto us a law is laid down" or "Unto us these teachings are handed down" or "Unto us a statement of faith is delivered." The peace of God, the peace that passes all understanding, is this: a baby swaddled in a manger. Our joy, a joy unspeakable and full of glory, is this: a laid down and living Lord.

> If someone proved to me that Christ were outside the truth and it really were that the truth lay outside Christ, I would prefer to remain with Christ than with the truth.
>
> —DOSTOYEVSKY'S FAMOUS CONFESSION OF THE 1850s[22]

Is Christ a noun or a verb in your life? If he's a noun, you may be capable of intellectually comprehending that the Lord is good. But only if he is a *both* a noun and a verb are you able to "taste and see that the Lord is good."[23] A verb means Jesus is alive and active in the flesh. He is an experience and an embrace. Paul's very personal metaphor of Christ's "circumcision of the heart" promises a life where God's truth is chiseled on a heart more than with ink on a page or chalk on a blackboard.[24]

Shakespeare's plays were not written to be studied, but to be acted. The reason why we read the Bible is not simply to study the text or to understand the words on the pages. The reason why we read the Bible is to live, understand life, and know Jesus. "I decided to know nothing among you except Jesus Christ, and him crucified," Paul said.[25] In coming to know Jesus, we come to know ourselves and others, as well as God. Jesus himself warned us not to confuse knowledge of the Scriptures with knowledge of God. In belittling the Pharisees' vaunted scholarship, he said, "You search the scriptures because you think that in them you have eternal life; and it is they that testify on my behalf. Yet you refuse to come to me to have life."[26]

The text is not the absolute. The text can only point to the Absolute. Readings of the Scriptures within different Christian communities will reveal different meanings. There is not just one reading of the text that exists for all time. For example, Paul's Romans sermon is different if it's being exegeted in Galatia as opposed to Guatemala, in Tarsus as opposed to Tokyo. The only "once for all" is Jesus.

For many years I found Matthew 7:22 utterly incomprehensible: "Many will say to me on that day, 'Lord, Lord, did we not…in your name…perform many miracles?'" Or, as the NRSV reads: "Many will say to me, 'Lord, Lord, did we not prophesy in your name, and cast out demons in your name, and do many deeds of power in your name?'" Here you have people confessing Jesus and calling him rightly "Lord." Here you also have leaders who are successful in their ministries and doing great things for God. Not just a few people, and not just a sporadic good deed. But "many" people doing "many" incredible miracles in Jesus's name.

But Jesus doesn't praise them or bless them or even thank then. He *rejects* them. He doesn't criticize what they did. But he does say "I never knew you. Away from me, you evildoers!"[27] Why were they ushered out of his presence? Because they didn't "know" him. Because they weren't in a relationship with him. Because they possessed the right principles, but they weren't possessed by the Truth. They chose the cushy world of cardboard maxims and creedal diagrams in place of the terrifying world of revealed mysteries and unpredictable relationships. This is why Jesus says: "Unless your righteousness surpasses that of the Pharisees and the teachers of the law, you will certainly not enter the kingdom."[28] A technical, dutiful, obedient righteousness is not enough. Jesus wants his disciples to engage him in a *relational* righteousness.

"Want to learn how to live?" asks Quan Yin. "Follow the feminine."

"Want to learn how to live," asks Krishna. "Follow the Lotus and chant the Gita."

"Want to learn how to live?" ask New Agers. "Follow your bliss."

"Want to learn how to live?" asks Buddha. "Follow mindfulness."

"Want to learn how to live?" asks Prophet Muhammad. "Pray five times a day and follow the Qur'an."

"Want to learn how to live?" asks Moses. "Follow the Torah."

"Want to learn how to live?" asks Chief Seattle. "Follow nature."

"Want to learn how to live?" asks Aristotle. "Follow my teachings."

"Want to learn how to live?" asks Confucius. "Follow my koans."

"Want to learn how to live?" asks Jesus. "Follow me."

NOTHING BUT THE TRUTH

If the life of faith is a consuming relationship with the Truth—the Whole Truth and Nothing but the Truth—then we need to acknowledge that Truth is always a two-edged sword. It has a double front.

As we face toward the Whole Truth, we see that its front is Jesus. But then there is another front. As we face toward Nothing but the Truth, its front is the Scriptures. It is impossible to have a true relationship with God without having a relationship with God's Word. We can't know God without the Scriptures. Ignorance of the Scriptures is an ignorance of Christ. But we can't truly know the Scriptures unless we know God. "We are the people of the Book and the Person," Chuck Smith jr., has written beautifully, "because Jesus and His Word are so interrelated there is no way to separate them. Without the Bible, we have no Jesus, but to follow the arrow of Scripture is to arrive at Jesus."[29]

There is no way to God's Story that does not involve the Bible, but the text is not the Truth. Black spots on white paper are not Beethoven's *Sonata Pathetique*. It's not until the ink marks are put into practice and performed, when life and sound are added, that the score takes on life and transports those who hear it.

The Bible is the score of a Creator who continues to speak to the church and point us to the Conductor in generative and life-giving ways. It's quite possible to know the Scriptures and not know the Truth. Knowing God and knowing the Scriptures are not the same thing. As Jesus himself put it, "You diligently study the Scriptures because you think that by them you possess eternal life. These are the Scriptures that testify about me, yet you refuse to come to me to have life."[30] Some people think we'll have Bible studies in heaven, but they're wrong. Heaven is the presence of God. We will no longer need the written description.

Do we believe in a book or a person?

—ROBERT E. WEBBER[31]

The Bible is like Prego's "100% Natural" pasta sauce. At least that's what the commercial suggests.[32] A guy walks into the kitchen and finds his wife pouring a can of Prego tomato sauce into a kettle. He says, "My mother made her tomato sauce from scratch."

In real life, one of two things would happen at this point. The wife would either say, "Then go to your mother's and eat *her* sauce." Or the guy would be wearing the sauce.

But in the commercial, the wife looks at her husband and demands, "And what are the ingredients in your mother's sauce?"

He begins to click off the secrets to his mother's sauce.

"Fresh vine-ripened tomatoes."

She reads the label: "In there."

"Oregano."

Again, reading the label: "In there."

"Onions."

"In there."

"Basil."

"In there."

"Garlic."

"In there."

"Parsley."

"In there."

"Salt."

"In there."

The same is true of God's Word. Everything we need to be in the GodLife relationship is "in there," in the Word of God.[33]

LOVE LETTERS (THE PREMIER LOVE STORY)

The Scriptures are many things—letters, parables, sermons, poems, histories, biographies, liturgies, songs. But behind all these multiple literary genres, the backdrop of everything is the greatest love story ever told. What if God means for all of Scripture to be God's love story to us? What if God never intended the Bible to be strip-mined for propositions, or dissected and analyzed like a stiff leopard frog pulled from a bottle of formaldehyde? What if God never wanted the Bible to be turned into an interesting library of varied and profound literature or a stringent code of conduct?

What if the Bible instead is our shoebox full of love letters, our living library of family scrapbooks and diaries that connect us to our ancestors, helping us know them so we can know ourselves and understand what our family name stands for? What if it's our storyboard of relationships from which we learn how to form friendships and deal with the people and problems we encounter?

The Bible is best read as a love letter from God,[34] not a question book or an answer book, not a systematic theology or a scientific textbook or a dogmatics dictionary. The main subject of the Bible is God's relationship with what God most loves—God's creation and creatures. The Scriptures are the story of God's relationship with us—the covenant of relationships established between the Creator and those God created. For Jews the story centers on a covenant. For Christians the story centers on a Person. The source of our identity as Christians is a love story—or more accurately, a collection of love stories simple enough to be read by children, complex enough to elude total human comprehension.

> We must return to the Scriptures for the story that it is and stop approaching it as if it is an encyclopedia, looking for "tips and techniques."
>
> —JOHN ELDREDGE[35]

Living as a Christian, or claiming membership in the family of faith, is not a matter of being bad or good, or right or wrong. It's a matter of being dead or alive. The Christian message is not a timeless tablet of moral principles or a code of metaphysics. The Christian message is the greatest love story ever told of love come down from heaven to earth, a love so vast and victorious that even hatred could not keep it down.

Humans can't help but tell stories. In everything we do—science, music, architecture, literature—we tell stories, even the same stories, over and over. We tell stories because we are created by God, and God is a Storyteller. As with any love letter, Scripture tells stories about its Author, a God whose character is revealed in human form most wholly in the manifestation of Jesus the Christ, the greatest Lover the world has ever known. Our best comprehension of Truth, the Whole Truth, comes from the Greatest Love Story, as it reveals itself in Scripture, in tradition, and in the church.

Christianity is a storied spirituality. It creates a culture of storytellers. You and I are important parts of the story, but it's not our story. It's God's Story. The Greatest Love Story does not begin with us, and the story does not end with us. God is Alpha and Omega, the beginning and the end. Each one of us is a new telling of God's unending love story. And each one of us has in us the story of Adam and Eve, and every other biblical story. Each one of us also has in us the story of all other possibilities.

God's story doesn't just describe our reality. Biblical stories also help *create* our realities.[36] We find who we are when we find who God is.[37] This makes the first task of storytelling to be truthtelling. Our lives are so laden with lies and bad stories that without God's Story, our soap-opera lives never become grand opera, much less GodLife. Only in relationship with God's Story can life be lived with operatic intensity.

To fully experience the GodLife relationship, we must be fully immersed in God's Story.

OPEN YOURSELF TO GOD'S STORY

How to Allow Scripture to Shape Your Life

> Let our gardener, God, landscape you with the Word,
> making a salvation-garden of your life.
> —JAMES[1]

W e become like what we like. Just as the kinds of friends we choose decide the kind of person we become and the direction life takes, the stories we relate to most closely structure our identities. Some of the most important choices we make are our companion stories—the stories we choose to live with. It takes only a few basic stories, or what scholars call "deep structures," to organize human experience. The reason why there are as many as thirty thousand Christian denominations in the world is because our different relationships to these stories structure our realities differently.

OPEN YOURSELF TO GOD'S STORY

To choose the right companion story and to be shaped by it for a lifetime, you need to get into a real relationship with the Bible. What does this mean? I can think of five things it means:

1. Memorize and live out its stories.
2. Fall in love with a new passage every day.
3. Take it to bed with you.
4. Talk to it and hear it talk to you as you wrestle with the text.
5. Become a fifth gospel, a third testament.

Memorize and Live Out Its Stories

"Five chapters a day keeps the pastor away." With these words I was encouraged as a child in the daily reading of the Scriptures. No way did I want to invite pastoral intervention in my family. When I was a teenager, competition in "sword drills" kept me reading the Bible and honed my skills in finding obscure verses and remembering the exact locations of Zechariah and Zephaniah.

"Twelve verses a week for twelve straight weeks gets you a week at summer camp." With these words I was encouraged to memorize Scripture. At a very young age, my parents enlisted me in a program called Bible Memory Association (BMA). Beginning at age five, I memorized a certain number of Bible verses a week, and at week's end recited them to a "hearer." Every couple of weeks, if my hearer signed my sheet, I picked from the pages of a catalog my prize of godly merchandise. When I reached a certain age, twelve weeks of flawless recitation was rewarded by a week at one of BMA's Miracle Camps.

> The true test of whether or not one belongs to God's people is neither the observance of dietary laws and Jewish festivals, nor the cultivation of superspiritual experiences, but whether one belongs to Christ, alive with his life.
>
> —BIBLICAL SCHOLAR
> N. T. WRIGHT [2]

I thank God for this grounding in the Scriptures. But I learned how to memorize and recite Bible verses, rather than how to memorize and recite Bible *stories*. I could recite yards of verses, but nary a yarn or complete story line.

I now realize that my best theological education in Sunday school was what I used to think was my worst: the chalkboard, the flannelgraph, the skits and bathrobe dramas. For it was here that I learned God's stories.

The Christian life is the sum of relationships with stored-up God-stories, not the accumulation of verses or the dutiful checking off of biblical ordinances. For the Christian, dogma is story, not proposition. This is important, because a story is ongoing, affecting your life constantly, shaping and guiding and enlightening you. The GodLife is a story yet unfinished, a story God has framed but that we are invited to have a hand in coloring.

In order for us to keep Jesus's words in our heart, as he directed, we must not only know his words—we must also be able to tell his stories. We sing songs to help us tell the story and use biblical references to help us remember the story. Memory is not just a function of the brain, it's a function of the whole body. Remembering involves *all* our senses, including our physical senses and our social senses.

Fall in Love with a New Passage Every Day

It's time to end the theological error of talking about how to make the Scriptures "come alive." The Word of God *is* alive. It's we who must "come alive" to the Scriptures.

God has planted time-release explosives throughout the Scriptures, and at various times in history, including the history of each one of us, certain portions of the Bible "go off." Our job is to plant our lives in the passages of the Bible that are exploding so that their power will explode in us. Or in the words of the psalmist, "You thrill to GOD's Word, you chew on Scripture day and night."[3]

Your most exciting relationships with the Word of God are in the future. Nobody wants to "settle down" in a relationship, so keep traveling. Keep reading. Keep blood flowing to your imagination and your soul.

One of the most thrilling sensations in life is the sensation of being at the beginning of something. Just as there is nothing more exciting than a new relationship, so there is nothing more exciting than a new relationship with a biblical story—seeing it fresh as if for the first time. If we could only get as excited about a new day of living in "the round" of God's Word as poet Stanley Kunitz does about a new day of living in "the round" of the world:

> I can scarcely wait till tomorrow
> when a new life begins for me.[4]

As with any new relationship, there are joys and dangers. For one, there are the joys of discovery. Is there anything more exciting than to be reading a book (or living in a world) where we are still discovering things? The Scriptures, like real people, reveal different sides according to the depth of our relationship and our capacity to understand them. The most surprising discovery of all is ourselves. In the Scriptures we find our identities and come alive to who we are. I once was dead, but now am alive; I once was lost, but now am found.

But there are dangers, as well, in discovery. If you, like Abraham, are journey laden, you will be heavy laden, and no more "burdened" than walking with a friend. One of the reasons we shun relationships is that every link leaves us with a limp—feet to drag, ears to ring, hearts to break, tongue to burn. Sometimes love doesn't feel like we want it to. You never know where a relationship will lead, what new directions and new ambitions it will bring, how it will change you and the way you live.

The Bible is hazardous to your status quo. When you place something new "in focus," you blur what you previously focused on. The Word of God can totally upset your life. The Scriptures are the greatest change agent in the world. We need to learn to read not only the lines of the Bible but between the lines and behind the lines and below the lines and across the lines. We need to learn to read the Bible as if our life depended upon understanding it, because it does.

> Christ isn't going to give you a rosy picture. He is going to give us peace about what's happened, hope for eternity with him, the Spirit that speaks to me and comforts me—but not the winning lottery ticket.
>
> —NOVELIST BRETT LOTT[5]

Every passage needs a passage. Every life passage needs a story to help you get through it. Associate certain passages with passages of your life, and tattoo your Bible with markers and mementos of these transitions. Don't be afraid to write on white.

Take It to Bed with You

Stories have the power to change the world. But only if you take them to bed with you.

Homer's *Iliad*, a manual in the art of combat and courage, was recognized as a classic even in its own time. Alexander the Great's prized possession was a copy annotated by Aristotle, and he took it with him on his march to world conquest. When he went to bed at night, he placed a dagger under his pillow and often stuffed alongside the dagger his well-read copy of the *Iliad*.[6] It wasn't taking the book to bed with him that altered the course of history. It was Alexander's internalization of the story of his hero Achilles. But stories aren't internalized until they make it into your dreams.

"A professor is one who talks in someone else's sleep," poet W. H. Auden contended.[7] As your primary professor, the Scriptures need to slip under the door of your consciousness. Some people don't pause long enough in the vicinity of God's Word to be trapped by its truth. Others don't open the doorway that leads into the hidden rooms of their heart to let the Word work its magic in the deep recesses of their being. Only if you put out the welcome mat and invite the Word into your life will it "do its work on you."[8] Even if we are busy reading, are we at the same time busy listening and welcoming?

Just as it is good for your body to eat food every day, it is good for your soul to integrate some Bible story or parts of a story every day. Develop nightly as well as daily routines of Bible feeding. The psalmist encouraged us to "thrill to GOD's Word" by "chewing on Scripture day and night."[9] Chewing the text (ruminating) releases juices that bring joy and energy to life.

What biblical characters are you most drawn to? Which one is your alter ego? Keep your biblical companions close at all times—including overnight. Along with a verse for the day, why not a story or a metaphor for the night? Decide when you're brushing your teeth what story you will brood over. Two of my favorite nighttime mantras are the angel's blessing "Peace on earth" and the familiar Sunday-school song "Into my heart, into my heart, come into my heart, Lord Jesus."[11]

> When your head droops at night, let a page of Scripture pillow it.
>
> —SAINT JEROME[10]

At night, when you can't sleep, instead of counting sheep, call the Shepherd…and recall ghost stories—Holy Ghost stories.

When the rabbis talk about a love for the Torah that makes the heart beat faster and flutter with joy, we think it's a cute metaphor. It's not. It's a literal description of how the Scriptures want to work on us from birth to death. In the Eastern Orthodox tradition, icons depicting the dormition (falling asleep) of the saints often show the revered in their caskets with hands folded over their favorite gospel.

I want my hands folded over the entire Bible. And not just when I die.

Talk to It and Hear It Talk to You As You Wrestle with the Text

Communication, especially fresh communication, keeps a relationship alive.

We like to define disciples of Jesus as people who live "by the book." The phrase "by the book" suggests people who know the correct procedures, who have mastered the policy manual. It should mean people who are living masters of relationships and experiences and interactions. "By the book" means a relationship with Scripture in which you talk to it and you hear it talk to you.

Read every word as if it is spoken to you. Because it is. As you listen to God's story, put yourself in the story. Instead of, "What life lessons can I learn from the text?" explore the life you can encounter while being in the text. Instead of asking, "What answers can I find in this text?" ask, "What voices of truth can I hear today?" You're not seeking abstract meaning. You hunger instead for the transforming power of an encounter with Christ.

Standing on a London street corner, G. K. Chesterton was approached by a newspaper reporter. "Sir, I understand that you recently became a Christian. May I ask you one question?"

"Certainly," replied Chesterton.

"If the risen Christ suddenly appeared at this very moment and stood behind you, what would you do?"

Chesterton looked the reporter squarely in the eye and said, "He is."[12]

If we're in GodLife relationships with the Scriptures, we admit to hearing voices. The stories of Scripture are the voice of God speaking to us. Every story in God's Story meets the needs of our own lives and times. When we read the story of the Two Lost Sons, we hear God saying to us now, as the father said to the elder of his two prodigal sons, "Everything I have is yours!"[14]

> Being a Christian is more than adding Christian principles to our lives. Jesus requires full allegiance to his teachings, but being a Christian means having our lives radically transformed by the Gospel and God's Spirit within us.
>
> —PERRY G. DOWNS[13]

Rekindle past relationships with stories that have grown too familiar to still have an impact. Even while you expand your friendship base with the Scriptures, be open to revisiting your relationships with texts that have carried you in the past. The word *Hebrew* literally means "one who crosses over a river." This is what it means to be a child of Abraham: to trust the One who carries you across life's rivers.

Show your appreciation to God for this dynamic, life-giving relationship with the Scriptures. Ask forgiveness for having underplayed your pleasures in the GodLife relationship. Voice your gratitude, and express your gratitude with others.

Some stories you don't approach alone, especially when they draw you into what Paul called "the deep things of God."[15] Even Peter admitted that many things Paul wrote were hard to understand.[16] The first principle of swimming is this: "Don't go into deep water alone." Develop a buddy system that you can draw from. Remember that Bible study is best done in groups, in relationship with the Scriptures' community of interpretation.

The Scriptures are accessible to both the unlearned and the learned, the "uneducated as well as the educated"[17] as the *Westminster Confession of Faith* puts it. Too much of an " 'expert' ethos" has stifled Bible reading,[18] as if only biblical scholars could correctly handle the word of truth.[19]

Become a Fifth Gospel, a Third Testament

Our lives are to become texts (stories, letters) for others to read. Or in Paul's phrasing, "living epistles." When the Word of God becomes such a part of your life that it is more than a lamp unto your feet and a light unto your path—it is your very feet and path itself—then your life has become a fifth gospel, a third testament.[20] Texts need to be interpreted in such a way that others can read and comprehend them. When a life hasn't become a text, there is little to interpret.

Just as God the Father lived God's life in Jesus, so God the Son lives his life in you. "It is no longer I who live, but it is Christ who lives in me," the writer of Galatians claimed.[21] What kept Christian faith alive for Paul? Not the teachings of Jesus so much as the same Spirit of God that was alive in Jesus and is alive in us. Paul referred only infrequently to Jesus's teachings and ministry.[22] What he referred to most often was the power of God to make Christ alive in us.

In fact, the promises spoken to Abraham "and to his seed" proved to the writer of Galatians that we live by grace through faith and not by law. The Hebrew Scripture doesn't say "and to his seeds" (suggesting many) but "and to your seed" suggesting one—Christ.[23] The Law of Moses, which came centuries after the time of Abraham, did not invalidate the promise God made to Abraham. Our inheritance comes by faith, by trust in a covenant, not by law, by obligation of a contract.

Many years ago, I remember a country preacher at a camp meeting in Denton, Maryland, building a sermon on "The Missing *S*." His text was Galatians 3:16-18. He spent the entire sermon exploring the significance of the absence of a final letter *s* from this word *seed.* God made a faith covenant with

Abraham and with Christ, Abraham's seed. By not saying "and to your seeds," the preacher argued, God was excluding Abraham's entire lineage, meaning all the patriarchs, Moses, Joshua, the prophets. The promises were made to Abraham and to Jesus.

When you skip from Abraham to Christ, who is the most important person you skip over in those two thousand years? Moses. Paul leaps over Mosaic law. And in so doing he intimates that the inheritance based on the law of Moses was a deviation from the true inheritance based on God's promise of grace to Abraham. In short, Paul says, "Don't talk to me about Moses. Talk to me about Abraham and Jesus. Talk to me about the God who promises to 'remove from your body the heart of stone and give you a heart of flesh.'"[24]

God performs a heart transplant in each one of us. God gives us a new heart and puts a new spirit within us, one in which "the word of Christ dwell[s] in you richly."[25] We have yet to come to terms with that word *dwells*. We love to quote "The Word became flesh." But we lop off the rest of the sentence, "and dwelt among us." To "dwell among us" and to "dwell in us richly" suggest it's not a matter of more information, but more *indwelling*. Jesus is more than a template for our lives. Jesus wants our lives to become a temple in which God can dwell.

In the GodLife relationship, every Christian becomes a gospel story. Martin Buber liked to tell the story of a grandfather who was paralyzed. One day one of the man's grandchildren asked him to tell about an incident in the life of his teacher, the great Baal Shem. So the grandfather began telling how Baal Shem, when he was at prayer, used to leap about and dance. The more into the story the old man got, the more he became Baal Shem until he stood up from his wheelchair and, to show how the master had done it, began leaping and dancing. From that moment the grandfather was cured.

Buber went on to say: "That's the way to tell a story."[26] You become what you tell.

When you tell the story of Jesus's forgiving his enemies, you become someone who forgives his or her enemies. When you tell the story of Jesus's crossing the street to help an outcast, you cross the street to help the nearest outcast.

Christians live the story of Jesus. Christians don't just tell the story of Jesus.

When it comes to stories, there is always more to tell. You have never fully arrived in a relationship with a biblical text. There is always more there. Just when you think you understand a story, suddenly you find that it surprises you once again. Just as you keep inviting your neighbor over for coffee—learning something new with every visit—keep visiting your companion stories. Know that your best relationships with the Scriptures are in the future.

Sadly, for some Christians the story has stopped. God has done all that God is going to do, and God's voice is embalmed in a book. This turns the work of evangelists into being the salesmen of a tradition, not Christ-introducers and life-connectors to an ongoing, never-ending story.

For some, the stories are frozen awaiting a future Parousia. The problem with freeze-dried stories is the same with anything that has the living water drained out of it: They taste dreadful, feel like brickbats, and crumble when you hold them too tightly.

For some the story has run out of steam and needs revision and reinvention—as if God didn't get it right the first time. This turns reading the Bible into minesweeping the Scriptures for hidden detonations. For some not only is there nothing new under the sun. There is no Sun.

For some the story is an addendum to their own story, like some guilt outing to Disney World that's crammed into a calendar so that everyone can say, "We did it." It is only when our story gets grafted onto God's story, the story that came as a gift and grace, that our own story comes to life.

For others the stories of God are not entries in their family diary, but laws for living passed by some divine legislature. This is the biggest reason why Jesus's storytelling was deemed sheer madness, dissed as mere children's stories. Where was the Law of Moses? Where were the words of the prophets and ancestors? Where was even God in these parables of his?[27]

Evangelism is the practice of out-narrating the world by telling a much better story, a story that can win the hearts and minds of the world's peoples, a story of love, harmony, and peace. People are being seduced by the wrong stories, partly because we don't know how to tell the Truth, the Whole Truth, and Nothing but the Truth.

Evangelism is not convincing other people to accept the propositions you believe. Evangelism is inviting other people to begin a relationship with

Jesus—to go on a journey with him and make his story their story. If the basic issue of evangelism is how we help people meet Jesus, then evangelism is not doctrinal transactions but spiritual interactions.

THE ULTIMATE TEST

In part 2 we focused on the test of Abraham and how it became a test of relationship. This chapter on God's story ends with a theological meditation on the Christian meaning of "test."

The word *test* comes from the Latin *testum,* which stood for an earthen vessel. During the Middle Ages, the French term for "test" denoted a shallow, porous cup or cupel used to examine and evaluate precious metals. Impure gold or silver was heated in this cup, and it was the function of the "test" to absorb the impurities from the metal, leaving behind a pure bullion of gold or silver. The terminology was borrowed into Middle English, and by the late sixteenth century, the word denoting this cup was used figuratively and called a test. When something was "put to the test," the genuineness of the precious metal was determined.

The Bible says, "For you, O God, tested us; you refined us like silver."[28] Ditto these words from Proverbs: "The crucible is for silver, and the furnace is for gold, but the Lord tests the heart."[29] And consider this from Zechariah: "I will refine them like silver and test them like gold. They will call on my name and I will answer them; I will say, 'They are my people,' and they will say, 'The LORD is our God.'"[30]

The good news in all this? Jesus is the Way, the Truth, the Life…and the Test. The Ultimate Test.

Jesus is the answer to the test. Any test. He is even more. He is the Great Test itself. Like the ancient test which absorbed the impurities of a precious metal, Jesus absorbs the impurities of sin and filth in all who place themselves in his cupped, nail-scarred hands.

Jesus is the ultimate test that enables us to be all we can ever hope to be, all we were ever meant to be. The test that allows us to live and love in relationship more wonderfully than we could ever dream. The test that absorbs all our hurts and ills, our impurities and imperfections, and that multiplies our strengths like the fish and loaves, uses them in ways we cannot even begin to imagine.

Let's not grade Abraham's test, or the disciples' papers. Let's take our own test.

For us the question is: Are we up to the Test?

PART IV

OUR RELATIONSHIP WITH OTHER PEOPLE OF FAITH

LOVING THE "ONE-ANOTHERS"

When Being Right Is Just Plain Wrong

In the same way I loved you, you love one another.

—JESUS[1]

Tom Wiles served a stint as university chaplain at Grand Canyon University in Phoenix. A few years ago he picked me up at the Phoenix airport in his new Ford pickup and whisked me away to keynote a leadership conference at the university. Since I was still mourning the trade-in of my Dodge truck, we immediately bonded, sharing truck stories and laughing at the bumper-sticker truism: "Nothing is more beautiful than a man and his truck."

As I climbed into his 2002 Ranger for the ride back to the airport a day later, I noticed two big scrapes by the passenger door. "What happened here?" I asked.

"My neighbor's basketball post fell and left those dents and white scars," Tom replied with a downcast voice.

"You're kidding! How awful," I commiserated. "This truck is so new I can smell it."

"What's even worse is my neighbor doesn't feel responsible for the damage."

Rising to my newfound friend's defense, I said, "Did you contact your insurance company? How are you going to get him to pay for it?"

"This has been a real spiritual journey for me," Tom replied. "After a lot of soul-searching and discussions with my wife about hiring an attorney, it came down to this: I can either be in the right, or I can be in a relationship with my neighbor. Since my neighbor will probably be with me longer than this truck, I decided that I'd rather be in a relationship than be right. Besides, trucks are meant to be banged up, so I got mine initiated into the real world a bit earlier than I expected."

Dead Right

Tom's wisdom has stayed with me. How many times have I sacrificed being "in relationship" for the personal satisfaction of being "in the right"? How many times have I won the argument, but lost a friend or damaged a heart? I have a friend whose wife warns him that if he thinks he has to be "always right," then he can be "dead right."

When he was practicing law, Abraham Lincoln was hired to sue someone over a $2.50 debt. He didn't want to do it, but his client insisted that it was a matter of principle, even though the person being sued was a friend.

So Lincoln asked for a fee of ten dollars, to be paid in advance. He then gave half to the defendant, who promptly paid his debt.

And what about Christians as a group? Does the church lack credibility with the culture because Christians would rather be right than be in relationship with one another? We'd rather be right about our positions, right about our condemnations, right about having the "right" interpretation of Scripture. We'd rather score points than secure relationships with others who share the Christian faith.[2]

I see sobering parallels between the church in the West and managed health care—an institution that is almost universally reviled. Rush your bleeding three-year-old to the emergency room, and the first thing you hear is not "What's wrong?" but "Where's your insurance card?" Likewise, a visitor's experience with the church often is less one of relationship ("How can we love you?") than one of being in the right ("Do you believe in the deity of Christ? Do you stand up for the inerrancy of Scripture? Do you hold to a premillennial view of the end times?"). The church has deep convictions, but do the convictions crowd out friendships? Jesus was familiar with the religious rules regarding what could not be done on the Sabbath. He ignored the rules and healed a sufferer. God didn't put us here to serve the rules, Jesus explained. It's just the opposite. The rules exist for our benefit.[3]

Relationship Rules

Did Jesus come to teach us "right" theology or did he come to redeem our relationships with God and with one another? Jesus's own "prayer report" in John

17 revolves around his stewardship of his relationships.[4] Significantly, Jesus's last act before his death was to arrange for the care of his family.

Family is another word for relationships. Jesus taught that family is more soul and sweat than blood and burg. Jesus saved the world by teaching twelve partners how to be family—how to get along together and belong to one another. And even then, he failed with one of them.

Surveys continue to show that family is rated as the greatest source of happiness. When adults are asked to rate five aspects of their lives (relationships, health, personal fulfillment [defined as personal growth and job satisfaction], financial status, and leisure activity), relationship to others and oneself consistently is ranked as the number one ingredient in a quality life.[5]

This shouldn't surprise disciples of Jesus. Relationship is pivotal to Christian theology, because God is Love, and Love is impossible outside of relationships. Relationships are the ecology of God's kingdom, the new creation. The Holy Spirit is not a gift to individuals. The Holy Spirit is a gift to the body of Christ. We have no choice but to live with, listen to, and learn from one another.

> No one would choose to live without friends, even if he had all other goods.
>
> —ARISTOTLE[6]

A handful of relationships reveal God to us—beginning with our relationship with the "one-anothers"—other people in the body of Christ. God indwells us both individually and collectively. God creates both new persons in whom Christ can live and a new people (the body of Christ) in whom the divine life can be reproduced and dispersed.

In the modern era, people came to church and asked, "Who is God?" But today, if people come to church at all, they ask, "Who are God's people? How does Christianity cash out in community and in practice?"

Christian philosopher Stanley Grenz argues that the spiritual quest for postmoderns is found more in their multifaceted relationships with one another than in finding a "home alone" with God.[7] When the church gathers, a relationship with God is possible that is present in no other arena of life. You can't have Jesus without the church. But it's not, "Where the church is, there is Jesus." It's just the opposite: "Where Jesus is, there is the church." If God is present and in touch with us when we are in community, what does that look like? Another way of asking this question is: What do dynamic, growing relationships in the body of Christ look like?

Just Because You're Right Doesn't Make You Right

Why did so many early Christians lay down their lives for this new religious movement? Because they agreed with a certain account of Jesus's death and resurrection? Or because early Christianity offered a framework of relationships for their lives that offered spiritual redemption and a road to social, psychological, and intellectual betterment that enabled their trust in Jesus to deepen and grow?

In the past, we would have answered by talking about the authoritative and binding "rules of relationship." Instead of rules per se, I want to use the word *rule* with a meaning that is in tune with its original intent.

Kanon ("sphere" or "area") is the Greek word for *rule*. It is translated into Latin by *regula*, which means "straight stick" or "bar." Benedictine monk David Steindl-Rast has revealed that the root meaning of *regula* is "trellis," a scaffolding that enables a plant to grow upward and reach toward the sun. When the plant can't support itself, the trellis enables it to continue climbing heavenward. Thus, the original Rule of Saint Benedict and the call to a "ruled life" was to provide a framework for spiritual growth, a pattern for living that enabled a climber to reach higher and that freed the "ruled" person for greater service to God and solidarity with others.[9]

> If you submit to a common rule, you can only do so on account of Christ and the Gospel.... [The rule's] purpose is to free you from useless fetters, the better to bear responsibility and exercise all the boldness possible in your ministry.
>
> —Brother Roger,
> prior of Taizé[8]

An Argument for Growth

I understand the tarnish on the "growth" paradigm—the idea of unending improvement through expansion—which clamors loudest through the corridors of power. I share the backlash both in the culture and in the church to the mentality of growth as the first and highest good.[10] One scholar has argued that "sustainable growth" is an oxymoron.[11] The notion that we can grow our way out of balding forests, falling water tables, melting icecaps, dying coral, encroaching deserts, disappearing wetlands, eroding soil, and vanishing clean water is now rightly seen as a delusional optimism.

Unlimited growth brings to mind cancer cells, epidemics, future disaster, extinction. What before was the measure of progress has become a sign of our biggest problems.[12] "Developed" land is now "destroyed" land—stripped of maple trees to make room for strip malls and named after what they killed (Maple Tree Mall). Talk to anyone who lives in a growing city and you will hear about the exhaustion of resources and the grinding of life to a gridlock standstill.

But in nature, things grow: organisms, forests, individuals, gardens, and families. Jungian psychoanalyst James Hillman has defined a different view of growth that is more in keeping with the relational nature of reality.[13] Instead of abandoning the concept of growth in favor of alternative models, such as "sustainability," "no-growth," and "zero-sum" models, let's rework the reality of growth into more relationship-oriented categories. It is biblically impossible to get around the growth metaphor. In fact, Paul's notion of "perfection" means "full grown"—a life that makes room for growth, maturity, ripeness.

The most significant discovery unearthed by the leadership literature of the past twenty years is that two signs indicate successful leadership: improving relationships, and the improving stories that are spawned by the improving relationships. Interestingly, these signs of successful leadership constitute two of the three "signs of the Spirit" that were so central to early Christianity. The early church touted three tests of authenticity, or as it called them, "signs of the Spirit."

First, and the one missing from the leadership literature of the past twenty years, is the Lordship of Christ and the centrality of an apostolic witness.[14] For the Christian, everything else pales by comparison to the preeminence of Christ.

The second sign of the Spirit consisted of manifestations in the life of Christians of "fruit of the Spirit."[15] James exhorts us to "humbly accept the word planted in you."[16] The Word of God bears fruit, not when it is comprehended, but when it is lived—implanted and transplanted. And the fruit of the Spirit is proven in relationships. When relationships get worse, things go bad. When relationships get better, things improve. This is true in the corporate world[17] just as it holds true when Christians relate to one another in the church.

The third sign of the Spirit was the usefulness of spiritual manifestations to the churches.[18] In other words, when relationships get better, there are stories to back up the improving relationships. Relationships, not numbers, show if growth is biblical, healthy, and truly fruitful. Perhaps it's time to declare a moratorium on statistics in the church. What if the only thing we reported was the answer to this question: "Is spiritual fruit in evidence in your church? Give me the stories, not more statistics." My dream for the church? God's people telling more God stories than golf stories. An authentic Great Awakening is when people can't stop talking about what God is doing.

Rituals of Right Relationships

Our Life Together Requires More Than Principles

Nothing could more surely convince me of God's unending
mercy than the continued existence on earth of the church.

—Annie Dillard[1]

Christianity offers a relational repertoire of resources that attracts people today as it did in the first century. Authentic spiritual relationships with "one-anothers" occur in a relational matrix with five interweaving strands. In light of this, let's examine five "relationship rules" of one-another living that form the framework for spiritual development:

1. Relationship is deepening.
2. Relationship is intensification.
3. Relationship is shedding.
4. Relationship is repetition.
5. Relationship is emptying.

With a trellis as our rule, how does growth lead us to God in relationship with the one-anothers? Taken together, these five rules form the trellis on which to grow and lattice relationships of integrity and truth in a world of broken relationships and fractured truth.

1. A Growing Relationship Is Deepening

Deepening relationships go downward, and when you go deeper you get dirty. Pastor John Ambrose Wood was the father of author Catherine Marshall. He spent his entire ministry serving rural congregations. One day he called on a new member in Keyser, West Virginia. When the pastor extended his hand in greeting, the man, a worker on the B&O Railroad, apologized: "Can't shake hands with you, Reverend. They're too grimy."

With that the pastor bent to rub his hands in the coal dust and then offered his blackened hand to the worker. "How about it now?"[2]

James Hillman defines deepening growth as "work in the dirt."[3] Plants can't grow heavenward without first growing downward. Colorful blossoms are the by-product of bland, down-and-dirty roots. Relationships that blossom are knee-bending, hands-dirtying digs into the bedrock issues.

It is sometimes hard to see this downward direction as positive. We like to think of God as being above us, not beneath us, a God "overarching" not "underlying" us. But if our relationships are to bear fruit, they first must become rooted in the soil of the Spirit. Any growth, whether inner or outward, doesn't mean taking charge by ripping the roots out of the dirt. It's just the opposite. It means constantly returning to the roots for their nutrients and energy. Fruits come from roots.

The ultimate fruit is Jesus, who yields the taste of love. In some early Christian writings, Jesus is described as "this fruit" that comes from the "tree of knowledge" in paradise. When we are grafted into Christ, we bear the fruit of love which enables the kingdom of heaven to break through and grow on earth. The church and its sacraments are the "first fruits" of this growing kingdom—a community of the vine and branches. In this community, a healthy relationship is defined as an ever-deepening knowledge of one another.

> Great little one! Whose all-embracing birth…stoopes heav'n to earth.
>
> —CAMBRIDGE SCHOLAR AND POET RICHARD CRASHAW[4]

Scripture tells the story of a God who was not afraid to get hands dirty in a relationship with us. Our God takes the initiative and "comes down." In the greatest come-down of all time, the very being of God came down and became one of us.[5] Or in the words of Ephesians: "He who descended is the very one who ascended."[6]

The incarnation was the greatest deepening of relationship in history. What gravity is to the natural world, grace is to the spiritual world, lifting us up by getting us to the bottom of a relationship. But it was not enough for Jesus to come down from heaven to earth. The divine come-down was not complete until Jesus embodied the extent of God's deep love in his getting down and washing his disciples' feet. *Foot* was a four-letter word in the first century—the dirtiest part of the human body. No first-century rabbi other than Jesus ever washed his disciples' feet. It is impossible to wash feet without getting hands dirty and wet. Far too many of us are trying to keep our hands clean when the question at Judgment Day is going to be "Show me your hands. How dirty and wet are they?"

Jesus reverses the moral grounds of the master-and-servant relationship: "I tell you, he will fasten his belt and have them sit down to eat, and he will come and serve them."[7] The master of all is the servant of all. The word *servant* literally means "to wait at tables." When the church would rather sit at tables than wait on them, the church's service is bad. And when the service is bad, the table is empty, no matter how good or plentiful the food.

If you're concerned about your dignity, think about this: Where's the dignity in being hung naked on a tree? Where's the dignity in kneeling down to wash the dirtiest parts of someone's body? Where's the dignity in being born in a manger?

A second aspect of deepening relationships is that we get rooted. The church is a root community of people who live connected lives—relationships intertwined with God's story and intertwined with one another's stories.

The church is, of course, other things in addition to a root community. It's the place where Christ's forgiveness is enacted. It's a sacrament of Christ's presence. It's a gift-giving space where people can exchange their gifts and grow their gifts. It's an apocalyptic, *arrabon* ("down payment") community, which is different from an *enechuron* ("pledge") community where no money is put down. It's a foretaste of God's dream for the future. It's a place the Spirit of Christ circulates but sometimes transcends—the Spirit can work as much against as within Christian communities.

But most of all, the church connects us to our roots—our ancestors, our traditions, our "apostles' teachings," our stories, and our songs. If you can sing "When Peace Like a River" without crying, you don't know the song's story. If you can sing "Amazing Grace" without shivers, you don't know the gospel story. If you can say the Apostles' Creed without straightening up, you don't know the church's story. In a world that is constantly in flux, our roots are the Jesus Rock—a rock more solid than any Jurassic rock, yet a rock streaming forth with more living water than any artesian spring.

2. A Growing Relationship Is Intensifying

Sobonfu Somé grew up in Dano, a West African village where entire families share living space and multiple generations spend their lives together. When she told her family that she and her husband, Malidoma, were living alone in a big house in USAmerica, her family felt sorry for her. In fact, Somé's mother shook her head and cried out in a where-did-we-go-wrong voice, "What are you doing this for?"

Somé says, "I explained to her that everybody has his own place and there's no village to go to. There's no family where we live. I told her, 'You might want to come and live with me.' And she said, 'No, not under those conditions.'"[8]

We live in a culture that worships the big and showy. That explains why notions of growth that are based on miniaturizations rather than magnifications, intensifications rather than expansions are as inconceivable as big empty houses were to Somé's mother.

> Snowflakes are one of nature's most fragile things, but just look at what they can do when they stick together.
>
> —VESTA M. KELLY

When there is intensification of relationships in the body of Christ, two things are happening—there is more resonance and there is more conversation, both of which "magnify" the Lord.[9]

To enter the world of true success is not to open doors to numbers and results, but to navigate spheres of resonances, connections, and presences. The ultimate in success is to be out of sync with and ahead of what the culture defines as success. Real success is the presuccessful uncovering of what physicists call "strange attractors"—truths hidden within the everyday, waiting to be revealed. When they emerge they generate strong resonances. At first you don't know what to make of them or what to do with them, but they begin to rock the world with their resonance.

Major advances in history are brought about by agents of resonance. The 1840s obstetrician Ignaz Philipp Semmelweis discovered a "strange attractor": hand washing. Semmelweis became convinced that one reason why women were dying in such large numbers in childbirth was because doctors weren't washing their hands. Even though his hygienic measures reduced deaths from childbirth from 9.92 percent to 1.27 percent a year, he was laughed out of

Vienna and hounded out of medicine.[10] No one in the 1840s could conceive what a doctor's washing his hands had to do with preventing fever in a patient.

A few decades later Louis Pasteur announced his discovery of the same "strange attractor." He argued that infectious disease was caused by microbes. So strange was this attractor that a fellow scientist challenged Pasteur to a duel. The Academy of Medicine in France was so embarrassed by Pasteur that they expelled him from their membership.[11]

Christianity has its own strange attractors. The wages of sin is death. But the wages of righteousness can be deadly, in the form of persecution, humiliation, ostracism, and isolation. Check out what Jerusalem did to Jesus and what the church did to Galileo.[12] Spiritual truth is not revealed by counting votes or nodding heads. In Christianity, the moral victory often belongs to the losing side.

The popular meaning of "success" is winning or leading the pack, getting ahead, being first. But the word *success* also means following behind or coming after. When you "succeed" someone, you fall in behind another person, guarding his or her legacy. Sometimes experiencing success for Christ is nothing more than falling in step behind him.

For Jesus, success is *kairos*—an ancient Greek word that described that moment in archery when an arrow that will successfully reach its target is released from the bow. The arrow hasn't yet reached its destination, but the magic moment, pregnant with the future, has been released on its journey. Agents of resonance help people hear the future (and God) speak to them. The agent of resonance could be a smile, a joke, a hug, a metaphor, a book, a discovery—anything that helps the voice of Truth resonate within us, the resonance of God's presence. Resonance is the sound of truth received that amplifies the truth in one's own soul.[13]

In addition to resonance, intensified relationships produce conversations—interrelated and spidery interconnections. The more complex the interconnections, the higher the possible intelligence. There is virtually no distinguishable difference between a squid neuron and a human brain cell. What separates the two is that humans have more of them wired together. There are 100 billion neurons in the human brain, with at least 1000 interconnections between neurons, or 100 trillion connections. The less isolation there is in various portions of the brain, the more intelligent the species.

When speaking of a community, be it a faith community or a corporation, high intelligence resides not in isolated individuals but in nodes of relationships—groups, networks, communities. Intelligence is the direct result of connectedness and communication: True communication is a conversation.

But not just any conversation. Compare what passes for conversation in today's talk radio with eighteenth-century coffee houses, where a gentleman was defined as a "man of conversation" and which raised conversation to an art form in which it became true that you can make things better by talking about them.[14] As Abraham discovered in his argument with God over Sodom and Gomorrah, the best conversation partners are those you can argue with, or against, but never without.

> Jesus was short on sermons, long on conversations; short on answers, long on questions; short on abstractions and propositions, long on stories and parables; short on telling you what to think, long on challenging you to think for yourself; short on condemning the irreligious, long on confronting the religious.
>
> —AUTHOR AND PASTOR
> BRIAN MCLAREN[15]

On 19 September 1931, a three-way conversation took place between Hugo Dyson, J. R. R. Tolkien, and C. S. Lewis. After dinner, these three friends strolled the Oxford campus talking myth and metaphor and Messiah. All three of these brilliant scholars were so enthralled by the exchange that they were moved to write about it later. Tolkien was the first to "break up the party"—at 3 a.m.

Lewis and Dyson talked until dawn. They listened to each other's fears and hopes and desires, and each found himself drawn closer to God. In fact, twelve days later Lewis wrote a friend that "I have just passed on from believing in God to definitely believing in Christ.... My long night talk with Dyson and Tolkien had a good deal to do with it."[16]

The best conversations lead us to change our way of thinking and our way of living. In the best conversations we are forced to face the truth.

3. A Growing Relationship Is Shedding

A growing community of Christians should be a shedding church. Anything that grows, sheds. Some shedding is constant and predictable, such as the shedding of skin. Other shedding is sudden, catastrophic, and uncertain, like the forest fires of betrayal, divorce, or death.

The best way to prepare for life's forest fires is to do some advance burning or strategic shedding. If intensification is a process of greater complexity, then shedding is simplification. It was said of Marian Anderson, one of the great singers of the twentieth century: "She hadn't simply grown great, she had grown great simply."[17] My theology is getting thicker and more complex the older I get, but my faith is becoming simpler as it crystallizes around some very simple words. One word in particular: Jesus.

All shedding needs sheds, places where the shedding can take place in relative safety. For planet Earth, Antarctica is a simplifying shed. Antarctica drains heat from the global atmosphere. It reduces everything to a single substance (water) in a single state (ice) and gives off a single by-product (oxygen). Without the simplifying tendencies of the icecaps and the rainforests (Earth's two sets of lungs), the planet could not breathe and grow.

I grew up around three sheds, each with its own special use: a potting shed, a potty shed, and a tool shed (that also served as a woodshed). Perhaps these can serve as metaphors for the shedding that needs to take place in preparation for and in the service of real growth.

Potting Sheds for New Learning and New Growth

Potting sheds are places where new growth is cultivated or where old growth is transplanted in fresh soil and into larger pots, giving the roots room to grow.

One of the closest relationships in my life has been with someone I first met when she was almost ninety. I was in my midthirties at the time, and I had just become president of a seminary. My first week on the job I heard about two octogenarians who were celebrated as "the two grand dames of Dayton." Both were towering presences in the life of a city they loved deeply. Both were major philanthropists. And both names went to the top of my list of people to meet.

My overtures to one were immediately rebuffed. But my overtures to the other, Marie Aull, went quite differently. Marie liked to surround herself with people of all different ages. Her stable of "old friends" was extensive and influential—but she realized that to prevent her days from becoming a long procession of hearses, she needed to bring new friends into her inner circle. As long as her mind was still hers (she lived to be 105), Marie spent her life in potting sheds.

The word translated "disciples" in the Great Commission ("Therefore go and make disciples of all nations"[18]) is the Greek noun *mathetes*.[19] It is the gospels' favorite word for a follower of Jesus, and literally means "learner, student, apprentice." The goal in a relationship with Christ is not to be become learned, but to become lifelong learners, open to new knowledge, new friends, new places. And to incorporate our learning into our living.

Before Jesus's arrival on the scene, a person's stance before God's anointed leaders was not disciple but servant. Those who "followed" Moses, Elijah, or Elisha were servants. But the word *mathetes* means even more than "learner" or "student." When used in the New Testament, it conveys a sense of "a close and definitive relationship with one person," even to the point of sacrifice and death.[20] A disciple is a learner whose relationship with a Teacher goes all the way the Teacher leads. Jesus promises his disciples an entire life of learning with a divine Mentor: The Holy Spirit "will teach you everything, and remind you of all that I have said to you."[21] The Jesus School never graduates us from the potting shed. Wisdom is a lifelong pilgrimage.[22]

In marriages that are growing, both partners are always learning things about each other for the first time. Of course, we often ask stupid questions of each other, and even of God, as do all learners. Think of the stupid questions asked by Jesus's first students: "Can I sit on your right hand? Can we call down fire onto that city that rejected us? How many times do we have to forgive?"[23]

Shedding learnedness is a process of simplification. Paul was afraid that the Christians in Corinth were allowing their minds to be "led astray from the simplicity and purity of devotion to Christ."[24] The spiritual path is one of increasing simplification and shedding. The greatest words ever uttered were spoken to everyday people in the simple language of fishermen and farmers, and saved for the ages in koine (common Greek). The greatest prayer ever modeled has simple words in simple sen-

> Basically, I know only three things. And of those three things I can remember only two at any given time.
>
> —DEVELOPMENTAL PSYCHOLOGIST BRUNO BETTELHEIM[25]

tence structures. In the first English translation of the Greek New Testament, William Tyndale wrote for the "ploughboys." In the first German translation of the Greek Bible, Martin Luther wrote for the "butchers and cobblers." Florence Nightingale said the whole of religion can be found in two sets of four one-syllable words: God's, "Lo, it is I" and in our response, "Here am I, Lord."

The more complex the world, the more simplicity we need. Only simplicity can navigate complexity. Einstein used only three letters and one number to unlock the mysteries of the universe: $e=mc^2$.

Tool Sheds for Relearning

Some of the biggest shedding—learning and relearning—in my life took place in the tool shed, which doubled as the proverbial woodshed. The tool shed is where I was confronted as a child with the mortal folly of my rule-breaking, boundary-crossing ways. When my life did not line up with my learning, it was time for some relearning. The instrument of relearning was a leather strap. These lessons took place not "because you do not know the truth, but because you do know it."[26]

Woodsheds are less places of punishment than places of relearning and retooling. There is a wonderful story of the desert fathers who went to one of their elders and asked what they should do if they caught a brother dozing during services. "Should we pinch him?" they asked.

The elder answered, "Actually, if I saw a brother sleeping, I would put his head on my knees and let him rest."[27]

Where do we get the notion that God is eager to punish us? How did the church communicate an image of God so that, as one Christian admitted when someone said, "God is near," the first thing he thought of was, "and He's armed and dangerous"?[28] The biblical metaphors of God's view of us could not be more intimate: a father's child, a husband's wife, a shepherd's sheep, a groom's bride.

One of my favorite woodshed stories involves the friendship between Ludwig Wittgenstein, a great Christian thinker of the twentieth century, and Bertrand Russell, one of the greatest atheist philosophers of the twentieth century. In 1911, a young Wittgenstein arrived in Cambridge to be mentored by Russell, the English philosopher. After five terms of study and deepening friendship, however, Wittgenstein concluded that he could not continue in the friendship.

Over the course of two letters, the younger man wrote:

> I can see perfectly well that your value-judgments are just as good and just as deep-seated…as mine…and that I have no right to catechize you. But I see equally clearly, now, that for that very reason there cannot be any real relation of friendship between us…. *We ourselves* are not *so very* different, but our ideals could not be more so. And that's why…we shan't *ever* be able to talk about anything involving our value-judgments without either becoming hypocritical or falling out.[29]

How history might have been different if Wittgenstein, a Christian, had chosen to remain engaged in a relationship with Russell, who wanted to be his patron and even wrote an introduction to the very work that attacked him. Instead, Wittgenstein decided to be "right" rather than to be in relationship. Without any woodshed relearning, Wittgenstein closed the door to further conversation and spiritual exchanges.

Woodshed relearning results in looking at things differently and doing things differently. Historian Stephen Ambrose, in one of his last interviews, told the story of Andrew Jackson Higgins, who built landing craft in World War II. Higgins refused to hire graduates of engineering schools because he was convinced they were creativity killers. Instead, Higgins Industries hired engineers who were self-educated and self-motivated. At the beginning of the war he had twenty employees. By the middle of the war he employed thirty thousand people who ultimately turned out twenty thousand landing craft. President Dwight D. Eisenhower told Ambrose personally, "Andrew Higgins won the war for us. He did it without engineers."[30]

It doesn't take an "expert" to live as a Christian. But it does take a lifetime of woodshed and toolshed relearning.

Potty Sheds for Unlearning

I am just one generation removed from the outhouse. Some of my earliest memories of staying at the Boggs family homestead in Alvon, West Virginia, are of getting up in the middle of the night to visit the two-holer.

For relationships to grow, sometimes we need to unlearn things. We need learning dumpsters like potty sheds to get rid of learning that is dated and to let go of grudges and gripes, misunderstandings and misperceptions that are blocking our system. And sometimes we need to shed relationships that are destructive.

We've all experienced gridlock when trying to get to work. Thoroughfares turn into miles-long parking lots. There is such a thing as mental and spiritual gridlock that can be even more difficult to get out of than a traffic jam.

The need to shed learning is more acute now than ever. More information has been collected in the past three years than since the beginning of time.[31] We live in a world that puts "information at your fingertips but tends to keep wisdom out of reach."[32] One reason there is greater distance between the amount of information being generated and our ability to alchemize that information into wisdom is that we haven't done our *unlearning* homework.

In a lifetime of seventy-five years, a person today is closer to being three hundred years old in terms of knowledge, experience, and travel. We're all on the move, whether we're in a new marriage, the parent of a teenager, or the son or daughter of an aging parent. Every relationship changes and relocates. Relationships are dynamic and sometimes need to be renegotiated based on fresh knowledge.

Some of the things we believe about relationships and the life of faith need to be disposed of in potty

> The better a man will have known his own ignorance, the greater his learning will be.
>
> —MEDIEVAL MYSTIC, THEOLOGIAN, AND CHURCH REFORMER NICHOLAS OF CUSA[33]

sheds so we can be receptive to new and better ways. The one thing I am sure of when I get to heaven is that I will have to edit my theology.

4. A GROWING RELATIONSHIP IS REPETITION

Familiarity can breed contempt. But even more, familiarity breeds contentment and care.

Children get this right—we just don't listen to them. Think about a child who insists on *Goodnight Moon* at bedtime for the umpteenth time. Or ask any needlepoint artist, whose craft gets more polished with every passing precision. Or ask any homemaker, whose routines make sanctuaries out of drywall and wood. Without repetition there can be no beauty.

Indian popular cinema is called "Bollywood." It is known (and sometimes ridiculed) for its formulaic character. But repetition and familiarity have a special, almost sacrosanct role in Bollywood filmmaking. In fact, it is the sense of familiarity that engenders the delight of the moviegoers. Every Bollywood film is not so much a standalone movie as a flower in a wreath that links people together in the Bollywood universe.

Growing relationships require repetition. Especially our relationship with the divine and with the one-anothers. In the Christian tradition, repetitions are called rituals, which open us to the sacred. Rituals are the realignments of relationships through actions that restore harmony to distorted thinking and dissonant living. Rituals force us to see everything in relationship. For example, sickness is not simply a biological issue; it's also an issue of your lifestyle, your family, your community, your job. Through ritual we unleash the past and release new futures.

Rituals come in a variety of forms. The repetitive reading and rereading of the Scriptures, for example, is called *lectio divina.* The recitation of repetitious prayers is called a rosary. The recitation of creeds (Apostles' Creed, Nicene Creed) is called a litany. In fact, repetitious prayers like the Lord's Prayer help one become a pray-er, a person who desires to turn one's entire life into a "Lord's prayer."

> It's not the opening in the gallery that makes the painter (although it may make his or her career); it's the repetitious actions in the studio.
>
> —Jungian "soul-maker" psychoanalyst James Hillman[34]

Prayer is another name for relationship. Jesus taught that the first "principle" of prayer is relationship: We talk to God on the basis of an at-ease relationship and call God "Abba."[35] Of course, some people are more formal in their relationships, even with parents, and prefer prayers found in prayer books or prayers inherited from the saints. Others are more spontaneous and prefer ad hoc prayers. But the Christian tradition is unanimous in the understanding that praying requires that the body, mind, and spirit all be in relationship.

Monks of the medieval era would whisper the psalms they had memorized so that their bodies were engaged in the conversation of prayer. Prayer involved a change in body position so that the heart, head, and hands would be engaged and in alignment. There was not one "right" posture—kneeling, standing, bowed down—just as there was not one right way to pray. In fact, the greatest theologian in the history of Christianity admitted that he didn't know how to pray ("we do not know how to pray as we ought") but that rather than rely on special techniques we ought to trust the Spirit who "intercedes [for us] with sighs too deep for words."[36]

When Jesus died on the cross, three things were expelled from his body: breath, water, and blood.[37] Jesus's breath became the church; his blood became the eucharist; and his water became our baptism. The living proof of the gospel, according to Saint John, is the threefold legacy of the dying Christ and the ongoing threefold repetition in the life of the church: the breath, the water, and the blood.[38] The rituals of the church drew adherents into relationships with water, blood, and breath.

Rituals of Water

The Bible begins and ends with water.[39] In between are wave upon wave of water stories, water invitations, and water rituals.

Jesus's favorite image description for his ministry was water: a well, a stream, a river, the "living water."[40] "Let anyone who is thirsty come to me, and let the one who believes in me drink. As the scripture has said, 'Out of the believer's heart shall flow rivers of living water.' "[41] In this, one of Jesus's most famous water quotations, he is citing a passage that no one can find in the Hebrew Scriptures; it appears only at the end of the Bible.[42]

A Christian is known both by the watermarks and the water table. The watermarks of baptism signify the seal of the covenant, a cleansing and rebirth into a new way of living and dying in the world. As Jesus went through the "deep waters of death," as the tradition puts it, like him we are invited to be "baptized into his death"[43] so that we can emerge, like the children of Israel through the Exodus, into new life on the other side of Jordan. The watermarks of baptism constitute a "living by dying" strategy for success—we die to self by drowning and emerge to eternity.

We wash in the water to obtain our watermarks, but we also need to drink water to live. Christ is the water table from which we slake our thirst.[44] No matter how terrible the dryness, no matter how shrill our cries at our private wailing walls, there is always the watering hole of the Spirit, which issues in rivers of living water. Watermarked people are called to become water tables for others.

Rituals of Blood

The essence of the evangelism practiced by Jesus and the disciples was not taking stands on issues of the day, or teaching propositions, but performing signs that opened the doors of the senses to experiences of the divine. The gospel is not about what Jesus stands for. The gospel is about what Jesus does. In shedding his blood, he frees us from sin and death and makes us into new people. Jesus didn't die for principles. Jesus died for people. Jesus existed for no other purpose than to deliver a message from God: That message was his death on a cursed cross and his resurrection from a sealed tomb.

The eucharist[45] is a feast that brings together two opposite extremes: the worst of sin and death and the best of grace and life. The paradox of the Last Supper—commemorating defeat and death that was also a celebratory feast— was not easy to understand. In fact, over and over the disciples didn't understand. But later they remembered. At the First Breakfast they "got" the Last Supper. Their ability to "remember" most often took place at a meal. Hence the importance of eucharistic rememberings, where we live the paradox of the gospel. The good news is that in the depths of human defeat you can find the triumph of God.

Is "Do this in memory" a command to perform a ritual or an invitation to let the life of Christ become your life? The eucharist (literally "thanksgiving") is a sacred family meal at which we kneel and give thanks for the lightning-rod singularity of the Cross. It draws people into a closer relationship with the divine and makes Christ's power and presence so real that, in Jesus's words, "You should do as I have done for you."[46]

The distinctly Christian ideals of sacrifice, redemption, and community send Jesus's disciples into the world to give blood and become "living sacrifices," feeding others without any expectation of return. In the words of the apostle Paul, we are "not only to believe *on* him, but also to suffer *for* him."[47]

Rituals of Breath

The church speaks with the breath of blood and the breath of water, which together comprise the breath of life. Humans live "in-spired" lives only if we breathe in what God breathes out. Our breathing must be in sync with God's breath. Adam was created when God "breathed" into an ugly clump of clay on a wheel called Earth the breath of "lives" (plural—male and female).

One of the key words for Paul is *spirit,* which comes from the Latin *spiritus* which has the original meaning of "breath" or "wind." God's work in the world comes from God's breathing. "Inspiration" means literally "breathing into" or "blowing upon." We are told by the psalmist, "Let everything that has breath praise the LORD."[48]

The church's holiness depends on the church's breathing patterns. The Jewish temple was turned into a "den of robbers" and a "market"[49] because it hyperventilated and sucked in its own halitosis. Indoor environments are some of the most toxic sites around, causing symptoms ranging from headaches, lethargy, and raw eyes to asthma, high blood pressure, and cancer.[50]

The breath Jesus bestowed on the apostles gave them the power to bind and loose sins. The fresh breath of the Holy Spirit turns toxic dead zones into life zones. An "in-spired" church is exciting and unpredictable because its breathing is in sync with the Spirit who invades our lives in ways that surprise us. The modern church made "inspiration" to be all about biblical inspiration and not about other kinds of in-spiration: to create, to imagine, to love, to praise.

The most holy breath ritual is the kiss. In the early days of Christianity, the church was known as "The Community of the Kiss." Its kissing ritual was not the kind of air-kissy false intimacy that we see all around us. When the early Christians brushed up against people, they planted kisses on the faces of the diseased, the scorned, the downtrodden.[51]

Jan Winebrenner was raised in a Navajo community, where she learned not to point with her finger. In Navajo culture, finger pointing is deemed an act of violence. "The hands are deceptive things without brains and are hired things without souls," is how a Navajo elder put it. So a Navajo will never point a finger at anything. Instead, the Navajo gesture by using their entire body, especially the head. But most often with a movement of the lips much like a kiss.[52]

Rituals of breath help us exchange finger pointing for kissing. Right breathing enables disciples of Jesus to give up weapons of violence including gossip, envy, and lies. We take up arms against one another when we should put our arms around one another.

Perhaps you can't bring yourself to kiss; but if you can point a finger, you can hold a hand.

5. A Growing Relationship Is Emptying

Jesus came to us empty-handed, dirty-handed, and openhanded. If your hands are empty, dirty, and open, they are the hands of Jesus.

The gospel path is one of self-emptying, which is why it's narrow and difficult. In emptying himself on the cross, Jesus was raised to glory and he raised us with him. The biblical phrase for emptying is *kenosis,* and the ultimate act of kenosis is the Incarnation: "…though he was in the form of God, did not regard equality with God as something to be exploited, but emptied himself, taking the form of a slave."[53]

Kenotic moves are essential to relationship building. God's creation of a world with which to be in relationship was itself a kenotic move. Simone Weil called creation the greatest act of humility, for it was when God ceased to be everything so that creation can be something. God's restoration of relationship with a rebellious world was another kenotic move. When a relationship is broken, the injured party is the only one who can heal it because only the injured can forgive. Our sin cut our connection with God; God forgave our sin, and sent Jesus to restore the connection.[54]

Relationships grow through giving and receiving. God gives; we receive. For us to receive what God has to give, our hands need to be empty. All whole relationships are based on mutual disclosure, revelation or emptying of self in conversation with another.

Embrace Absence

Emptying is fundamentally the awareness of what isn't there, which makes absence a determining force in presence. Novelist John Updike observes how "cold is an absence, an absence of heat, and yet it feels like a presence."[55]

Absence and presence are the both/and of all relationships. Jesus needed to go away so that he could be present in a more powerful and universal form—"It is for your good that I am going away."[56] Sometimes the best thing you can do for someone is to be absent from him or her. Relationships can grow fastest and strongest in the wake of absence than of presence.

> Every morning you should wake up in your bed and ask yourself: "Can I believe it all again today?" … At least five times out of ten the answer should be No because the No is as important as the Yes, maybe more so.
>
> —PRESBYTERIAN NOVELIST AND ESSAYIST FREDERICK BUECHNER[57]

Even the absence of faith, or the presence of doubt, can leave us with stretch marks from growing in the Spirit. Madeleine L'Engle wrote something early in her career about her own quarrelsome friendship with truth: "Sometimes I just know that I am going to come down with an attack of atheism again. It's like the flu. Spiritual flu, I call it. I get ready to endure three or four days of doubt and deep distance from God. Then through the grace of God, I find myself spiritually well again."[58]

Embrace Chaos

Chaos is another name for emptiness. In our relationships we crave order and shun chaos. But we should prize chaos more than order. Ordered relationships are stable and comfortable, but they aren't growing relationships. Only chaos brings forth new ideas, new experiences, and new energies, because only chaos is open and receiving, ready for change.

How many times have you said or heard said, "I only wish things could return to normal." Normalcy is never good. In fact, what some relationships need more than anything is stirring sticks that can upset the normal, empty the predictable, and bring some chaos.

See chaos in your kid's room? See positive, not negative.

See chaos on your desk at work? See positive, not negative.

See chaos in your relationships? See potential and possibility and creativity.

Order is what already is; it's status quo. Chaos is what can be; it's phase transition. There is no healing without the waters being stirred up, emptied of their stillness. Seek the order within the chaos, not the order imposed on the chaos.

Margaret Mead was married to an equally renowned anthropologist, Gregory Bateson. One of my favorite Bateson stories comes from his consulting contract with a zoo. The otters were in trouble. Their physical health was fine. But these animals that loved to frolic were sitting around all day, lifeless and lethargic. Bateson was brought in to diagnose the situation and offer recommendations. He spent several days observing the sleepy otters. It seemed to him they were depressed.

So he took matters into his own hands. He took the paper on which he was prepared to write his report, hooked a long string at one end of it, and dangled the paper above the area where the otters were slumbering. Soon one of the otters noticed the paper, began playing with it, and caused it to sway in the air. This awakened the curiosity in another otter, who also started pawing it, and the two otters started competing. By now the entire otter population joined in the frolic.

When Bateson retrieved the paper, the otters kept playing. They were "cured" and never went back to their listless life.[59]

The magic of a dangling piece of paper was not the paper but the stirring stick that shook up the otters' environment and introduced some novelty that energized their interactions. When relationships get too comfortable and predictable, the intervention of stirring sticks is imperative if growth is to take place.

Embrace Ignorance

Jesus makes knowers out of us. A knower is not a thinker. A knower is not a feeler. A knower is an *experiencer.* Knowing is experiencing the thing that you know.

But humans are defined by what they don't know as much as by what they do know. Someone once compared learning to an island in a lake. The shoreline of our island is our border of ignorance. The bigger the island of learning gets, the more our knowledge increases, and the larger our borderlines of ignorance become. It's your awareness that you don't know anything that enables you to know everything.

> If only I knew then what I still don't know.
>
> —SCOTTISH POET
> DOUGLAS DUNN[60]

Abraham knew what he knew, and what he did not know. God told him to leave his home and set out on a journey. That's what Abraham knew. But where was he going? That's what Abraham knew he didn't know. Upon nothing more than a promise and a hope to bring blessing to "all the families of the earth," Abraham turned his back on the familiar and known and embraced the unknown. He did this not as an act of belief but as an act of faith. An act of belief is stepping forth based on what you know. In contrast, an act of faith is stepping forth as you admit that you don't know.

Relationships can take our breath away because they open us up to parts of one-anothers and ourselves that we didn't know existed. Do people want others to know them as they really are, or as they are trying with varying degrees of success to be?

Embrace Disappointment

Every relationship is doomed to disappoint. In the Garden of Gethsemane, Jesus was lonely and needed support. He begged of his disciples, "Remain here, and stay awake with me."[61] They soon fell asleep. Every one of them.

Why do more than 80 percent of couples who experience the loss of a child end up divorced? Because it's easier to start over with someone new—without the pain—than to embrace each other's pain and embrace each other amid the pain. We

> I want to sing like no one is listening
> to dance like no one is watching
> and to love as though I had never
> been hurt.
>
> —ANONYMOUS

tend to flee from relationships that are difficult or unfulfilling, because we're afraid of being swept away or wept away by the hurt.

Relationships can miscarry. They also can bring great delight, taking us by surprise. The problem with prenuptial agreements, for instance, is that they focus on what could go wrong rather than on what is right. And they assume there is another relationship always possible around the next corner.

All relationships have wrinkles that you can't iron out. Some are better than others, but no relationship is perfect. All relationships have failings, but all relationships don't have to fail. The promise is that you can achieve a détente with imperfection and that the organizing honesty of the Heidelberg Catechism—guilt, grace, gratitude—can be the organizing honesty of all your relationships.

Embrace Conflict

To say "relationship" is to say "conflict." This is perhaps the biggest reason why men tend to be more relationally challenged than women: We shut down when dealing with conflict. Relationships die without communication, and communication is hardest in the midst of conflict.

Authentic community is more crazy than cozy, more porcupine than teddy bear. It's weird and odd and ragged. Archbishop of Canterbury Rowan Williams talks about living in the body of Christ as "profoundly hard work." We are stuck together with people we may think are "dangerously deluded in their belief about what [is] involved in serving Christ."[62] That's why the church needs to resurrect its relationship rituals of repentance, reconciliation, and forgiveness.

Superhuman feats aren't leaping tall buildings in a single bound or doing a triple flip on a wakeboard. Superhuman feats are astounding acts of forgiveness, awakening acts of courage, bridging acts of betrayal, overcoming acts of fear, rejecting acts of rejection, releasing acts of love, transcending theological disputes. How can people know that Christ is alive if Christians don't love one another? Whenever the phrase "peace of Christ" occurs in the epistles, it does not refer to something inner, but to living in harmony with one another.[63] Consider the world's view of the church: a place of warehoused anger and theological infighting. The pettiness can be unmatched by anything you find in the world.[64]

Seventh Day Adventist theologian Peter J. Prime proposes that the challenge of the church today is the same as the one facing the church at Ephesus, where Christians "loved doctrine at the expense of the doctrine of love."[65] Relationships trump principles. The early church confounded the world with better relationships: "Look how they love one another." Jesus taught that everyone would know by the church's love for one another that he had been sent.[66]

I know a church in California whose prominent pastor stands before the congregation preceding every communion service and reads the names of people dismissed from membership along with detailed reasons for their dismissal. Contrast that kalashnikov community with the witness of the three epistles of John, written to a koinonia community fractured and frustrated by competing theological tenants and schismatic behaviors. How remarkable, therefore, that they are most known and remembered for their words about love. The writer of 1 John confronted the potentially disastrous nature of some wrong ideas of perfection that were circulating among the churches. Yet he did not speak first about right beliefs or right teachings. Instead his most often-repeated theme, his most central concern, is to impress upon these communities the centrality of the Christian mandate to love.

Embrace Constraints

Everyone needs limits. Give people free rein and people will do more to erode than ennoble society. "Freedom of choice" is isolating because it stresses the individual apart from the consequences of one's choice on others. Without relationships, freedom of choice becomes suicidal. The more freedom of choice there is, the more connections there need to be. The "right partner," the "right path," the "right" anything is almost impossible to choose outside the constraints of connections.

But are we bound to one another by rules, or are we bound by relationships? Jesus argued that relationships are more binding than laws. Relationships raise the standard of discipleship higher than any external and hieratically enforced morality could ever do.

"You have heard that it was said to the people long ago, 'Do not murder…,'" Jesus said. "But I tell you that anyone who is angry with his brother will be subject to judgment."[67] "Thou shalt not kill" is more than obedience to a law. It is a spiritual relationship with others that is nonviolent—no hatred and no jealousy. Rules and regulations reform us, at best. But resurrection recreates us. Besides, we are living in a time when the lines between "right" and "wrong" are being blurred and when rules aren't yet written for what people are facing.

Jesus made a distinction between lip service and life service. Paul called it the difference between law obedience and heart obedience, a rules morality versus a relationship morality. It's not what you stand for, it's what you live by, that counts. Both Moses and Jesus taught a "way of life" or a "way of living in relationship" more than a way of thought.

The Ten Commandments are not best titled "Rules to Live By" but "Rituals of Right Relationships." The Ten Commandments are designed to show us the art of relationships and the hows of friendship. The seventh commandment is more than a proscription about sex outside of a marriage; it's about any act that weakens a committed relationship. The sixth commandment goes beyond not doing something that would destroy oneself; one should not do things that destroy one's relationship with oneself.

Is koinonia committed to principles, policies, polities—or to Christ and to one another? One of the problems people have with "living in community" is that they're trying to live out their principles rather than their relationship with Christ.

Paul reintroduced the yoke image, first introduced by Jesus, to help us picture freedom in Christ. The yoke was a despised symbol of slavery, of being under someone else's control. Egyptians put yokes on Hebrew slaves. Farmers put a yoke on a team of oxen to force them into certain routines and routes.

Yet Jesus said, "Take my yoke upon you and learn from me, for I am gentle and humble in heart, and you will find rest for your souls."[68] The yoke of Jesus is the leash of love. "Submit to one another out of reverence for Christ."[69] The "love of Christ constraineth us," Paul testified.[70]

Why don't I lie to avoid an awkward moment or to advance my own cause? Do I choose not to lie because I fear getting caught, or because my relationship with Christ makes me want to live an honest and honorable life? It's the relationship that keeps me honest.

Christians don't avoid "bad things" because we're afraid of crossing over a line that separates right from wrong. We've all crossed over the line. Thomas Martin, former manager of a Jack in the Box restaurant, reported that he'd been robbed of $307 as the store was closing. He provided police sketch artist Jack Lee with a detailed description of the suspect. When Lee put his pad down, he observed that the drawing looked just like Martin.

Martin confessed.[71]

In the words of Paul, "All have sinned and fall short of the glory of God."[72]

It is the yoke of Jesus, also known as the "love of Christ," that constrains us to move forward in Godward directions—to dwell in the GodLife relationship. Relationships are like yokes: They keep our heads up, our spine from shaking, and our bodies moving forward.

The yoke of a relationship with Christ is liberating and soothing at the same time it is more constraining than all the rules and regulations in the universe. Ethics is rooted in relationship. Paul was less concerned about breaking a commandment than about violating his GodLife relationship.

When the rule of law reigns, life's greatest fear is to incur God's wrath. When the rule of relationship, the Law of Love, reigns, life's greatest fear is to break God's heart.

PART V

OUR RELATIONSHIP WITH THOSE OUTSIDE THE FAITH AND WITH THOSE WHO ARE DIFFERENT

Loving the "Others"

Why Jesus Preferred the Ragged over the Right

It's just so easy to do the goat dance.
Yeah, but it's hard, it's so hard...
to love somebody.
—SINGER-POET GREG BROWN[1]

Romance and mystery lead the pack among book publishing's biggest sellers. People are looking for someone to love and some mystery to live. And it should come as no surprise that both of these involve relationships.

Relationships fill our lives with both romance and a mystery, offering connections as well as intrigue. Relationships make life enjoyable, or at least bearable. Remember the reports of phone calls made from the two United Airlines flights and the two American Airlines flights on September 11, 2001? Realizing that their planes were going down, passengers who managed to call left one message with their spouses and children: "I love you."

Love gets us out of bed in the morning. Yet it remains one of the great mysteries of life. In particular, human friendship is beyond our comprehension. You can't find the equivalent of friendship relationships anywhere else in nature. Friendship is species-specific to those created in God's image.

It's a difficult thing we do, living with others on this earth. It becomes even more difficult when we can cybertravel our way through life, avoiding actual human contact for long stretches of time. Technology makes it too easy to avoid high-maintenance relationships like friendships.

CLOSE ENCOUNTERS OF THE "OTHER" KIND

God's invitation to us isn't, "Shut up and listen!" but, "Walk with me and help me serve others." God's greatest desire is to love us so that we can love God and others. God's greatest hope is that we will join God in a relationship that turns others around, that turns people who are "accidents waiting to happen" into "people who make things happen."

"I want final say and sway in your life," God says, "but talk to me, wrestle with me, be my friend as we wake up this world with some really good news."

Christian mystic Leanne Payne says faith is walking alongside God. But it's so much easier just to walk alongside myself. Walking alongside Jesus demands that I make others the focus of my relationship with the divine. In contrast, when *I* am the focus of my relationship with God, then I can relax and just concentrate on attending to my own needs. It's so much simpler when others aren't involved.

At the memorial service for country singer June Carter Cash, Johnny Cash's daughter Rosanne celebrated her stepmother as someone who knew only two kinds of people: "Those she knew and loved, and those she didn't know...and loved."[2] The purpose of love is to love others. My guess for the open-sesame question at the Pearly Gates? "Who have you brought with you?"

Holocaust survivor and philosopher Emmanuel Lévinas calls the question of the "other" and the claim "others" make in our lives *the* religious question. Lévinas upsets the philosophical applecart by insisting that ethics, not metaphysics, is the "first" philosophy. There is something more fundamental than "being." That is "being in relationship."[3]

The metaphor that Lévinas used for the "other" is the "face" *(le visage)*. When we insist on integrating "otherness" into our own preconceptions and preexistent categories, we "deface" the other, demean his or her integrity, and diminish that person's contribution to our understanding of the world. We are not called to fit someone else into our own story, but to encounter and experience the ways that God is in the other person's story. Only in a listening relationship can the other be truly "faced" and not "defaced." The critical test of any faith thus becomes "does it make space for otherness?"[5]

> I believe we can change the world if we start listening to each other again.
>
> —LEADERSHIP GURU
> MARGARET WHEATLEY[4]

My oldest son made me a grandfather twice at once. My grandsons are twins, and I can't tell them apart. Only their parents can tell Caden from Conor. Why? Because they are deep in relationship. Only in the depths of relationship can the "otherness" of others be appreciated and added to your learning curve.

The key to evangelism is to be receivers of others—ushers to the Other, not users of others. In receiving others, we enter into their world of abundant otherness—their experiences, their thought patterns, their stories. In using others, we treat people as objects and hope to get something out of them (a conversion, a donation, their acquiescence to our argument). One can receive others and celebrate their stories without buying into their every perspective. This is how the early Christians dealt with the multiplicity of faiths in the ancient world. They did not blast away at other religions. They simply made the ultimate claim for Jesus as the Son of God with everything that was in them.[6]

Since every disciple is commissioned as an evangelist, we all could learn something about evangelism from photographer Jan Phillips, who refuses to take photographs of people she hasn't spoken with.[7] In a Beijing hotel lobby, Phillips met a British photographer who showed her his newest toy: a lens that allowed him to photograph others at a ninety-degree angle. "I can point my camera straight ahead and get a secret shot of someone at my side," he explained. Phillips wondered why he would be so proud of such a thing. She wanted her images to "reflect some connections, no matter how brief or limited. That connection was the healing part."[8]

There is a midrash that says God spoke to the Israelites on Mount Sinai not "face to face" but "face after face." To one observer, God appeared standing. To another witness, God appeared as if seated. To one, God seemed as a young man, and to another as an old man.[9] God shows us many faces: a joyous face, comforting face, laughing face. Likewise, it is our privilege to show God our true faces, if we will but do it. The fact that Abraham kept his head down on the three-day hike to Mount Moriah, refusing to show God his face, speaks volumes about his vacating of his prior intimacy with God.

KNOWING GOD THROUGH OTHERS

As Christians, we know ourselves in relationship with the Other, and also in relationship with the "others"—those not of the household of faith. We discover the Other and ourselves through our relationships with the others. I move toward God by moving toward others. Jesus never separated soteriology from neighborology—the artistry of how to be a neighbor to another.

During the last week of his life, Jesus was teaching in the temple. The keepers of the tradition, the Pharisees, tried to trap him with the question: "Teacher, which is the greatest commandment in the Law?"

The answer, of course, everyone knew: "Love the Lord your God with all your heart…soul and…mind."

Then Jesus revolutionized the world by putting another scriptural passage next to it. "And the second is like it: 'Love your neighbor as yourself.' All the Law and the Prophets hang on these two commandments."[10]

The "hanging" goes both ways. We hang on them for dear life. And they hang us with their judgment. Not working on the Sabbath is not enough. Not lying is not enough. Faith involves a relationship with the world, which means a relationship with those who are not "of the faith." Not until you're in a relationship does a person behind the uniform (or whatever it is they're hiding behind) become a real, live person. And when we're in such a relationship, we see that God becomes human in the stranger.[11]

GETTING CLOSE IS GETTING STRANGER

The classic passage of welcoming the stranger is Abraham's hospitality to the three strangers at Mamre.[12] Immersed in prayer with God when the strangers appeared, Abraham interrupted his prayer to prepare a meal. He later found that the strangers were angels bearing a message of a future far different from the one Abraham and Sarah dreamed possible. It was this meeting that the writer of Hebrews had in mind when he counseled, "Do not forget to entertain strangers, for by so doing some people have entertained angels without knowing it."[13]

God came to Abraham in the guise of a stranger, ate at his table, and called him his friend. God appeared to Abraham through strangers, which reminds us that dignity must be extended to the "other." As the praying Abraham discovered, prayer doesn't plunge us deeper into ourselves, but deeper into others. The early church looked on prayer as a conversation[14] with God that brings us into greater intimacy with God and others. Prayer is not what you do to get God's attention. Prayer is what you do to bring yourself to attend to God and to pay attention to others.[15]

Can you think of a better definition of the Incarnation than this—God leaving the Godhead and going "into the world to...carry the divine life into it"?[16] In incarnation, God becomes "other"—no longer God in heaven but God in mortal flesh. God became human to engage us, the "other," in relationship. This is indeed a strange statement. To say that God became human is like saying that a circle is a square.

The apostle Paul believed that disciples of Jesus are "predestined" or "called" to "extend hospitality to strangers."[17] Two Greek words for hospitality are primarily used in the New Testament. One is *proslambanomai,* which means to "take aside" and "take with"—in other words, to select and bring along. The other is *philoxenia,* which means more than simply welcoming the stranger, but loving the stranger.[18]

Jesus could hardly talk about "selecting strangers to love" without talking about the dinner table. Jesus used the table as a primary setting for teaching and faith formation. To launch his earthly ministry he turned water into wine at a wedding party. When Jesus debuted his ministry at that wedding celebration, where food, faith, and festivity were linked, he telegraphed the trajectory of his entire ministry. The last thing the pre-Resurrection Jesus did with his disciples was to serve them bread and wine. And after the Resurrection, the most intense encounters with the risen Lord occurred at meals. In Emmaus it was the act of eating with Jesus that revealed who he was.

Two things stand out in Jesus's table hospitality. First, he didn't like to eat alone. Second, he ate with anybody. These two features of Jesus's ministry were lashed together and used as a whip: "Here is a glutton and a drunkard, a friend of tax collectors and 'sinners.'"[19] In contrast with John the Baptist, who didn't come eating and drinking and whose approach to sinners was censure, Jesus was always eating, drinking, and welcoming sinners as table companions. He couldn't seem to resist it.

Jesus Didn't Like to Eat Alone

Jesus often did things alone, but it seems he didn't like to eat alone. He invited strangers and friends to eat with him without preconditions and accepted meal invitations from almost anyone. Jesus was as hungry for people to share a meal with as he was for food.[20]

Eating together builds relationships. It's no accident that the oldest surviving recipe in the world is for a social beverage: beer.[21] The greatest single indicator of healthy relationships in a family? Shared meals. The family that eats together (five nights a week) stays together.[22]

> Thank you, Lord, for another crack at togetherness.
>
> —HOMER SIMPSON,
> THE SIMPSONS

Jesus used meals as a means of introducing people to God and inviting them to join him "on the way." Table fellowship was not the reward for entering a love relationship with God. Table fellowship was an invitation to embark on a love relationship with God.

Over and over, Jesus told food stories and enacted food rituals that invited people to reflect the hospitality of God.[23] In fact, Jesus loved food so much he defined his ministry as "food."[24] Soul nourishment comes to us only as we do God's will. That's our food. When people dine with Jesus, bread is *always* on the menu, the Bread of Life. In his *Confessions,* Augustine tells of a voice from above saying, "I am the food of fully grown people; grow, and you shall feed on me. And you will not change me into you as like the food your flesh eats, but you will be changed into me."[25]

Eating disorders are primarily caused by relational disorders. Bad eating corrupts good relationships, and vice versa. Our binge-and-purge approach to relational intimacy evidences the difficulty we have in sustaining relationships both with one-anothers (those who are part of the faith) and with others (those outside the faith and those who are different). Anorexia is a symptom of a culture that resists depth and intimacy in relationships. Bulimia is a symptom of an eat-on-the-run culture that briefly takes in, and then quickly releases, all types of relationships. We leap into love and then upchuck our way out. Obesity is a symptom of a fast-food, channel-hopping culture (two out of three USAmerican adults are fat[26]) that is undisciplined in its relationships, supersizing expectations and gorging itself on fantasies of celebrity love. Hollywood images are the number one export of USAmerica to the world, and obesity is now the world's biggest public-health problem. The World Health Organization named obesity a global "epidemic" in 2000.[27]

In our avoidance of those outside the faith, and in our insistence that they first conform to our beliefs to earn our friendship, we all have eating disorders.

Relationship with the "other" implies shared risks and resources. Honest relationships involve conflict, misunderstanding, tension, and make-up periods. But we don't allow ourselves to engage in these perfectly normal dimensions of relationship. Instead, when someone makes us mad, we run. When someone confronts us, we either fight or hide. When someone does us wrong, we remain silent and grow bitter about it later. Some of us will do almost anything to avoid a confrontation with another human being.

Humans find it quite difficult to live with one another even during the best of times. Some of us aren't emotionally wired for intimacy. Some of us have crippling flaws that make relationships difficult. In fact, some of history's greatest contributors have been relationship-challenged. As an adult, Isaac Newton shunned personal intimacy in all its forms, preferring his laboratory of the mind to living specimens. Henri Nouwen, who inspired many of us to move deeper into relationships with God and one another, had trouble himself developing intimacy with others. Relational disorders abound among creative people.

During the Second World War, while they were both in Yugoslavia, English satirical novelist Evelyn Waugh and his friend Randolph Churchill (son of Winston) got in constant fights. Churchill one day exploded, "I thought you were supposed to be a Christian and a Catholic." To which Waugh replied, "And think how much worse I would be if I wasn't."[28]

But we live in a culture that makes relationships harder while stimulating the hunger for relationships.[29] The more globally the market economy structures itself, the more relentless the assault on all nonmarket social relations. This makes the church's role in strengthening the social and ecological webs in which humans live all the more important. Unfortunately, the culture seems to be more aware of this than the church. The most highly visible people addressing the impoverishment of our relationship skills are "relationship ministers" such as Dr. Phil, Dr. Laura, Oprah, and (my favorite) Delilah.

Consider some contrasts between what we experience and what we long to experience:

- My parents taught me how to play Scrabble with them. Parents today are more likely to teach their kids how to play Solitaire.
- One third (35 percent) of USAmericans today say they have been through a romantic breakup at least once in the past ten years.[30]

- More than one in ten USAmericans (12 percent) spend Friday nights alone.[31]
- And today, one in four USAmericans lives alone.[32] For the first time in history, more USAmericans live alone in single-person households than there are families comprising a husband, a wife, and one child.[33] The voice at the other end of the cell phone—"Hello? We're breaking up!"—might well be the motto of our era.

Norma Jean Mortenson spent much of her childhood in foster homes. In one of those homes, when she was eight years old, a boarder raped her and gave her a nickel. He said: "Here, take this and don't ever tell anyone what I did to you."

> We're all in this together—alone.
>
> —HUMORIST LILY TOMLIN[34]

When Norma Jean went to her foster mother, Gladys Baker, she was badly beaten for telling what had happened. Norma Jean was told: "Our boarder pays good rent. Don't you ever say anything bad about him!" At the age of eight, Norma Jean learned what it was to be used, given a nickel, and then beaten for trying to express the hurt and loneliness inside her.

Eventually she escaped to Hollywood and took the name Marilyn Monroe. When her handlers told her they would make a "sex symbol" out of her, she confessed she didn't know what a symbol was. Dumb-blonde roles were invented by Marilyn Monroe, and in spite of her beauty, everyone on the set hated her. She kept crews waiting for hours. They thought she was preening. Most of the time she was in the dressing room throwing up because she was so terrified.

She went through three marriages and kept asking: "Did you notice I'm a person?"

On a Saturday night when she was thirty-five, Marilyn Monroe took her own life. When the maid found her body, she noticed the telephone was off the hook.

In one of Father John Powell's books, the Jesuit theologian tells the story of Claire Booth Luce's question: "What really killed Marilyn Monroe, the love goddess who never found any love?" For Claire Booth Luce, the dangling telephone was the symbol of Marilyn Monroe's life.[35] She died because she never got through to anyone.

We just keep breaking up. Our relationships mirror what is inside us. Wealth and fame, rather than freeing us up for better relationships, often tie us down. Materialism has become the top secular religion. Studies show that the more you identify with your possessions (including your pocketbook), the greater will be your foul moods, negative attitudes, and disabled relationships. In fact, the primary reason why the "happiness" charts fail to keep up with economic progress is because the good things in life are not good "things" but good relationships—friends, family, loved ones.

We aren't relational because we have relationships in the same way that we have a new SUV. We are relational because only in connection with others does life have meaning. It is only in relationship that we are known and that we know love. As Joe Myers reminds us in *The Search to Belong*, our true "belongings" are not our possessions but our relationships.[36]

One person can make a difference. But a person does not make a difference because he or she is one. People make a difference because they are connected. It's better for us to make decisions with more connectivity, rather than with more certainty. The future belongs to those who help people make connections and those who enhance relationships.

The more access we have to official information—and our levels of access are unprecedented—the more valuable is informal communication. Information technology that delivers up-to-the-minute data threatens to crowd out the knowledge and wisdom we gain through casual, face-to-face conversation. The informal network is now so rare it has become more valuable than the formal one.

But the relationships we're searching for are different from networking—where human interactions are business opportunities, where we focus on winning by having the right friends in the right places at the right time.

True relationships with others decenter the self. They get us outside ourselves and teach us that the world is not just about me. And relationships with others break down the boundaries that separate us. Every time we partake of the eucharist, are we not embracing boundary-breaking, relationship-building lives? Every time we overcome fear of the other, isn't our own faith strengthened? Is there a pastor or theologian who doesn't know the truth of Martin Luther's admission that he did not have as much faith as others thought he had, but that in talking about faith with others and one-anothers, his faith grew?

For too long our vision of others has been based on the notion of a Unitary Self—a fixed, stable self that goes through life in one form. We are just now beginning to understand that a human being, who is created in the image of the Triune God, is a trinity of selves: head, heart, and hands. Put another way, a person is a community of selves. When we shoehorn the self into a fixed, singular container, we fail to understand the complex web of relationships within which our sense of self operates. A healthy "self" is the harmonious relationship of constantly moving internal parts and processes.

Every person needs a range of relationships, some casual and fleeting, some soul deep, some that stay for a lifetime. We face not one big death in life, but a series of minideaths. Relationships come and go, and we don't always get to choose which ones get restored.[37]

All relationships require cultivation and care. If each one of us dedicated a half hour (or even fifteen minutes) every day for connecting with our friends, especially our closest confidants (which translates in the Russian idiom as "kitchen friends"), how different would life be?

And while relationships deliver rewards such as the enjoyment of companionship and a sense of belonging, relationships also generate weeds and unwanted growth. Every relationship causes pain and suffering. Fault lines run through every relationship that are not our fault. Just as nowhere else in nature do you find "friendships," so human beings are the only species to weep. Perhaps having friends and having to cry are more related than we realize.

The word *vulnerability* comes from the Latin word *vulnus,* which means "wound." To be human is to be capable of being wounded. Every friendship has a history of "some-things-were-said" scenarios. But the friend who holds your hand and says the wrong thing is more precious than the one who stays away and says the right thing or says nothing. There is no relationship without communication, and there is no communication without ongoing conversations.

> I will find that special person who is wrong for me in just the right way.
>
> —AUTHOR AND ACTIVIST
> ANDREW BOYD[38]

Every relationship has griefs. But we can choose not to let these harden into grievances. A long human lifetime lasts only 650 thousand hours. That's all the time we get. Life is too short for grudges and grievances.

Jesus knew the value of friendship, just as he knew the deep hurts that can come at the hands of friends. Still, he hated to eat alone. He loved people too much not to share a meal and a relationship.

Jesus Ate with Anybody

Not only did Jesus dislike eating alone, but he also ate with just about anybody. He was an equal-opportunity relationship builder. It was in his DNA to invite the strange as well as the stranger into a table relationship. This makes sense when you consider Jesus's actual DNA. A Moabite woman (Ruth), a forbidden foreigner, stands at the start of the Davidic line of Jesus. The book of Ruth ends with the genealogy of David, where there is not just Jew, but Moabite. And when Jesus said, "Do this in memory of me," he was instructing us to do the same: share table companionship with Moabites and Levites, with idolatrous outsiders like Ruth and adulterous insiders like David.

Toward the end of the twelfth century, a prudish monk known as Richard of Devizes issued a stern warning to those unwary innocents who might be contemplating a visit to London.

> Do not associate with the crowds of pimps; do not mingle with the throngs in the eating-houses; avoid the dice and gambling, the theatre and the tavern. You will meet with more braggarts there than in all France; the number of parasites is infinite. Actors, jesters, smooth-skinned lads, Moors, flatterers, pretty boys, effeminates, pederasts, singing and dancing girls, quacks, belly-dancers, sorceresses, extortionists, night-wanderers, magicians, mimes, beggars, buffoons: all this tribe fill all the houses.[39]

These were precisely the types of people Jesus chose to invite to his table. British preacher J. H. Jowett called Jesus a "receiver of wrecks."[40] He gathered around him all the pariahs. What triumph is it to love the lovable? Jesus asked. What success is it to heal the healthy? Swiss psychiatrist Paul Tournier claimed that Christianity is the only religion that states that God loves the unrighteous more than the righteous. Christianity has much less to do with being "right" than it has to do with building right relationships—the strong protecting the weak, the rich serving the poor, the insiders making room for the outcasts.

Our choices determine whether we come to dinner with Jesus or refuse relationship. But the invitation is open to everyone—even to us. Jesus is most often gentle with those who are living rebellious, disobedient lives. He was accused of being a soft-on-crime Messiah. Jesus was most often harsh with those law-and-order types whose righteousness blinded them to right relationships with God and those outside the "right" group. Jesus was always arranging dinner dates between wrecks, weird people, and The Twelve.

> I will search for the lost and bring back the strays.
>
> —GOD, SPEAKING THROUGH THE PROPHET EZEKIEL[41]

Jesus removed his disciples from the isolation of village and family life and forced them into relationships with foreigners, strangers, children, women, lepers. The "kingdoms of the world" enclosed strangers within hostile fences, eroded trust levels, and limited cordiality to kith and kin. The "kingdom of God," in marked contrast, involved daily table sharing and hospitality with strangers, including sympathy for aliens and criminals and safe havens for the poor.

If our bodies are temples of the Holy Spirit, the early church reasoned, then we must see all others as temples and treat others with tenderness and respect. To hurt others is in some sense to attack God.

As with immigrants to a country, we can value strangers for what they bring to us—diversity, talent, industry, innovative cuisines, plus a renewed appreciation of our own homeland whose virtues are so great that "others" are drawn to us. Or we can fear strangers for what they might do to us—dilute our common heritage, fragment our politics, undermine our preferred culture. Isn't the real gift we receive from others precisely their "otherness"?

In the journeys of Bilbo Baggins through forest and dale, Bilbo and his companions came to rest in the house of Elrond.

> [Elrond's house] was perfect, whether you liked food, or sleep, or work, or story-telling, or singing, or just sitting and thinking best, or a pleasant mixture of them all.…

All of them, the ponies as well, grew refreshed and strong in a few days there. Their clothes were mended as well as their bruises, their tempers and their hopes.[42]

Can this be said of our houses of worship? Christ's mission in the world is to draw people into a GodLife relationship. God is trying to make friends. We are called into Christ's mission to befriend others.[43] Some social systems—even some church systems—are better at manufacturing strangers than making friends.

Is the church a place where we learn how to befriend the strange and estranged—to learn from them, to love them, to listen to them, to extend the generosity of the GodLife relationship? Think about the feeding of the five thousand: "They all ate and were satisfied, and the disciples picked up twelve basketfuls of broken pieces that were left over."[44] This is a story of utter scarcity and tremendous need. Thousands of hungry, weary souls had nothing to eat. And their need was met by the generosity of Jesus.

Of course, we know how much Jesus disliked eating alone. Can the same be said of the church?

Jesus and the Outcast

Finding God in the "Other"

> Whenever you did one of these things to someone over-
> looked or ignored, that was me—you did it to me.
>
> —Jesus[1]

Jesus really did have strange tastes. He especially liked being around the poor, the marginalized, the forgotten. Who should be invited to the table? The disabled, the outcast, the overlooked[2]—precisely those people excluded from the table by certain religious communities. For Jesus it was not "Poor people and other outcasts, find yourself a church"; it was "Church people, find yourself the poor and the outcasts."

The New Testament teaches that the church is the body of Christ. Jesus teaches that the victims of hatred and oppression are Jesus. "Whatever you did for one of the least of these brothers of mine, you did for *me*."[3] So if the church refuses to identify with the poor and forgotten, it is turning its back on Jesus. It cannot become one body with Christ.

Sadly, the church is too busy connecting people with the *memory* of Jesus, the Jesus who "once was" or the promise of a returning Christ who "is to come." Meanwhile, the church is neglecting the Jesus who "is right now," the Jesus who lives all around us in the lives of the poor, the sick, the disabled, the persecuted, and the dying.

THE REAL ATHEISM

Who is the follower of Jesus and who is the atheist? Catholic activist Dorothy Day constantly reminded her workers that the true atheist is the person who can't see Jesus in the face of the poor. It is popular to talk about poor people, as Mother Teresa often lamented. But it's not nearly as popular to talk *to* poor people. The issue is not on what principles of justice and freedom do you stand, but on what freedom roads are you traveling? Let's forget for the moment about the hard-core poor. Consider the working poor and those being paid poverty wages. How many maids, tellers, cooks, waiters, child-care workers, home health aids, hairdressers, and other low-wage workers are table companions at your church?[4]

Can God say about your church, as about Job, that you have eyes for the blind and feet for the lame, and that you're father of the poor?[5] Or are the words of Saint John Chrysostom more applicable to your church, words spoken to the prosperous Christians of Antioch:

> Your dog is fed to fullness while Christ wastes with hunger. When
> Christ is famishing, do you revel in luxury? Christ has nowhere to
> lodge, but goes about as a stranger, and naked and hungry, and you
> set up houses out of town, and baths and terraces and chambers with-
> out number, in thoughtless vanity; and to Christ you give not even
> a share of a little hut.[6]

The persistence of poverty in a world that is boundlessly rich is the scandal of our time. The richer nations will pay a heavy price for their neglect of the poor. In the words of a Nigerian tribal chief, "If you don't share your wealth with us, we will share our poverty with you." No one is "gated" from the poverty and despair of the people on the opposite side of the globe. If we learned anything from the tragedy of 9/11, it is this: The health problems of the developing nations are impacting the health of the world's rich. The economic problems of the poor are hampering the economies of the rich. Already the anger of the poor is restricting the freedoms of the world's rich.

The poor don't need our money or our resolutions so much as they need our relationship. Some studies have shown that foreign aid has proved to be an excellent method for transferring money from poor people in rich countries to rich people in poor countries.

RELATIONSHIPS, NOT RESOLUTIONS

Morals, values, and ethics are incarnated in relationships. The daily practice of what we believe makes a louder statement than anything we might say or put into writing. At Enron, ethics was a matter of official company policy. Enron boasted a cadre of ethics consultants and required new hires to sign an ethics pledge before they joined the firm. Enron is now a byword for the vilest betrayal of corporate ethics.

Johnson & Johnson took a different approach. Instead of developing a detailed official policy, ethics was embedded in the company's culture. Moral philosophy was a part of every decision-making process, and ethics pervaded the company's relationship network. Consider how Johnson & Johnson handled the discovery in the 1980s of seven packages of cyanide-laced Tylenol, its best-selling painkiller. The company immediately alerted the public and, at enormous cost, removed Tylenol from store shelves. This bold and ethical action helped make Johnson & Johnson a byword for the highest in standards of corporate conduct. Johnson & Johnson had no formalized ethics policy, but it did practice an ethic of relationship.

> Faith is not a set of recited formulae, even though we need them to stabilize our thoughts to think with, but an act of uncovering whereby the eyes of the blind are opened, the ears of the deaf are unstopped and those long silent find a tongue of fire.
>
> —BRITISH SOCIOLOGIST DAVID MARTIN[7]

Even with an official policy in place, those in power can violate the policy while deluding themselves into thinking they are above reproach. We are all sinners and hybrids. We all come from a land of "between." And in our muddleheadedness and hardheartedness, we easily forget that the church's primary religious function is relationships.

There's an old story about three African elders visiting the West. The visitors were asked: "How can you tell when night ends and day begins?"

The first man responded: "When I can distinguish the olive trees from the fig trees, then I know that night is over and day has begun."

The second answered: "When I can see the forms of the animals across the Serengeti, I know that the darkness is leaving and the light of day is arriving."

The third visitor took an entirely different tack: "When we can see a black woman and a white woman and call them both 'sister,' when we see a poor man and a rich man and call them both 'brother,' then the darkness of night has lifted and the light of day has come."

This man understood the deeper meaning of the question. The darkness lifts not according to the time of day, but according to the practice of relationship.

DOING GOOD TO OUR ENEMIES

We are called to be—like Jesus—the friend of sinners. That means building relationships with people who reside outside the orbit of our moral universe. It means becoming their friend and loving them. It means accepting them and their differences and being willing to be enriched by those differences. It involves discovering Jesus in places and people we don't expect Jesus to be.

If you knew your next meal were going to be your last, who would you want to join you? Wouldn't you want this to be a time of circling the wagons and drawing strength from your friends? The one person you *wouldn't* want at the table is your sworn enemy—the person whose betrayal caused this to be your last supper on earth.

Not Jesus. His last supper was open to his worst enemy and to other betrayers, including Peter and even to self-centered disciples who were less concerned about Jesus than they were about who was going to get the greatest seats in the kingdom. Pastor Steve Ayers issues a needed reminder: "Never forget that Jesus loved Judas. This is the relational understanding the church needs to move to in the twenty-first century. We must love a culture and a nation that looks more like Judas than the faithful disciple."[8]

> It might be possible for a person to love without risking danger—but this is not the case with us.
>
> —BISHOP OF CONSTANTINOPLE ST. JOHN CHRYSOSTOM[9]

In my life, Jesus is often more the problem than the solution. Jesus says: "Take on the sufferings of others. I call you to self-sacrifice more than self-fulfillment. Self-preservation is not the highest value." The world says: "You're not the savior of the world. You only need to worry about saving yourself. If you're not going to look out for yourself, who will?"

Whose advice do you think I'd prefer to follow?

But the biggest headache I get from following Jesus is from what may be the most unexpected of all his teachings: "I tell you: Love your enemies."[10]

The hatred of the world and all things in it, especially your enemies, was a cardinal tenet of the Essene community at Qumran. Even to this day in Pakistan, it is the norm for farmers to talk about themselves in these terms: "my wife, my land, my children, my cow—and my enemy."[11] The "enemy" was such a component of a person's identity that there was a saying: "Tell me who your enemy is and I'll tell you who you are."

The airways are crowded with Christian ministries that have discovered that the best way to increase donations is to define yourself as fervently engaging in battle against an enemy. Osama bin Laden is a firm believer that the best way to solidify the collective character of a religion is to identify who your enemy is and make war against that enemy.

That's why Jesus's instruction to love your enemies was and remains so radical. That's also why the biblical picture of Abraham on his knees begging God to spare his enemies from destruction still shocks us. We are more prone to beg God to punish our enemies and to show us ways to get even with our enemies than to love our enemies.

It's not just politicians who maintain an enemies list. Picture the person who ranks as number one on your own enemies list. Now consider this: Jesus died for that person. And Jesus calls you to love that person.

Loving Our Enemies

God never limits his faithfulness to his friends. God is faithful even to God's enemies. Abraham was both God's friend and God's enemy.

Our worst enemy is always ourselves. We all fail by being unfaithful to the dynamic relationship that our Lord desires to have with us. Yet God keeps coming at us, always finding a way to stay close. We wrestle even with the love that comes when we don't want it.

"What if some were unfaithful?" Paul wrote. "Will their faithlessness nullify the faithfulness of God? By no means!"[12] Even though we have proven untrustworthy, even though we have betrayed God, God's faithfulness triumphs over our faithlessness. "If, when we were God's enemies, we were reconciled to him through the death of his Son, how much more, having been reconciled, shall we be saved through his life!"[13]

If we don't love our enemies, we can't love ourselves. We have met the enemy, and he is us. There's a little of Judas in all of us. Abraham was constantly falling short: He dishonored Sarah, trashed Hagar, sacked Ishmael, sacrificed Isaac. Again and again, Scripture shows us that God decides not to choose special people. God chooses, then people become special. The story of Abraham is more about God's faithfulness to Abraham than it is about Abraham's obedience to God. God's chosen people weren't chosen because they were special. They were chosen because God is special. And it is through their relationship with God that they become special.

Michael Lindvall tells about a friend named Fuad Bahnan, an Arab Christian pastor in Beirut after the last Arab-Israeli war. In 1983 Israeli armies drove into Lebanon, and members of the church began to buy all the canned food they could to survive a rumored Israeli siege. West Beirut was totally cut off. The session of the church met to decide how to distribute the food they had purchased.

Two proposals were debated. The first was to distribute food to the church members, then to other Christians, and last—if any was left—to Muslim neighbors. The other proposal was different. First food would be given to Muslim neighbors, then to other Christians, and finally—if any food was left—to the church members. The meeting lasted six hours. "It ended when an older, quiet, much-respected elder, a woman, stood up and said, 'If we do not demonstrate the love of Christ in this place, who will?' and so the second motion passed."[14]

Eve's Leaves, Adam's Fall, and the Naked Truth

One of my favorite fragments of ancient Persian wisdom is this bit of advice: "Do not welcome elephant trainers into your tent unless you are prepared to entertain elephants." Anyone who keeps an open table had better be prepared to deal with the invisible elephant: sin. The ugly underside of the soul is never far from the surface.

In the best-selling advice book *Dear Gangster,* we find the following exchange:

Dear Gangster:
There's something awfully wrong in this world but I just can't figure out what it is. Love seems to be so slippery—no, greasy—no,

slimy. I can't get a grip on it. Can't get it in a headlock, can't make it scream for mercy. What is it that's wrong in this world? Sum it up for me, will ya?

—Two Words or Less Would be Good

Dear Two Words or Less:
    You & Me.[15]

The writer of Ecclesiastes spelled it out: "Surely there is no one on earth so righteous as to do good without ever sinning."[16] You and I are the reason why the world is the way it is. During the announcements at Saint Andrew's Presbyterian Church in Newport Beach, California, Dr. John A. Huffman Jr. sometimes offers this welcome:

> Welcome to Sinners Anonymous. We at Saint Andrew's are a group
> of men and women who do not claim perfection in our own right. We
> may be all dressed up and look pretty good, but the fact is that every
> one of us is a sinner and daily needs the help of our 'Higher Power,'
> Creator, Sustainer God, who, through the work of Jesus Christ, His
> Son, offers grace and forgiveness, and through the power of the Holy
> Spirit the strength to get through one day at a time.[17]

Both the Beauty *and* the Beast live inside every one of us. Both Cain and Abel are the ancestors of the human race, and the unmasking of each of us reveals penchants for jealousy and murder and greed. We are all both victims and crucifiers. We lie, we cheat, we gossip, we hoard. Methodism founder John Wesley suggested that it is impossible to hold a conversation lasting more than thirty minutes without saying something that shouldn't be said. We all have flaws. Even the best among us go horribly awry (you don't want to read Martin Luther's 1543 polemic, *The Jews and Their Lies*).

We shudder at the 160 million war-related deaths in the twentieth century.[18] We cringe to learn that 23 million people have been killed and 60 million injured in one hundred fifty major conflicts since the Second World War. But violence, cruelty, sadism—these are not deviations from the "norm," but normal vectors of human nature. Evil lurks inside every one of us. My favorite twentieth-century poet Denise Levertov acknowledges in her first Christian poem the force "which stays/our hand,/our murderous hand."[19]

Someone once observed that there are two kinds of people: drains and radiators. We'd rather surround ourselves with the warmth of heaters than tinker with the underworld of damp, cold, dirty sewer lines. But a big part of the church's ministry is in the drainage business. One of the greatest twentieth-century preachers, Austin Farrer, tells this story about the plague that broke out at Constantinople:

> The Christian Emperor consulted the Christian Patriarch and they
> ordained ceremonies of expiation and of national repentance to avert
> God's punishment. In saying that the people deserved the divine
> wrath, the clergy were, of course, on safe ground. The people always
> do deserve it. No observation can be more safely ventured in any age,
> than the observation that there is a lot too much wickedness about.
> But there was a physician in the imperial city who aimed at greater pre-
> cision of diagnosis. The particular wickedness, he suggested, by which
> the men of Stanbul had attracted the divine wrath was neglecting the
> drains: and since it is hypocrisy to confess faults we do nothing to
> mend, sanitary measures might be more pleasing to God than litanies.
> Such was the physician's suggestion. Did they agree with him? No, they
> put him in irons for his impiety. The shafts of plague are the arrows of
> God. Shall we hope to avert his judgements by cutting his bowstring,
> or by blunting his darts? No, we must fall on our faces and pray.[20]

Sometimes we are multiplying litanies and neglecting drains—the forgotten drains of sin. What a wrong journey it has been from "Sinners in the Hands of an Angry God" to "Low-Self-Esteem Clients on the Couch of an Understanding Therapist." Sin is more than self-disesteem and self-victimization. Reformed theologian Cornelius Plantinga puts it like this: Sin has "first and finally a Godward force."[21] This concept is missing in so many discussions where the sinful life has been supplanted by "sickness" or "addiction" or the "unhealthy lifestyle." What's missing is the "Godward force." Sin is an offense against God.

But there is a second feature missing in the church's "sin" talk. Sin is a relational concept. It is a violation of and damage done to our relationship with God and others and ourselves. God's grace is the gift of relationship. Both sin and grace are defined biblically more in relational than juridical terms.

Christianity has taken the same wrong turn that late Judaism did. It has attempted to turn God's covenant of promise, grace, and unconditional love into a contract.[22] In a contract, all loopholes are closed by both parties. In a covenant such as God's covenant with Abraham, and most especially the New Covenant of Jesus, there are open ends. We'd rather fixate on the knotting of loose ends than frolic in their openness and then just trust God.

Sin is not a breaking of *commands;* sin is a breaking of *relationships.* When we sin we do not break stone-bound laws, but heart-carved love. That's why the answer to sin is not better education or better willpower but a better means of reconciliation and restoration of relationship: the Cross.[23] Jesus doesn't let us off the hook. He doesn't just slap our hands and go on. Jesus sometimes holds our hands to the fire. But he holds our hands.

If sin is rightly defined as "wrongdoing" and sanctification as "rightdoing," then Paul was sinless before his conversion. "As to righteousness under the law," Paul wrote, "[I was] blameless."[25] Gerald Hughes quotes the inscription from an administration building urging people to "obedience, diligence, honesty, order, cleanliness, temperance, truthfulness, sacrifice and love of one's country." The inscription was found on the ceiling of one of the administration buildings in Dachau, the Nazi concentration camp, for prisoners to read frequently.[26] These words of "rightdoing" are not a call to repentance, but a call to idolatry.

Hughes then comes up with one of the best definitions of sin in the history of Christianity: Sin is a refusal to "let God be God in you."[27] Holiness is high-powered conductivity. When we plug in to make the next connection, sin is blockage to the conduction of power. Sin is that which blocks the flow

> Sin does not consist in wanting bad things: there are no bad things; all things are created by God. Sin consists in how you want small things. It is loving, for example, material possessions, which are good and created by God, at the expense of loving God who created a world in which what we do-not-and-cannot possess is greater than the things we can possess.
>
> —DOMINICAN FRIAR HERBERT MCCABE[24]

and formation of GodLife relationships. Repentance then is a return to relationship where we allow God, rather than ourselves, to shape our lives and our living. Repentance is the ceramic or copper "conductors" that permit connectivity with and conductivity of the divine.

Far Away Is Close at Hand

"There was a man who had two sons…"[28] Many have called this simple story the greatest short story ever told, or most commonly the Evangelism in Evangelio (the gospel in a gospel). The story has inspired some of our greatest artists—from painter Rembrandt, to composer Claude Debussy, to poet John Masefield, to choreographer Sadler Wells, to writer Charles Dickens, whose *A Christmas Carol* is a variation on the story of prodigals. Cold-hearted even to crutches, Scrooge eventually gets welcomed back into the human fold.

There is a heart of the gospel and permanent essence of Christianity that is found in the parable of the Prodigal Child.[29] It is a pattern of salvation that involves sin, repentance, and free forgiveness without any conditions other than repentance itself. In fact, the father doesn't bother to wait for any pleas for forgiveness; he runs to meet his son and hugs and kisses him. If more beautiful words than these have ever been written in a story line—"His father, when he saw him coming, ran out to meet him"—I don't know what they are.

Who is the real "prodigal" in this story? Is it the Prodigal Elder Brother? Is it the Prodigal Father? Is it the Prodigal Younger Son, who is probably the most preached about character in the Bible? Or maybe it's the Prodigal God?

Or maybe every character in this story illuminates a different feature of the word *prodigal.* In fact, maybe we are, each one of us, those two sons. Perhaps these two types of individuals do not exist as two separate people, but as two persons who reside inside each one of us.

It has become fashionable to see the elder brother as the true "prodigal." Coming in from his field, he heard all the ruckus and demanded: "What's all this music and dancing?" When told his younger brother had returned and their father had rolled out the red carpet and killed a calf (notice how many times "fatted calf" crops up in the elder brother's conversation) for a mega-party, he went ballistic.

It was hurtful for the younger son to ask his father for his inheritance ahead of time, a request that some scholars have interpreted as amounting to wishing his father's death ("Why don't you hurry up and die?"). What actually was the younger brother's sin? Not "loose living," but *nonliving* in relationship with his father. He valued more highly what he could get from his father than friendship with his father. In fact, the Greek text never uses the words "riotous living" or "loose living." In the words of Herbert McCabe, "English translators have been conned by the vindictive slanders of the elder brother later in the story. Here we are just told that he spent his money…'without hanging on to it'—as though there were no tomorrow. His sin does not lie in sensuality and harlots. His sin is much more serious. It is in the abandonment of his father's house."[30]

Besides, how did the elder brother know that his younger brother visited prostitutes? The elder brother made it his self-righteous duty to volunteer this information to his father—that this wastrel son of his had devoured "your living" with harlots. Even after his younger brother asked for forgiveness, the elder brother couldn't resist an opportunity to make himself look good. So he tore his brother down. But beware. Listen to what people are criticizing others for. It tells you a lot about what the critics themselves are up to. When you throw a stone at someone, you wound yourself.

The younger brother's request to "divide the living" was an extraordinary private insult to his father, but even more extraordinary was the elder brother's public insult when he refused to participate in the father's feast. All the prominent people of the village were there. For the elder brother to refuse to "come in" and join the party was a grave public insult. In fact, the agony of this rejected love created a rupture between father and elder son as severe as between father and younger son.

What kept the elder son away? What made him so problematic? He'd been obedient. He'd been faithful. He was dutiful and submissive. What more could any parent ask?

But his father wanted more. He wanted the companionship of a loving son. And when the younger son came home and said, "I want to be in a relationship with you once more," and the father got excited, the elder son went bonkers. From the principled position of the elder brother, it was the younger brother's own fault that he was homeless and penniless. He made his choice, so let him suffer the consequences. The elder brother worked like a slave for his father. And what did he get? The elder brother's self-righteousness and jealousy kept him from enjoying the party. He was the type of person who couldn't understand a Savior who said he didn't want servants. He wanted friends.[31]

The father in the story had been shamefully treated and taken advantage of. Yet he was forgiving and threw a party. The elder brother in the story had not been wronged. Yet he was the unforgiving one.[32]

Each of us at some point has gotten lost in a far country. There is fascination in the faraway land, and each of us has a different "far country." But you can get equally lost at home. You can stay home and be "good" and get just as lost as if you had gone as far from home as you could get. The elder brother who stayed home had every virtue but one—love. Anyone without love is as lost as you can get.

The role of the church is to throw parties for all prodigals. The role of the church is to proclaim: Wherever your far country is—either far away or at home—it is not too far for God to reach you and throw you a party. The parable of the Prodigal Child is a story about parties—the parties of the "far country" that are destructive and enervating, and the parties of the family that are true forms of merrymaking and celebration.

A festival consciousness provides the ligatures that tie us to God and to one another. Christianity's need for a festival culture is nowhere more apparent than in the USAmerican church, which is not much for parties. The church can weep with those who weep, but gets nervous when celebrating with those returning from far countries. Can we throw a party for our enemies—those not yet deemed "worthy" of having parties thrown for them?

The parable is not a rebuke for staying outside but an assurance that God wants others inside. It's about a prodigal God who has selfish children, children who are oblivious to their Father's feelings. Yet God loves each prodigal in a lavish, extravagant way. Whichever way you are prodigal—one of the self-righteous "elder brethren" or one of those "prodigal kids" out sowing wild oats—God comes out to meet you, as the father came out to both sons, and invites you to join in the family festivities.

> He may not deserve your praise, but he deserves to be treated as if some day he might.
>
> —JAMES RICHARDSON[33]

There are two ways of describing you—and the rest of us—at this moment. We are either away from God but drawing near, or we are near to God but drawing away. Which describes you? Which do you think pleases God more?

As the father said to the elder brother, "You ought to be glad and make merry." The most famous short story ever told ends with this statement: "So they began to celebrate." God wants people coming "from the east and the west, [so they can] take their places at the feast with Abraham, Isaac and Jacob in the kingdom of heaven."[34] What will it take to get you to come in and join the party?

Evangelism is inviting prodigals to a party. Evangelism is introducing others to a God who is waiting to welcome them home with these words: "Everything I have is yours." But if we insist on self-justification, if we prefer to maintain a broken relationship with God, how can we hope to invite strangers to the table of God's feast? How can those in God's family who have broken with the Father expect to attract others into a relationship with the Giver of the party?

Pursuing God-ordained relationships with those outside God's family requires that we understand that others are at the center of our own relationship with God, that we literally meet Jesus as we are in relationships with others, and that we are ourselves strangers and aliens. If we shun relationships with others, we are shoving Jesus out of our lives.

Donald Miller explains that he never found jazz music to his liking because it gave off alien sounds. Plus, its musical themes never resolved themselves, and the listener was left hanging. Then his view was changed:

> I was outside the Bagdad Theater in Portland one night when I saw a man playing the saxophone. I stood there for fifteen minutes, and he never opened his eyes.
>
> Sometimes you have to watch somebody love something before you can love it yourself.[35]

I have grown to love many things because the people I love, love those things. I have grown to love Avril Lavigne because of my daughter Soren's love for Avril Lavigne. I have grown to love Spongebob Squarepants by watching my son Egil's love of Spongebob Squarepants. I have grown to love Linda Ronstadt's voice from listening to my wife's love for Linda Ronstadt.

I've learned to love others deemed oddballs and odd couples because Jesus was a soft touch for lost souls and last-place finishers.

I've learned to love certain people because I've watched Jesus love them.

PART VI

OUR RELATIONSHIP

WITH GOD'S CREATION

GETTING RIGHT WITH DIVINE HANDIWORK

Loving What God Has Made

It is a mistake to think that God is only,
or even chiefly, interested in religion.
—ARCHBISHOP WILLIAM TEMPLE[1]

God and Abraham had a pedestrian relationship. They liked to take walks. One of the first things God did in this down-to-earth relationship was show off the sights and sounds of the rivers and lands that God promised to Abraham and his descendents.[2]

God's earlier covenant with Noah was made with "every living creature of all flesh that is on the earth."[3] Nature and humanity are inseparable. That's why God kept sending Moses back to negotiate with Pharaoh until the Egyptian sovereign could get it right. Pharaoh finally said, "Okay, the Israelite men can go and worship." Moses said, "Sorry, not good enough." For Moses, "the people" had to include women and children. And more.

"The people of the covenant" were to be defined as all creatures: "Not a hoof shall be left behind."[4]

When we meet God, we meet God's world. And what a world God has given us! We can only be with God to the extent we are in relationship with both the Creator and creation. The church's earliest theologians spoke of creation itself as a sacrament, a "sign" of God's presence, a divine language through which God communicates with us. Our spiritual ancestors also believed that all creation was involved in the redemption drama and was a source of the revelation of God—although not on the same plane with Scripture and tradition.[5]

Today, Christians expend a great deal of energy and effort learning how to rightly exegete Scripture. Such exegesis helps us comprehend and know God. But what about learning how to exegete nature—the handiwork of God? Take for example the "arboreal theophanies" known as trees.[6] Think about some trees in the Bible: trees in Eden, trees of Mamre, cedars of Lebanon, Zaccheus's sycamore tree.

Trees have deep theological meaning: They come out of the ground, they feed the world, they house the world, they oxygenate the world, they provide medicine. When you plant a tree, water it, and care for it, you begin a relationship with that tree. It becomes a friend—not like your spouse or a close confidant, but a friend nonetheless. What is the shape of your relationship with this part of God's creation—these lifelines that support us so lavishly? And why do Christians seem to have more problems with people who worship trees than with people who worship titles or things?

Jesus called our attention to one of the mysteries of relationships: They're involuted. We go "within" ourselves by getting "outside" ourselves. How do we "find ourselves"? Jesus says: "Lose yourself" in the other. "Other" can be people, but it also can be places. Intimacy with God is found, in part, through our involvement in the natural world and through relationship with God's creation.

> The whole sensual world is, as it were, a book written by the finger of God.
>
> —TWELFTH CENTURY THEOLOGIAN
> HUGO OF SAINT VICTOR

Jesus lived out this mystery of involution. He had favorite sacred places. Jesus needed the mountains, the desert, the lakes and seas to stay strong in his relationship with God. His favorite place of prayer? The two extremes of the wilderness and a garden.

We don't need to become Gaians to see that Saint Francis had it right: Nature (birds, trees) is our sisters and brothers. Not our gods, not our creators, but made of the same stuff of creation as we are. Saint Bonaventure's contrast between a vestige and an image is helpful as we think about creation. Every creature has a vestige of God, but only human beings have the image or "expressed likeness" of God.[7] This rich aspect of the Christian tradition is lost in modernity's disconnect between ourselves and the natural world. It was not Christianity that led to the domination and exploitation of nature. It was Enlightenment rationalism with its drive to control and subjugate everything it touched, removing the divine meaning, the evidence of God that is inherent to all of creation. Enlightenment thinking created the Sarumans of the world, described in the movie *The Lord of the Rings* as someone who "has a mind of metal and wheels" and "does not care for growing things."[8]

Loving the Earth

The African American theologian Howard Thurman defined the kingdom of God as another name for God's dream of a friendly world filled with friendly people under a friendly sky. Consider how unfriendly our skies are today. Indeed, they go beyond unfriendly to deadly—manufacturing melanoma with every ray of sun. This is just one sign of our failed relationship with creation. The Pentagon has now made climate change a "security" issue.[9]

When I was growing up, fish was the last wild food.[10] I heard stories of how supplies of cod were once so plentiful in the North Atlantic that people could almost "walk across the Atlantic dryshod" on the cods' backs.[11] But by 1992, the cod population was so decimated that Cape Breton's waters were closed to groundfishing so the fish could have a chance to replenish. Those waters have been closed ever since.

In April 2003, dead cod began surfacing in Newfoundland. Some suspect this was because of the trainloads of mustard gas that were dumped off the coast of Cape Breton after the Second World War, barrels that became so corroded they were now breaking up and releasing gelatinous clumps of mustard gas. The food inspector from the Canadian Food Agency nevertheless approved cod washed up on the shore for human consumption. In his words, "Other than the fact that they're dead, they're in excellent condition."[12]

No Christian has an excuse for not being an ecologist. Ecology is nothing more than the science of an organism's relationship to its surroundings. Religious leaders are "spiritual ecologists," responsible for maintaining a healthy and harmonious environment in sacred communities. Environmental ecology is the study and understanding of what maintains harmony of relationships in nature. It is not just the mystic who "beholds Creation with the Creator's eye."[13]

Current approaches to species protection fall short ecologically because they fail to view planet Earth in terms of its relationships. As a result, these efforts fail to protect the essential connections that exist. Growing a forest takes about eighty years. But growing a forest rich in relationships (that is, bio-diversity) takes about two hundred years.

Why are the fruits of some New World plants inedible, or harmful, or both (Osage Orange, Desert Gourd)? Why are the fruits of other New World plants palatable, but encased in a hull so huge and hard that no animal can get at them (Honey Locust, Cassia)? These fruits are stranded by abandoned relationships, waiting for the guts of megafauna "ghosts" like elephants, rhinos, hippos, giraffes, and dinosaurs to digest them in their cast-iron stomachs.[14]

My friend Brian McLaren has an unusual hobby. He's an advocate for the welfare of turtles and tortoises. A large portion of his basement and fenced backyard is reserved for the raising of endangered turtles.

In one of his books, Brian explains that tortoises need the right balance of nutrients and minerals. If they aren't fed the right mix of food, they get sick.[15] Brian makes a compelling case for the same need for a similar "mix" in our spiritual nutrition. But the real problem forcing the near extinction of many species, as Brian knows only too well since he's devoted his life to addressing it, is not the balance of nutrients. The real problem is our failure to cherish wild places. Turtles in the wild don't need nutritionists and heroic turtle protectors to keep them healthy. When they're sick, they know what plants to eat to get well. What Brian's turtles are missing is the web of relationships that keep them healthy.

Animals eat things for medicinal as well as nutritional reasons, a phenomenon called zoopharmacognosy—the self-medication of animals by eating appropriate vegetation. Animals eat dirt (geophagy), especially the clay in the soil, because clay detoxifies the poison produced by certain plants to defend themselves from being eaten.[16] Since the amount of toxins in plants increases the more tropical the planet climates, the amount of earth eaten by herbivores in tropical regions increases proportionately.[17]

The green plants that starlings weave into their potentially itchy nests, to cite another example, appear to be chosen on the strength of their mite-repelling properties.[18] Cattle refuse to gnaw on fresh bones that might still have flesh attached. Cattle will only nibble on bleached bones.[19] Cattle raised in captivity had no choice when they were fed bone meal in Britain in the early 1980s. Hence the human-engineered plague of mad cow disease. Blood tests have demonstrated that wild animals have a resistance to those viral and bacterial diseases due to their diet in the wild.[20]

The problem is not one of finding the right mix of nutrients to feed wild animals held in captivity. The problem is the zoo itself. Our failure to cherish wild places, wildlife, and wild things is evidence of our tendency to divorce the wild from the sacred. Giving turtles food and shelter is necessary but not sufficient. Giving turtles a chance to reproduce is necessary but not sufficient. It's the matrix and milieu of relationships that make a turtle a turtle. And by not honoring God's creation, we have dissolved the matrix.

> We must beware lest we violate the holy, lest our dogmas overtake the mystery.
>
> —RABBI AND THEOLOGIAN ABRAHAM HESCHEL[21]

Barry Lopez and Richard Nelson, two of the best nature writers of the twentieth century, took part in a discussion about the nature of "wildness." Lopez argued that a bear taken out of its habitat and placed in a zoo is still a form of mammalian life, but, "It's not a bear." Nelson countered: "Even if it's in a zoo, it's still a bear." Lopez kept insisting, "It's not a bear."[22]

It's not a bear if it can't forage for blackberries and if it can't range over a vast expanse of territory. It's not a bear if it can't pick its own cave for the winter and if it's not free to select its own mate. It is the relationships and connections that make a bear a bear. Likewise, it is the relationships and connections that make a Christian a Christian.

German author Johann Wolfgang von Goethe created a "hero" that made him famous in the 1770s. In *Die Leiden des Jungen Werthers (The Sorrows of Young Werther),* the main character was a friend of the new parson's wife. The woman had "pretensions to scholarship," which led her to cut down all the walnut trees in the vicarage garden because she needed "more light" to read her studies of higher biblical criticism.[23]

It's not a Christian if he or she can't see how "the heavens declare the glory of God"—not to mention how walnut trees and "the skies proclaim the work of his hands."[24]

The CEO of a major multinational corporation was interviewed by a reporter who, when ushered into the executive's office, was overwhelmed by the inspiring view of the Rocky Mountains from the man's office window. "I don't look at it very often," the CEO confessed. In his case, the company's messy past keeps his eyes focused downward on the papers atop his massive desk.[25] Sadly, this man, like many others, had lost touch with the blessing and refreshment of God's creation. It's not a Christian if you fail to lift up eyes "unto the hills, from whence cometh [your] help."[26]

GOD'S GRACE REFLECTED IN CREATION

We are spiritual beings in physical bodies. And our biological selves need nature. There are huge health benefits to living in GodLife relationships—including relationship with creation. Contact with nature can heal, whether it's a walk in the woods, a drive on a scenic route, or even peering at framed nature photography hanging on a wall. Small contacts with creation—gardens and other green spaces—have a cumulative impact. People who view a nature video after a stressful event can reduce their pulse rate, skin conductance activity, and muscle tension after as little as five minutes. Following surgery, those who get a room looking out on trees heal faster and need fewer painkillers than those who look out on brick walls.[27]

A study at the University of Michigan's Institute for Social Research tracked the relationships of 423 elderly couples for five years, during which time 134 of them died. Those who had giving relationships (helped friends, did child care, assisted in errands) had half the mortality rate of those who didn't.[28] A giving spirit comes with free health benefits. It's interesting that the benefits don't accrue to those at the receiving end of the relationship, only the giving end. We need to give in order to meet one another's needs, and this need in us is so basic that "lack of religious involvement has an effect on mortality equivalent to forty years of smoking a pack of cigarettes a day."[29]

Our planetary as well as personal existence depends on our ability to be in relationship with creation. Jesus warned that whatever we do with the "least of these," which includes all living things, we also do to ourselves and to God. Soviet cosmonaut Vladimir Kovalyonok told how an orange cloud that formed from a dust storm over the Sahara and eventually settled in the Philippines as rainfall taught him "that we are all sailing in the same boat."[30] If we're all sailing in the same boat, the one billion earthlings living in first-class cabins can't expect not to be bothered by intrusions and incursions from the two to three billion living in the hold. If we're all sailing in the same boat, the emergency reports of leaking and sinking at the low end can't be met with high-end arrogance: "Why are you complaining down in steerage? All's well at our end."

Both affluence and poverty use too much of the planet's resources. Both overload the boat, forcing it to sit too low in the water. We shake our heads in disdain at Elvis Presley's taking his private jet in 1976 from Memphis to Denver and back to Memphis, using 5,500 gallons of fuel, just to eat a sandwich made from a loaf of bread slit down the middle and layered with peanut butter, bananas, and a pound of crisp bacon.

But we accept without objection the fact that when a 120-pound person takes a 3,500-pound car to the local convenience store to buy a loaf of bread or a pound of bacon, the energy efficiency of the trip is more wasteful than the Elvis trip and slightly worse than that of international travel on the supersonic Concorde jet, when measured per passenger mile. We are all sitting at the same table, with both ends dying, one from pigging out and the other from starving.

I cringe every time the local seafood chain restaurant advertises an "all-you-can-eat" shrimp special. Every time the waiter brings you a platter of peel 'n' eat shrimp, he also brings to the table an *invisible* platter of rays, eels, flounder, butterfish, and other miscellaneous "bycatch"—a term the fishing industry prefers over "trash fish" to describe untargeted species snagged by long lines and dragnets and then discarded at sea. Also snagged by the shrimpers' nets is a large unweighed and unreported "bycatch" of starfish, batfish, crabs, urchins, coral, sponges, and horse conchs.[31]

The impact of humans on planet Earth has been described as "the human asteroid."[32] In fact, the impact on the planet of even one human can look like an asteroid. When you replaced your old computer with a faster, more powerful model, how did you dispose of your earlier computer? Most computers contain mercury, cadmium, and up to seven pounds of lead, toxic elements that can contaminate groundwater for decades. Thomas Midgley, a USAmerican research chemist, has been described as having "more impact on the atmosphere than any other single organism in earth history." In 1921 he invented leaded gasoline, marketed in 1923 as ethyl gasoline, one of the worst pollutants around. Then in 1930–1931 he invented Freon, an inert gas useful in refrigeration and air conditioning but destructive to the ozone layer that shields living organisms from ultraviolet radiation.[33]

We are living in what one theologian calls an "ecological eschaton."[34] Sir Martin Rees, a Cambridge University astrophysicist and Britain's Astronomer Royal, has wagered one thousand dollars that "bioerror or bioterror" will kill one million people by the year 2020. "I think the odds are no better than 50-50," writes this world leader in cosmology, "that our present civilisation on Earth will survive to the end of the present century."[35]

God hasn't placed planet Earth in our laps and then left us holding the bag. But the Scriptures do give us fair warning that one basis on which God will judge each person is: How have you treated my Earth?[36] We are the ones God chose to be caretakers of the planet, but do we care? Have we been care-full? Or are we being care-less? Are we looking for apocalyptic raptures to save us from our sin of not caring for what God has made?

"Consider the ravens," Jesus said. "Consider how the lilies grow."[37] His word *consider* does not mean giving something a "passing note" or "pleasing contemplation." It means giving life's lilies and ravens *everything you've got.*

> And it was really God for whom
> The beasts had made a little room.
> —RALPH A. LEWIN[38]

In other words, be in relationship with flowers and birds.[39] It's time we own up to our ambiguous place in nature as both creature and creator, as both a part of nature and apart from nature. By being in relationship with lilies and ravens, we are in relationship with the One who is "over all and through all and in all."[40]

When we "proclaim the gospel to the whole creation,"[41] we are living the somatic connectivity between Christ and all creation. "When I am lifted up from the earth," Jesus said, "I will draw *all things* to myself." The correct translation from the Greek is not "all people" but "all things."[42] Paul says that we are called to participate in Jesus's reconciliation of the whole world to himself.[43] The risen body of Christ includes the new heaven and the new earth.

The Bible portrays the earth as morally sensitive: The earth throws up at Cain's murder of Abel; the rocks cry out for Jesus on the cross, as he prophesied they would if his disciples croaked. Just as the heavens opened at Jesus's baptism, the earth opened and was torn apart at his crucifixion. Along with the rest of creation, we humans share "his sufferings."[44]

In my first parish God healed one of the nastiest, most antagonistic parishioners I have ever ministered to. At that same church, I buried one of the most beautiful saints ever to bless my life. Why can't God be a nice God and heal the nice people? Why did my brother get polio, which left him limping for life? Why did my infant son get encephalitis, which has left him damaged for life? Why did my mother have to suffer so torturously before she died?

To be in relationship is to suffer. To have, you must give. To grow, you must suffer. To live, you must die.

That's it. Life is suffering. There's no use complaining about it. This is life.

We are instructed to seize every moment to speak a positive word.[45] We can talk about how suffering can make us more alive or how suffering can be converted into art or how suffering can be a school of instruction in life's virtues. All of those are true.

But no matter how many wonders and marvels I see in nature, no matter how many poppies and sunflowers inspire my reveries about God, nature is rampant with dark forces of destruction and decay and violence. The pervasive presence of cold in history, John Updike reminds us, "has the philosophical value of reminding men that the universe does not love us. Cold and absolute as the black tomb rules space; sunshine is a local condition."[46]

Every time I get out of bed to get dressed or sit down to eat or take out my Bible to read, I arm myself against those dark forces and the pervasive coldness. Our relationship with other forms of life is complex and mysterious. Life feeds on life. This can be a benign feeding. Consider that oxygen, the toxic waste product of one type of organism (green plants), is the lifeblood of other organisms. Or this can be a sacrificial feeding: For me to live, something must die.

Whether animal or vegetable, life sacrificed itself for me to eat. Have you noticed how menus in high-end restaurants increasingly describe exactly how our dinner died for us?

- Crispy, Line-Caught Wild Striped Bass, which means the fish were caught with a hook and line, not in a net.
- Day Boat Monkfish with Rosti Potatoes, Carmelized Cauliflower, and Lobster Bordelaise, indicating that the fishing boat remained at sea for only twenty-four hours.
- Harpooned Pumpkin Swordfish. This is, of course, a fish stabbed with a harpoon, not caught in a net with random companions.

- Oven-Roasted, Troll-Caught Alaskan King Salmon is nabbed through trolling, the same as line-catching except the boat is moving.
- Sautéed Trap Squid with Garlic, Tomatoes, Basil, and Andouille Sausage calls our attention to the fact that trapping the squid doesn't "bruise" the animal.
- Steamed Maine-Diver Sea Scallop with Olive Leek Emulsion means a human dove into the water to catch the sea scallop, and you're paying big bucks to eat it.

You almost need to know how your fish died to protect yourself. Ever wonder how the live fish in restaurant tanks got there? Divers with plastic squirt bottles inject liquid cyanide into the crevices of coral reefs. This either kills or dazes the fish, and the ones that don't die (roughly a quarter of them) are caught, placed in holding pens, and flown around the world to high-end restaurants where they will die anyway if they aren't eaten first.[47]

An animal sacrificed its hide for me to walk comfortably and safely over rough ground. Paul himself was a leather worker, as were his friends Priscilla and Aquilla.[48] My study Bible is basically tree sheets wrapped in dead cow. Each copy of the Gutenberg Bible (641 leaves) printed on parchment required the skins of three hundred sheep.

Loving Animals as Jesus Did

Jesus's relationship with animals deserves its own monograph. Jesus was born in a home for animals, not people. His baptismal bird was not a mighty falcon or eagle but a trash bird (a white pigeon with the poetic name of "dove"), and Jesus showed a special sensitivity for other nuisance birds of Jerusalem, the sparrows and the ravens. After his desert duel with the devil, he was ministered to by unnamed wild animals. For his "triumphal" ride into Jerusalem on a donkey, Jesus refused to separate the mother from colt, so had both brought to him.

At least part of Jesus's "temple tantrum" was his outrage at the abuses in the custom of animal sacrifices. In fact, animal sacrifice was never a part of the Christian tradition, and Christians were notorious for their opposition to the amphitheater games where gory beast hunts filled the morning and where people were treated as animals the rest of the day through public executions of criminals at midday, and gladiator fights to the death midafternoon.

The founder of Methodism, John Wesley, was an early creation theologian. In the eighteenth century, Wesley encouraged relationships with animals. In fact, he was convinced that we'd take our companion animals with us to heaven. If we take our wounds with us to heaven, he reasoned, why not our dogs and horses?

Disciples of Jesus look for the halo in every relationship and weave a halo of holiness around every relationship. Unnatural or unholy relationships with animals can curse us just as surely as natural and holy relationships can bless us. AIDS and Ebola came from apes in the half-logged jungles of Africa; SARS came from the civet cats raised for restaurants in bamboo cages in southern China; cholera came from rats drawn to excrement on the banks of the Ganges. The Alzheimer's-on-steroids disease known as bovine spongiform encephalopathy (mad cow disease) comes from eating mad cows, who got mad by eating sheep infected with scrapie.

Much of the church has still to comprehend how much animals are now part of the "family." Single-person households are giving birth to new meanings of the word *family*, now broadened to include a book club, a companion cat, a yoga class, or a chat room. This is not the traditional family. But it is a web of connections nonetheless, and the church must find ways to make itself a key part of people's "family." How many of our churches are "animal-friendly," even at Christmas when the animal-human relationship reached its holiest moment?

The Jewish concept of Shalom is a state of right relationships—peace and well-being, the offshoots of right relationships and harmonious interactions between humans and creation. For Jesus, the goal of life was Shalom, the natural state of creation before the Fall. "Peace on earth" is an image of

> I am because my little dog knows me.
> —NOVELIST GERTRUDE STEIN[49]

the harmonious relationships of the Triune God in the kingdom of heaven being practiced on earth. But Shalom is something that is not achieved; it is granted as a gift from God. If the Spirit produces in us relationships of harmony and peace, then our relationships with nature and animals should be characterized by harmony and peace.

The final vision of the Bible brings everything together in the success and victory of Jesus.[50] But Jesus's successes and victories are not conveyed in the language of politicians or philosophers, economists or generals. The language of victory is that of organic relationships (biology and psychology). In a world without borders or guards, a world without walls or gates, there's water once more ("the river of the water of life") and trees ("the tree of life") on each side of the river. There's growth and fruit and holiness and "healing of the nations"—a restored relationship among creatures, creation, and their Creator.[51]

But most of all, there is Jesus, our Peace.[52]

Our relationship with God by necessity includes our relationship with all that God created. If the creation joins in praising God and joins in the sufferings of Jesus, how can we disregard the importance of what God has created? If we are not in right relationship with God's creation, then we are not in right relationship with God.

One of the first stories I heard from my new friend Marie Aull after moving to Dayton, Ohio, in 1984 was the story of a bird named TV. In the late 1960s, at the Aullwood Audubon Farm and Learning Center in Dayton, an injured turkey vulture found healing and a home. Turkey vultures are not the most beautiful creatures in the world. But the only difference between an "ugly" turkey vulture and a "majestic" bald eagle is that one has a small head and weak claws, the other a big head and strong claws. Guess which one is which?

TV (short for Turkey Vulture) would sit on a window ledge at the Audubon Learning Center, watch the children being instructed in the mysteries of nature, and wait patiently until they were done. As soon as they came out, TV would jump off his window seat and walk with bowed and bobbing head to the kids for them to pet and greet him. He loved people, and this bowing and bobbing was his peculiar greeting to those who had brought him back to life and given him a home.

The Audubon Center mascot survived on road kill that was brought to TV by the Friends of Aullwood, a fancy name for the bluebloods and big givers who supported the gardens, the farm, and what became the largest learning center in the entire Audubon network. One can only imagine what passing motorists thought when these grand dames of Dayton would stop their Mercedes and Town Cars and pick up road kill for TV.

One Memorial Day holiday, TV was found dead, his head smashed to smithereens, at the entrance to the Audubon Center. The newspaper carried the story of TV's death on the front page. No one knows for sure what happened. But what seems most likely is that some visitor mistook TV's greeting for an attack and bashed his head in.

One wonders how many other greetings from nature we humans are mis-reading. One wonders how many other wonders of creation we humans are missing completely. One wonders how many other mysteries of life we humans are killing.

If we love God, we have to also love what God has made.

PART VII

OUR RELATIONSHIP WITH SYMBOLS, ARTS, ARTIFACTS, AND "THINGS"

The "Things" That Draw Us to God

Earthly Artifacts with Divine Meaning

> Painting or poetry is made as we make love, a total
> embrace, nothing held back.
> —ARTIST JOAN MIRO[1]

Can an artist despise the materials with which he or she works? Can God, the greatest Artist, despise the materials with which God works?

The universe is God's art. Our planet is God's best art form. Nature is God's best artwork. And humans are God's magnum opus.

The "stuff" of life is not the staff of life. But it's not the chaff of life either. We are living in God as we live in creativity and with created things. We are subcreators bringing beauty and grace to life in literature, film, music, and art.

Some have called Christianity the most "materialistic" of all religions because of its incarnational bent. You don't find God by fleeing from the matter of the world. You find God by entering the matter of the world. The word *mystery* comes from the Greek root *mysterion,* which means "sacrament." An incarnational understanding of God brings together mystery and sacrament, the invisible and the visible, the world of spirit and the world of matter. Remember, the Word became flesh. If the gospel doesn't connect us to the world, it's not the gospel.

Historians like to call this "lived religion."[2] The modern world uncoupled spirituality and "lived experience." But a religion that is limited to thought is not lived. It is pondered or imagined or discussed, but it is not real in the sense of life experience. In the wonderfully revealing words of anthropologist Meredith McGuire, "Without the full involvement of the material body, religion is likely to be relegated to the realm of cognitions [such as beliefs, opinions, theological ideas]. Embodied practices—including mundane and seemingly unexceptional activities like singing and preparing a meal—link our materiality as humans and our spirituality."[3]

Christianity is the ongoing life of the lived religion of Jesus. Jesus had a body, which means that people once had bodily contact with him. But the lived religion of Jesus's body created bodies of stories and practices, songs and rituals that continue that same lived religion into the present and thrust it into the future.

The self-emptying Incarnation means that God is known in the world through material, fleshly reality. As an artist is present in his or her art, God is present in stone, bone, silicon, glass, water, fiber. The personal is physical. To test the degree of gnostic antimatterness in your faith, ask yourself: *Why do I solemnly pray for "courage in this time of crisis" but laugh when someone prays for "help in getting this new job" or "finding my lost wedding ring"?*

A Collection of Rocks

One of my earliest relationship memories was with rocks. My mother collected one special rock from every place our family visited. When we were riding in the car she would suddenly exclaim, "Stop! Now!" My father would slam on the brakes and pull the car to the side of the road. My mother would jump out and claim her "memory." She scattered these rocks throughout the house and yard to remind her and us of the places we had visited together as a family. Objects such as this have a special power to bring to mind important images, memories, events. Thus, objects bring memory and meaning to the past.

Common things have a sacramental capacity, the ability to embody divine presence and purpose. Think of Rahab's window, Naboth's vineyard, Samson's hair, Potiphar's house, Shamgar's ox-goad, Balaam's ass, Moses's rod, Joseph's coat, David's pebbles, and Dorcas's needle. Relationships with these objects shaped the course of the entire Jewish-Christian tradition.

You and I are works of art, artifacts not mass-produced but handcrafted by God. Relationships with other handcrafted artifacts put us in a relationship with the Creator as well as with our fellow subcreators.

Art and artifact (created beauty) are less products than relationships with the holy. To reduce art to the level of product is "like praying in swear words."[4] To reduce economic exchanges like buying and selling to commodified, impersonal interactions without relationship is to prostitute our economic life. Our inability to help people develop healthy relationships with things has actually fueled consumerism and materialism. One reason Buddhism has done a better job than Christianity in not associating itself with misapplied materialism is because it has upheld the "real estate" of life as not property but relationships. The wealth the Bible talks about is relational wealth, creative and uplifting—a relationship of peace and revelation with God, relationships with other people, relationships with the world.

To be sure, the Christian community throughout history has had its share of Taliban types, iconoclasts who destroyed the arts, viewed the inanimate as devoid of meaning, and demanded that devotees say the right words and use the right formulas of faith or be burned at the stake. But in the best of the Christian tradition, the material is seen to convey the spiritual.

RELATIONSHIPS WITH THE ARTS

One of the first biblical texts to describe people's being filled with the Spirit of God lifts up the craftsmen Bezalel and Oholiab.[5] Artistic ability and skillful invention are gifts of the Spirit. To hang a painting in your house or church means more than displaying a framed rectangle of dried paint. When we surround ourselves with

> One thing I asked...
> to behold the beauty of the Lord.
> —THE PSALMIST[6]

material objects that are works of art, we are ringing our lives with the Spirit.

Art is a continuation of God's creativity through the human imagination. In fact, the church fathers associated the Holy Spirit with "both natural beauty and artistic skill."[7] It is often observed that in John 3:16's phrase "For God so loved the world," the Greek word for *world* is "cosmos." But "cosmos" can mean both universe/world *(cosmology)* and ornament/decoration *(cosmetics)*. Do we treat art as mere object or as beauty that reflects the beauty of God and the beauty that God creates and values?

No object is created out of nothing or made in isolation. Every object is born in community, accompanied by a whole host of other arts such as narrative, song, and dance, which then creates a new community that gives birth to more objects.[8] Creativity is less an act of the mind than an exercise of relationship: The mind midwifes the creativity, but the creative impulse is conceived from connecting dots and making connections with the world.

Art that transforms the world isn't without taints of contamination or compromise. Art enters a relationship with reality as it is—not our mental constructs of reality, but a true relationship that is obliged to deal with the world on its own terms. To transform the world, you have to enter it and engage it. For the church to transform the world, it must inspire fewer gird-your-loins responses and more get-off-the-grid responses to reality.

I share an incorporeal community with artists and writers. I talk to them every day. They speak to me from the shelves and walls where they hang. Howard Finster wants to talk to me about the New Jerusalem. Picasso invites me into a circle dance. Andy Warhol proposes new forms of walking shoes for my journey. An early cross hanging in my study has on it five circles, one for each wound of Jesus.[9]

Author and pastor Thomas R. Hawkins has hung a copy of Andrei Rublev's icon of the Holy Trinity, created in 1410, beside his kitchen table:

> Three angels, representing the three strangers who visited Abraham and Sarah, are seated around a table. These three angels signify the three persons of the Trinity. The three angels are placed in such a way that I can almost visualize the flow of energy and love between them. On the front of the table around which they are seated is a small square, an empty spot. We are invited into this empty space so that we may join the Father, Son, and Holy Spirit.
>
> As we eat beneath this icon, we hope that our table fellowship as a family mirrors these angels' table fellowship. As we share in their table fellowship, we become part of their intimate relationship and are transformed by it.[10]

The absence of the creative energies of art and culture are evident in any city, any mall, any suburb. All of them look alike. They are uninspiring, bland, boring. There is too much out-and-out ugliness in the church as well. Failure to bring beauty is an affront to the Spirit; absence of beauty is a sign of absence of Spirit. One theologian is brash enough to argue (though I wouldn't go this far) that "Those who destroy the beauty of God's creation or who create ugliness may be sinning against the Holy Spirit."[11] But as we consider beauty and ugliness, remember that God's aesthetics differ greatly from the world's aesthet-

ics. Christian understandings of beauty incorporate the foulness of foot wash-
ings, the rank riskiness of leper touchings, the ungainliness of donkey proces-
sionals, even the folly of crosses.

Both Simone Weil and Dietrich
Bonhoeffer are said to have been star-
tled by visitors who approached them
as they were transfixed, entranced by
the beauty of things around them. In

> The work of art which I do not make,
> none other will ever make it.
>
> —FRENCH RESISTANCE FIGHTER
> AND ESSAYIST SIMONE WEIL[12]

fact, Simone Weil argued that for people today, beauty is the most likely path
to God.[13]

RELATIONSHIP WITH FOOD

Ever sit at table with someone who ate so slowly that you were tempted to ask,
"What are you doing? Trying to get intimate with your food?" Or have you
ever sat at table with people who could not seem to leave the meal, so absorbed
were they in conversation?

It's hard to find a better description of the early church than this one:
"They broke bread in their homes and ate together with glad and sincere
hearts, praising God."[14] Indeed, food might be the clearest and most accessible example of the importance in the life of faith of our relationship with
artifacts, and of the power of artifacts to enliven faith and invite an awareness
of God.

When the first Christians met, they ate. Christianity was built around
tables, not pulpits or altars or books. Jesus forged the identity of his disciples
through ritual meals and the table talk that bound them together in his word
and spirit. Wherever Jesus reclined and dined, the meal became a festival that
knew no social distinctions and a festival that was supposed to continue on for
quite some time. In the book of Revelation, all things consummate in a feast.
Isaiah expects a banquet with fine wines:

> On this mountain the LORD of hosts will make for all peoples a feast of
> rich food, a feast of well-aged wines, of rich food filled with marrow, of
> well-aged wines strained clear.[15]

The Last Supper was Jesus's summary supper, the last in a series of suppers that punctuated Jesus's ministry. In between the Cana supper and the Emmaus supper, there were Mount of Olives suppers, Sea of Galilee suppers, desert suppers, garden suppers. In fact, there is a tradition dating at least to the sixth century that says Jesus held three suppers with his disciples before his death: one at Gethsemane, one at Bethany, and one on Mount Zion.[16]

Even today, there is abundant indication of the power of the artifact we know as food. There is a reason relationships grow faster around a table than anywhere else. The ideal size of a project team? The number of people you can seat around a table. Jesus's disciples didn't have meetings, they had meatings. In fact, the table became for Jesus a "primary symbol for the kingdom itself."[17] Our relationship with food reveals much about our relationship with others, with creation, and with God. To show up for meals is to show up for life is to show up for God.

Remember the saga of New Coke in the 1980s? Coca-Cola formulated a second recipe for its cola drink, based on marketing data that indicated soft-drink consumers preferred a sweeter taste. The newly formulated beverage was produced and distributed for retail sale, and the public outcry was fast and fierce. Coca-Cola learned something from the debacle. People have deep personal relationships with certain foods and products. Tastes can bring back memories that we cherish, and those who threaten those relationships have hell to pay.

Eating certain foods even helps me connect my story to the biblical story. For example, whenever I eat gazpacho I think of Jesus on the cross, since the history of gastronomy suggests that the drink the compassionate centurion raised to our Savior's lips as he hung from the cross was a spicy and refreshing gazpacho.[18] My love for turnips (best dished out at Niki's in Birmingham, Alabama) is a connection with "the poor, the crippled, the blind, the lame" that Jesus invited to his table, since turnips in the first century were the poor man's food. Meat was the most prized of all the foods, but meat was eaten rarely by the poor and only on special days by the rich. People lived off a menu of wheat bread and about thirty vegetables, the least highly rated of which was turnips.[19]

The most highly rated food of the ancient Hebrews was garlic, a food I love to hate. Garlic and ramps (the strongest onion imaginable) were among the foods the Israelites yearned for back in Egypt.[20] Jews loved garlic so much they were known as "garlic eaters," and the function of garlic as an early Via-gra was so prized that Friday evening was garlic night, the night of conju-gal duties. As someone who comes out of Appalachian culture, where in some counties you are forbidden to attend school within three days of eating ramps, ramps are a food I hate to love.

> On the first day he feeds him fowl, on the second fish, on the third meat, on the fourth legumes. Thus he gives him less and less until he serves him vegetables.
>
> —TALMUDIC EXHORTATION ON HOSPITALITY[21]

I like to eat fish on Friday be-cause that's when Jesus ate it growing up. What Sunday fried chicken was to my upbringing, Sabbath fish was to Jesus's.

My love of oatmeal connects me to one of the saints in my life, Marie Aull. Marie herself agreed more with Samuel Johnson, who called oats "a grain, which in England is generally given to horses, but in Scotland [feeds] the people."[22] But because she knew how much I loved oatmeal, the night before I would arrive for breakfast, Marie would put on the stove a pot of Irish oat-meal she purchased direct from a distributor, which simmered all night and was popping hot in the morning (and continued its popping in my stomach throughout the day).

Whenever bread or wine is placed before me, I try to remember the pain of the grain being crushed and the groaning of the grapes being squeezed and pressed out of shape, thereby maintaining a eucharistic connection with all life's bread and wine.

Relationship with Books

If you prefer to picture heaven as pearly gates and streets of gold and jasper walls and crystal fountains, be my guest. I prefer a heaven that looks like the reading room of the Library of Congress. My mansion in glory looks more like Dumbledore's "office" in the Harry Potter movies.

John Wesley, the eighteenth-century founder of Methodism, claimed to be a "man of one book." But he spent almost every spare minute reading books from every imaginable discipline and raged when his preachers resisted reading books other than the Bible. "If you need no book but the Bible, you have risen above Saint Paul," Wesley argued. To those who said they didn't have the money to buy "other" books, Wesley replied, "I will give each of you, as fast as you will read them, books to the value of five pounds."[23]

Winn Griffin is a colleague and mentor. The two of us share the same addiction. He tells of sitting in a room with a lot of strangers. It's his turn to speak. He rises and goes to the podium. "Hi, my name is Winn and I'm a book addict." They respond, "Hi Winn." He tells them his story, but admits "I'm not a 'recovering' book addict." My favorite president is Thomas Jefferson because he shared the same affliction Winn and I do: He couldn't stop buying books. Wherever he traveled, he was on the lookout for books. When he was in France, he acquired more than two thousand books, not including the ones he bought for George Washington, Benjamin Franklin, and James Madison.

Funding all his projects and building his beloved Monticello put Jefferson in debt (always). After the British burned the Capitol and with it the Library of Congress, Jefferson offered to sell his private library to the government. The debate in Congress was intense, but eventually both parties agreed on a price of $23,950. In April 1815, ten wagons carrying 6,707 volumes packed in pine cases departed from Monticello and became the nucleus of the new Library of Congress collection.[24]

So what did Jefferson do as soon as he got rid of his library and got out of debt? He started collecting more books.

The traffic lanes between literature and life are highly congested. My lived experience is colored by literary experiences and increasingly by a filmic eye.

> Love…friendship, books, the joy of art…
> keeps us tapping forward into the dark.
>
> —POET/NOVELIST
> STEPHEN DOBYNS[25]

My favorite episode of *Friends* has Joey Tribiani so terrified by Stephen King's *The Shining* that he keeps the book, whenever he's not reading it, in the freezer compartment of the fridge. Books have that kind of presence and power.

We are so attracted to movies that we can trace our life journeys in terms of celluloid sights and sounds. My childhood fascination with Lloyd C. Douglas's *The Robe* (1944) found expression in the costume designs of the movie *Spartacus*. My coming of age was marked by the tennis match in the movie *Blowup* (1966). The rebels and young Turks that did so much to shape my adolescence and twentysomething years— Spielberg, Scorsese, Coppola—are now becoming the grand old men of cinema.

RELATIONSHIP WITH TECHNOLOGY

I love certain garbage cans found at Burger King. You push open the can's door to deposit your trash. Some of the swinging doors even say "Thank You" on them, to which I have responded, "You're welcome." One day I realized what I was doing. *Sweet, you've started talking to garbage cans!*

The church could learn something from the hospitality of garbage cans.

I have a relationship, albeit a tumultuous one, with my computer. It's not as intense as the relationship Aldous Huxley used to have with his typewriter, which he celebrated as "the sole stay and comfort of my life."[26] But it's a relationship nonetheless. I spend more time than I care to admit thanking God for my computer. I spend more time with it than I do with any person in my life. My wife can't complain of being a computer widow because she has her own computer that she spends time with.

Are there more unexamined relationships in the world than our relationships to technology? In the future, chips and radio transmitters will be inside everything—shirts, shoes, staplers, refrigerators, rough-hewn beams, toilets, hairbrushes, and hairpieces—which means everything will have an "interaction" and thus some measure of intimacy. So we had better face our relationships with technology now, while it's still relatively easy to do so.

Try telling a NASCAR driver that people can't possibly have relationships with machines. Or tell a fighter pilot that a jet that becomes an extension of the pilot doesn't fly better than a jet that is treated as a mere object. You'll learn something.

I have a relationship with my car. I'm not the only one. A 2003 survey revealed that 63 percent of people talk to their cars, and 20 percent have given their cars names.[27] I've given a name to the voice on my GPS system: Matilda. I ask her if she'd like to go waltzing with me.

Starting with the fire and then the wheel, technology has always dramatically influenced our social relationships. What is different today is that the evolution of technology is so rapid that it is outpacing our social accommodations. In fact, human-to-human relationships are increasingly moderated by gizmos, implants, and other performance-enhancement devices with whom we are becoming intimate, even emotionally dependent. My computer is now functionally a part of my body. I call my computer case my "brain bag." When my computer goes down, I suffer brain damage.

> I found it more interesting and more significant to talk about an intimate relationship with prosthetics and gizmos than an intimate relationship between one human being and another.
>
> —NOVELIST AND FUTURIST BRUCE STERLING[28]

All technology cuts both ways—it is both our best friend and worst enemy. Some argue that computers will match computational capabilities of the human brain, an estimated 3.2 million instructions per second, in the second decade of this century. Blue Gene (IBM's biggest and fastest computer) will operate at one quadrillion operations per second when it becomes operational in 2005. Of course, my little IBM wouldn't know a good joke if one stared it in the face. It can't laugh with me or cry with me, but it *can* connect me to those who do.

But then there's our worst nightmare: What happens when computers are much smarter than we are? What happens when objects become more like subjects than objects? What happens when the visible and tactile difference between the born and the made disappears? You don't think that cell phones will one day be implanted in the ear? You don't think by then you'll want one of these electronic prostheses that replace the ringing of the phone with a tingle in the fingers? You don't think you'll also want to take advantage of all sorts of bodily responses—other than verbal—that will be available for communication?

If you don't think the future will be difficult to deal with, consider coming to terms with this one paragraph. We are almost at the place where we have to distinguish between "human" and "person." Very soon, the category of "human being" could be defined in purely biological terms, to distinguish it from "person." The category of "person" would denote something else, something relational, something spiritual.[29] The essence of "humanhood" would be biology. The essence of "personhood" would be synergic relationships, where the whole becomes greater than the sum of its parts. Consider our relationships with embodied selves (with "others"); our relationships of selves ("withness") to inner selves ("withinness").[30] All of these cyborgian relationships would be what make possible our relationships with the world and each other.

Was that paragraph as difficult for you to read as it was for me to write? The capacity of the human brain—and human intelligence—has brought us to the place where we're all cyborgs. We now are entering into deep and complex relationships with nonbiological tools and technologies—human to technological nonhuman.[31] But the scope of our relationships with cyborgs should be the subject of ethical deliberation, moral choice, and aesthetic judgments, rather than being foisted on us by engineers and technicians.

We can't conclude this discussion of technology without considering as well our relationship with the Internet. USAmerica has more public libraries than McDonald's restaurants, and 95 percent of these offer free Internet access. Ironically, the more involved you are in online chat rooms, the more likely you are to be a member of real-world communities and clubs. The more you surf the Internet, the less you graze your television channels.[32] Digital culture doesn't stimulate social isolation but social immersion in a complex array of communities. We aren't talking about disembodiment as much as we are new forms of embodied relationships.

The phrase "social capital" is another way of talking about the invisible connections that hold social groupings together or create new social networks. The development of the World Wide Web and dotcom technologies can actually enhance social capital and dissolve isolation. Do you think the person sitting next to you in the pew on Sunday morning really knows you any better than the person you're chatting with in cyberspace on Saturday night? People now share their minds and hearts more immediately and intimately with strangers across cyberspace than with strangers across the aisle. But that sharing on Saturday night only makes the hunger greater for in-your-face intimacy the rest of the week. The social capital created in cyberspace is being invested in face-to-face communities.

RELATIONSHIP WITH ANCESTORS

I have best friends whom I have never met. But I talk to them daily.

We need the dead to understand the living. And the words to me from my ancestors are "tongued with fire."[33] Their speech is Pentecostal, and they draw me into dramatic spiritual experiences. What I hear from them is beyond the spoken word.

There are authoritative voices in my life from both the living and the dead. I am part of a living tradition called Christianity. My identity is both fixed and fluid: I am living the tradition of the Christian faith by being in relationship with a whole host of ancestors. My identity is drawn less from my relationship with the teachings of the tradition than my relationship with the stories and art and people in the tradition—people who may not even be relationally connected other than that they, too, are living the tradition, and in living it, are re-forming the tradition.

We bind ourselves together by sharing the past and honoring our dead. Part of our identity as Christians is as inheritors and celebrants of the memory of our ancestors. In fact, one scholar has made the case for a "negative politics" that seeks to avoid repeating past mistakes by making sure they will not be forgotten.[34] As well as positive celebrations, we need memories and testimonies of injustice, humiliation, and pain. In the commemoration of our ancestors' hurts and mistakes, we find the courage and conviction to take a different direction.

However much bound together by a "tongued with fire" tradition,[35] many of these voices don't agree. Some are just-war voices, some are pacifist voices, some are inquisitory voices. There is no "orthodox" teaching about violence in the history of Christianity. Only a community of voices to which I am related and in which I myself have a voice. I live in multiple communities, communities in which I have no part in choosing members, communities that often exist in tension and conflict with one another.

In Daniel Zwicker's *Irenicum Irenicorum* (1658), he thanked the Lutherans and Moravians for introducing him to "the rudiments of reform and Christian freedom," the Calvinists for teaching him "the basic application of reason to the field of theology," the Remonstrants for their ideas on freedom of conscience, the Catholics for their views on good works and their esteem for the church fathers, the Mennonites for showing him "the lessons of Christ's life," and the Socinians for "their expertise in critical judgment." Zwicker based his proposal for reconciling diverse voices on the three guides of Scripture, reason, and tradition.[36]

The unvarnished truth about our great "cloud of witnesses" is that none of the voices is untarnished or unerring. Yet in the ancient words of the writer of Hebrews, time would fail to tell of all who had "conquered kingdoms, administered justice, obtained promises, shut the mouths of lions, quenched raging fire, escaped the edge of the sword, won strength out of weakness, became mighty in war, put foreign armies to flight."[37]

> Others were tortured, refusing to accept release.… Others suffered mocking and flogging, and even chains and imprisonment. They were stoned to death, they were sawn in two, they were killed by the sword; they went about in skins of sheep and goats, destitute, persecuted, tormented—of whom the world was not worthy. They wandered in deserts and mountains, and in caves and holes in the ground.[38]

Without the wisdom of these diverse voices, I would not be able to function in today's world where betrayal is more common than loyalty; a world where we spend most of our lives, not in the Promised Land, but in the wilderness. If we wait to live until we get to Canaan, we'll never live. So I learn from Elijah what it means to be left alone in the wilderness and still meet God. I learn from Jesus about how temptations in the wilderness can draw me closer to God. And I learn from the Israelite community about the perils and promises of spending four decades wandering in the wilderness.[39]

It also is important for me to remember the unknown saints, the unheralded "cloud of witnesses." Jesus told us in a variety of ways that those who appear first in the eyes of popular estimation may be last in the light of the kingdom.[40]

That is why I love so much the ancient Jewish tradition of the Secret Saints, the "Lamed-Vov." The Lamed-Vov are thirty-six Just Men

> It seems odd that certain men who talk so much of what the Holy Spirit reveals to themselves, should think so little of what he has revealed to others.
>
> —ENGLISH BAPTIST PREACHER CHARLES H. SPURGEON[41]

who through their deep love and devotion help the world to go forward. No one knows who they are. *They* don't even know who they are. This is similar to those Jesus described who lived lives of such service to others that at the Last

Judgment they have no memory of having clothed or fed "the least of these."[42]

The thirty-six Just Men exist anonymously among us. When one of them dies, another arises to take his place. Because their heartache over human sin and suffering is so great that even God can't comfort them, God allows the world to continue to exist. As an act of mercy toward them, "from time to time the Creator, blessed be His Name, sets forward the clock of the Last Judgment by one minute."[43]

During the Passover Seder, there is something called the ritual of the "open door." The door is flung wide open, and the participants say, "We invite Elijah to join Miriam at our Seder table, and to drink from his cup, Kos Eliyahu."[44] In a similar way, Christians need open-door rituals with their ancestors. I often open the door for John Wesley to sit at table. My tribal identity within Christianity is Wesleyan. I delight in eating some of Wesley's favorite foods (lemonade, candied orange peel), because thereby I honor his presence and authority in my life.

So, too, I open the door, not just for a historical community but for a literary community. I invite Tatian, Tertullian, Augustine, Hildegaard of Bingen, Joachim of Fiore, Teresa of Saint Lisieux, John Bunyan, George Herbert, Emily Dickinson, Malcolm Muggeridge, W. H. Auden, Denise Levertov, G. K. Chesterton, Brian McLaren, and many others.

RELATIONSHIP WITH CREEDS AND CONFESSIONS

If you cut the head off a cricket, it keeps on chirping. Some people are like that. Their brains are disengaged, but they keep talking.

The engagement of head, heart, and hands in Christian history has yielded a rich tradition of things that come out of the mouth: creeds and confessions. Our faith has developed through history, and this faith has expressed itself through confessions of faith. Faith needs the creeds like a body needs clothes. But a creedal faith is more relational than propositional. The key doctrines of the church (the Trinity, virgin birth, authority of Scripture, bodily resurrection, Parousia) are more interactions than transactions.

Christianity is much more than a mastery of texts and traditions. But that does not minimize those texts and traditions. The richness of Christian theology is expressed through relationships more than doctrines. But that does not denigrate the pastoral guidance that doctrines give. Beliefs are not the narthex to relationships, but the sanctuaries in which relationships develop and deepen. Creeds and confessions help us get an intellectual grip and put things together into a Big Picture.

> The Church is the part of the world that confesses the renewal to which all the world is called.
>
> —MENNONITE THEOLOGIAN JOHN HOWARD YODER[45]

If you dedicate your life to following Jesus, won't you also develop a philosophy as to why your dedication is worth the bother? It matters how our ancestors who were intellectual titans made sense of their relationships with God. It matters that our framework of understanding, how we organize our knowledge, is in formats that are transferable and teachable. Creeds and confessions, by virtue of their intellectual power, communicate the fruit of learning and originality in deceptively simple formulations.

Lists need not leave people listless. For your soul's health, you need to know some lists and be in relationship with them. Here are a few to get you started:

- one baptism creed (the Apostles' Creed)
- one daily prayer (the Lord's Prayer)
- three transcendentals of being (beauty, truth, and goodness)
- three parts of penance (contrition, confession, satisfaction)
- four last things (death, judgment, heaven, hell)
- four cardinal virtues (courage, prudence, temperance, justice)
- five relational fields in which we experience the Holy Spirit (the five fields of synergy according to the Apostles' Creed after "I believe in the Holy Spirit" are [1] the holy catholic church, [2] the communion of saints, [3] the forgiveness of sins, [4] the resurrection of the body, and [5] life everlasting)
- seven deadly sins (pride, envy, gluttony, lust, anger, greed, sloth)
- seven contrary virtues (humility against pride, kindness against envy, abstinence against gluttony, chastity against lust, patience against anger, liberality against greed, and diligence against sloth)
- seven corporal works of mercy (feed the hungry, give drink to the thirsty, give shelter to strangers, clothe the naked, visit the sick, minister to prisoners, and bury the dead)

- Ten Commandments[46]
- sixteen daily agenda items:

> A God to glorify, a Christ to imitate,
> A soul to save, a body to mortify,
> Sins to repent, virtues to acquire,
> Hell to avoid, heaven to merit,
> Eternity to prepare for, time to profit by,
> Neighbours to edify, a world to despise,
> Devils to combat, passions to subdue,
> Deaths maybe to suffer, and judgement to undergo.[47]

The Spirit goes ahead of the disciples in the Acts of the Apostles, but the Spirit is always linked to Christ. Truth is not invented, but transmitted. Its point of origin is Jesus. The revelation received upon which Christianity is based was not a rationality but a person. "In seeking to place everything Christian in terms of secular rationality," one scholar has warned, "Christians set themselves at risk of losing their Christianness."[48]

But we need other "looks" at Jesus to attain the "full stature" of Christ. Just because Jesus is the full revelation of God doesn't mean we can't learn from creeds and confessions. We learn even in contrast to the dogmas of other religions. Jesus tied our own learning to the church's mission to other cultures with other religions. It's the very "strangeness" of the other that opens up new learning about God.[49] The church needs to address the intellectual climate of its age: The vital theological task of every age is the formulation of views that are credibly held and creedally honest. There is no room or excuse for theological laziness. In George Marsden's recent biography of Jonathan Edwards, the greatest theologian USAmerica has produced is portrayed as a dedicated parish pastor who had one eye on the texts and tradition and the other eye on the trends of the times, always trying to connect the two.[50]

But we need to be careful about our confessionalism. Biblical faith does not make rational sense and never will make rational sense. The gospel does not fit within the canons of reason or logic. In fact, in some ways biblical faith is the critique of reason. Truth is revelation. And revelation, by definition, often does not correspond to quantifiable reality. Revelation may even create contradictions to what we think we "know" about reality. For a perfect example, try to explain the Trinity to anyone's logical satisfaction: God is One and God is Three. The empty tomb on Easter morning was a revelation, not a symposium.

It's Already Broken

Here are words of wisdom for all of us: "The nature of things is that if they don't get lost, they get stolen, and if they don't get stolen, they get broken, and if they don't get broken, they fall apart. This law applies to teacups, cars, people, sweaters, pets, computers, earrings, and just about everything you can touch or buy or have."[51]

No relationship is perfect because no person is perfect like no teacup is perfect like no sunset is perfect. All artifacts are already broken. All artifacts break down. There is no "perfect disciple." Rather than fret over imperfections, know that the moment is what matters. Concentrating on the preciousness of the moment makes our flawed earrings or our needy relationships all the more special. To be "in the moment" with our artifacts is to allow them to put us in touch with God.

There are some things you can't make disappear. Take spam on the Internet, mistakes in a book, mosquitoes in the backyard, moods in the person you love the most. You just have to live with certain things. Unlike school children who constantly make and break friendships, authentic relationship requires recognition and respect for people's varying intimacy capacities and thresholds.

God doesn't love nonsinners more than sinners. Nor does God love weak, lazy, and dumb people more than strong, hard-working, and smart people. God doesn't play favorites with love.

A man who had no children asked a father of four, "Why do you love your children the way you do?" The father thought for a second and said, "Because they're mine!"

Why does God love you and me, as flawed and needy as we are? God answers the question: "Because you're mine!"

PART VIII

OUR RELATIONSHIP WITH

THE SPIRITUAL WORLD

CLEAR SIGNS OF UNSEEN THINGS

Losing Yourself in the Mystery of God

Where shall my wondering soul begin?
—CHARLES WESLEY'S CONVERSION HYMN[1]

For more than two years early in this century, an exhibit on Albert Einstein's life and science toured New York, Los Angeles, and Jerusalem. The first greeting as you entered the exhibit was a warning sign with no words. In the center of a video screen was a dark blob, which morphed like a lava lamp into strange shapes with each new museum visitor. The blobs showed how each one of us might appear if light reflected from our person were distorted by a black hole—whose existence Einstein's theories predicted.

The curator of the exhibit at New York's American Museum of Natural History translated the wordless warning in this fashion: "From the minute you step through the front door, we will twist your view of space and time and what your entire vision of the universe is like."[2]

There could have been no better greeting to an Einstein exhibit than this one. At age five, young Albert was sick at home. His father brought him a compass, and the young boy was transfixed with the fact that wherever he went in the room, the needle always pointed north. "Something deeply hidden had to be behind things," he concluded.[3]

As Albert Einstein and the New York museum curator discovered, we live in an unseen universe. And as Abraham discovered in the Old Testament, faith stretches the soul until your life turns upside-down and twists inside-out, including your views of "normal" and "madness," as well as what the "good life" is.[4] In fact, the Bible delivers a warning sign on every page, saying: "Beware all who enter. You can never be the same again."

CHAPTER THIRTEEN

GLORIOUS STRANGENESS

The gospels immerse the reader in the strangeness of a relationship with Jesus where those who are gentle inherit the earth, enemies are embraced, strength resides in the broken places, second miles and second chances are the norm, and people live nothing that resembles an ordinary life. Christianity needs to be defamiliarized to make room for this strangeness. Much of what we think we know about the Christian faith we need to forget, or at least to set aside for now, so we can be converted by the glorious strangeness of the GodLife relationship.

"We will first understand how simple the universe is," physicist John A. Wheeler argued, "when we recognize how strange it is."[5] How strange is strange? The empty space of outer space is not filled with nothing. Instead, space is filled with invisible somethings, which some call "dark energy." At least 90 percent of the universe can never be observed because it consists of dark matter or high-energy radiation. In other words, scientists can only study 5 to 10 percent of the mass of the universe with standard scientific methodologies. The remaining 90 percent is unknowable by known procedures.[6]

> My own suspicion is that the universe is not only queerer than we suppose, but queerer than we can suppose.
>
> —J. B. S. HALDANE[7]

The spiritual quest is an adventure in the unseen world of the spirit. Moderns wanted to know more about God and to "think God's thoughts after him."[8] Postmoderns suspect there is more God to get to know than moderns ever imagined, and they want to get to know that unseen, queer, and strange God.

Episcopal bishop John Shelby Spong speaks for modern theologians when he claims, based on a long-defunct physics, that "our world is not one of miracle and magic in which virgins give birth, wise men follow a wandering star, or resuscitated bodies walk out of a tomb three days after burial."[9]

Postmoderns reply, "Oh, but it is!" To say "theism" is to say "supernatural." You can't have one without the other.

Ray Peacock, president of Crestmont College in Rancho Palos Verdes, California, tells of a seminary professor who taught doctrine. When she couldn't answer a question posed by a member of the class, she would always say, "It's a mystery." Her students jokingly determined they were in Mystery 101 rather than Doctrine 101. The truth is, that's exactly what class they were in. Every course on doctrine is a course in mystery. Christianity is a world to be explored, not a puzzle to be solved. If there is not dazzling mystery to the doctrines and dogmatics, they are not Christian doctrines and dogmatics. In the words of Gregory Wolfe, "Dogma are not so much efforts to give logical accounts of the mysteries of revelation as they are a process of creating a tabernacle for the shining mysteries within."[10]

THE WINDBLOWN GOD

Those who sold out to modernity tried to empty the church of its mysteries. Then, when they had largely succeeded, they wondered why the church felt so empty. One author argues that the reason Nietzsche, the son and grandson of Lutheran pastors, reacted so strongly against Christianity was because he saw it as systematized idolatry where "believers" were more in love with their theology than with God.[11] Moderns created God in the image of their propositions rather than losing themselves in a relationship with an unpredictable, dangerous, Real-Thing God who can resuscitate bodies and impregnate virgins and muster stars. The ultimate in a bad hair day? No hair-raising experiences of the divine. If you haven't gotten lost in some mystery today, it hasn't been much of a day.

There is an ancient fable in which a hunter asks a woodcutter if he has seen any lion tracks in the area. "As a matter of fact," the woodcutter says, "I can lead you right to the lion himself." The hunter, surprised at the possibility, demures. "It's...it's the tracks I'm looking for," he stammers, "not the lion."[12]

The tracks of God, and the tracks of others on the trail of God, no longer suffice. We have settled for eating the menu when all along we could have been eating the meal.

One reason the phrase *organized religion* falls so unheavenly on the ear is that it sounds too much like the oxymoron *organized truth*. Ever try to organize Truth? God the Infinite, the Eternal, the Unsearchable, has never shown much interest in being organized or systematized by humans. There's an old story about God and Satan walking together when God bent down and picked something up. Curious, as always, Satan inquired of the Lord, "What is that you have there?" As the Lord gazed at the thing, glowing brightly in the Lord's hand, the Lord replied, "This is Truth." Whereupon Satan reached out for it, saying as he grasped it, "Here, let me have it. I'll organize it for you."

My favorite phrase for spiritual leaders is based on the word *astronaut*. *Naut* means "sailor" and *astro* means "stars." An astronaut is a "sailor of the stars"; a cosmonaut is a "sailor of the cosmos." Spiritual leaders are "pneumanauts"—sailors of the Spirit—based on the Greek word for "spirit" *(pneuma)*. The Scriptures say that there is one thing predictable about those who are born of the Spirit: You can't tell where they come from or where they're going.[13] The only thing that's predictable about pneumanauts—the living masters of the invisible—is that they're unpredictable, they're windblown, they're pneumaorganized. How unpredictable is your life?

Being blown by God is scary stuff. Oftentimes we go to great effort to shut out the first little draft, never giving God's gentle breezes a chance to form, much less making allowance for the Mighty Rushing Wind. But pneumanauts have awakened senses for windbursts of marvels and enigmas, wherever they may be found.

Jesus, in his windblown nature, was unpredictable in almost everything he did. Take his healing ministry. There is little sameness to his miracles. In each case and with each person, Jesus adapted his style, his manner, his attitude. He had no canned responses, only windblown approaches to each person.

When a Roman centurion sent some Jewish elders to ask Jesus if he would heal the centurion's slave, Jesus responded immediately. Not knowing the man or his slave, he nevertheless set out for the centurion's home.[14] When the centurion later sent an emissary to intercept Jesus and tell him that he need only order the healing for it to be done, Jesus praised the man's faith and cured the slave from a distance, as requested.

But when Jesus's close friends Martha and Mary implored him to return quickly to their home because Jesus's best friend, Lazarus, was ill, Jesus stalled.[15] In fact, Jesus delayed so long that Lazarus died and was in his tomb four days before Jesus arrived. The miracle Jesus then performed was no mere healing. It was a resuscitation. But why did Jesus hustle to the aid of an unknown slave at the request of a Roman centurion, and then seemingly disregard the urgent plea from his dearest friends?

When the woman with the hemorrhage secretly touched Jesus to receive healing, he confronted her and then praised her for her faith. Yet when the Canaanite woman politely asked Jesus for her daughter's healing, she was sub-jected to much scrutiny and a spir-ited debate before Jesus responded to the woman's request.

Each situation was different, and each context elicited a different re-sponse from Jesus. Where he was,

> The soul should always stand ajar, ready to welcome the ecstatic experience.
>
> —EMILY DICKINSON[16]

who he was with, and the circumstances of the request all combined to help determine the path Jesus would take. Do we expect any less of Christ today? How open are you to surprises? Are you willing to take paths that Jesus is blaz-ing and follow him as he hacks a way in the wilderness?

The Spirit of Christ walked a new path with Paul and brought the Gen-tiles into the body of Christ.

The Spirit of Christ walked a new path with Saint Francis and brought all of creation into the body of Christ.

The Spirit of Christ walked a new path with Martin Luther and turned the altar toward the people, who are the body of Christ.

The Spirit of Christ walked a new path with John Wesley and strolled out into the streets and the fields to find lay leaders who would lead the body of Christ.

The Spirit of Christ walked a new path with Charles G. Finney, and an industrial, urban world was claimed as part of the body of Christ.

The Spirit of Christ walked a new path with Billy Graham, and a multi-racial, multinational, multicultural world was affirmed as part of the body of Christ.

What new path is the Spirit of Christ walking with you and with your church? In the words of British sociologist and lay theologian David Martin, "Everything depends on whether you believe the universe is reducible down-wards to nothing but covering laws operating in closed circuitry or gives rise to emergent properties opening on to the human, the unique and the unrepeat-able."[17] How open is your life and your church to alternative realities? We want to pin God down to some fixed position, to some single-point perspective. But if you're committing your life to anything, it isn't fixed doctrines or single-point principles but paradoxical mysteries and "manywheres"[18] perspectives.

Is there just one Christian response to all issues? What is the truly Christian response to prayer in public schools? What is the one Christian response to capital punishment? What is the sole, reliable Christian response to war? Is there an end-all-be-all response to any of these issues? Set out to draw a line and it turns into a circle. At any rate, the point of a point is not a point, but a circle—even a many-mansioned matrix.

Unseen Dimensions

The science of chaos and nonequilibrium physics is based on embracing uncertainty and unpredictability while knowing that underlying everything is a fundamental interconnectedness, purposefulness, and endless possibilities. Superstring theory hypothesizes the existence of multiple dimensions of existence far beyond our local space-time continuum.

We call three dimensions home. But there are many more hidden dimensions all around us. The world as we know it has "cracks" in it—as one or more dimensions of this ten-, eleven-, or as many as twenty-six dimensional universe crack open and "leak" into our three-dimensional space, filling it with the wondrous, the mysterious, even the miraculous. A pneumanaut cultivates relationships with more dimensions of reality than our three-dimensional space-time world can accommodate. Pneumanauts sail the Spirit, who can do nothing less than crackle with mystery.

The implications of superstring theory are actually nothing new. Our ancestors inhabited a very similar world of nonclaustrophobic relationships. The world of ancient Israel was not one where God "entered" from somewhere else but where what was ordinary turned out to be extraordinary. God is close, engulfing, surrounding. The biblical world has "little cracks in it here and there," according to James L. Kugel. "That is the whole point of the fog—donkeys start talking, perfect strangers seem somehow to know your wife's name, fires burn on and on, and so forth."[20]

> Before I formed you in the womb
> I knew you.
>
> —God, speaking to
> the prophet Jeremiah[19]

It's hard to talk rationally about hidden things, about things that are beyond reason, about cracks in consciousness, without seeming, well, cracked yourself. Consider these unknowns and allow yourself to think about them rather than immediately dismissing them as irrelevant, unexplainable, or simply not worth your time:

- the mystery of why the Twin Towers went down together, just as they went up together
- the mystery of why, as biology and other sciences learn more and more about life, we seem to know less and less what life really is
- the mystery of how all people alive today can be traced to a single, common ancestor[21]
- the mystery of how every person who will ever live is present now among us[22]
- the mystery of how no one gets hurt when one hundred tons of extraterrestrial material enters our atmosphere every day[23]
- the mystery of why the decisions we make today affect the entire universe's history
- the mystery of how part of your body, actual electrons, may be outside your body right now[24]
- the mystery of sighs too deep for words
- the mystery of things we are not yet ready to hear or bear

Apart from a few notable exceptions—for example Michel Henry's insistence on a phenomenology of the invisible,[25] Rupert Sheldrake's morphogenetic fields, and Merleau Ponty's last book *Le visible et l'invisible*—to speak of the invisible in the twentieth century was to risk being seen as having joined the dottier brigade. With only the lens of reason to give them sight, it's no wonder moderns were waiting for God but settled for Godot. Truth without reason is no truth. But truth without relationship is untruth.

MYSTERY RELIGION?

Being a Christian is more about relationship with God than beliefs about God; more about the presence of God than the proofs of God; more about intimacy with truth than the tenets of truth; more about knowing God's activities than knowing God's attributes. It is time to move from a religion that seeks to comprehend God to a relationship that seeks to encounter and be a home for God—to move from points and propositions and moralisms to mystery and paradox and participation in the divine life.

Relationships only stay alive by retaining the mystery. Once something is fully known, it dies. Relationships need strangeness and unpredictability. It's the same with our relationships with God. All relationships are dances of communication and concealment.

Anyone who talks about God doesn't know what he or she is talking about. God is another name for mystery.

Moses to God: What is Your name?

God to Moses: I will be what I will be.[26]

Moses spoke to God face-to-face, "as one speaks to a friend."[27] But Moses wanted something more than God's face. Moses wanted God's mind. Moses wanted more than just seeing and experiencing God. Moses wanted to go into the mind of God.[28]

And God said no because ultimately God is unknowable. If we knew everything, we would no longer be strugglers with God. Until the day we will see God face to face, we will only know "in part" and at best through a glass dimly. Until then, we will never know all that we want to know. We will never understand all that we want to understand.

The paradoxical nature of biblical truth, where the relationships between opposite extremes is the essence of truth,[29] should make Christians quite at home with contradictions and contritions. Philosopher Nicholas Wolterstorff pushes pneumanauts into the seas of paradox with this jolt: "Some of what God wishes us to believe may be fit and proper for us as his 'children' to believe, yet strictly speaking false. For all we know this may lead to theories which, though fully satisfactory for our human purposes, are also strictly speaking false."[30] In other words, God may want us to believe some things that appear contradictory. To deny either contradiction would be to deny the truth. In Christianity, when you perceive a truth, look for the opposite truth. Heresy is a truth that has lost its opposite.

It is true: "Without any doubt, the mystery of our religion is great."[31] Instead of talking about God or "thinking God's thoughts after God," theologians ought to be participating in God's life, experiencing God's flow, living the mystery that is God. All right answers lie in God, not in us. In the words of one Greek Orthodox theologian, "We see that it is not the task of Christianity to provide easy answers to every question, but to make us progressively aware of a *mystery*. God is not so much the object of our knowledge as the cause of our *wonder*."[32] God is as much to be found in creeks as in creeds, in canyons as in canons, in silence as in statements, in experiences as in edicts, in conversations as in convictions, in heart as in head.

The "secret" to holiness is "drawing near"[33] to the Mystery that always has about it the uncomprehended and the incomprehensible, the Truth that never exhausts its shadow and secrecy. But just because God is life's ultimate Mystery doesn't mean God is ultimately incomprehensible. For in Christ "are hidden all the treasures of wisdom and knowledge."[34]

Christianity is a mystery religion. When you've wrung the mystery out of Christianity, you've wrung its neck.

But Christianity is the opposite of what we've come to think of as a "mystery" religion. It's not one that keeps secrets. It's one whose secret has been revealed, but it still retains its mystery: God has openly revealed the "mystery of his will, according to his good pleasure that he set forth in Christ, as a plan for the fullness of time, to gather up all things in him, things in heaven and things on earth."[35] Christianity's mystery is an open secret.[36] If the secret is hidden from anyone, it's the

> God is not only at work in every particle of his creation and in all our human experience, but he makes his home in us.
>
> —GERARD W. HUGHES[37]

wise and proud. The secret is revealed most powerfully to "little children."[38]

To embrace Jesus is to embrace and declare mystery. We are instructed to "declare the mystery of Christ."[39] And that declaration is this: "The mystery that has been hidden throughout the ages and generations but has now been revealed to his saints. To them God chose to make known how great among the Gentiles are the riches of the glory of this mystery, which is Christ in you, the hope of glory."[40] Some people say we don't know what we have until we lose it. But it's more true that we don't know what we've been missing until it arrives.

The embarrassment of Christianity is also its richest mystery: Christ in you. "The Spirit of him who raised Jesus from the dead," Paul said, "is living in you."[41] The kingdom of God lives in you, Jesus said.[42] Jesus is living his resurrected life in and through you. Just as God the Father lived God's life in

Jesus, to the point where Jesus said, "Whatever I say is just what the Father has told me to say,"[43] so God the Son lives his life in you. "Greater is he that is in you, than he that is in the world.[44] Greater things will you do," Jesus said.[45]

Jesus said: "Anyone who has seen me has seen the Father."[46] Jesus says to his church: "If people see you, they've seen me." We are commissioned into this mystery, not to begin a new ministry, but to carry on Christ's ministry. The perfect tense in the verse "As the Father has sent me…"[47] means that Jesus is continually being sent, that he exists in a state of "sentness." The Ascension does not mean that he is no longer the "sent one." We don't take over Jesus's ministry. It is still his ministry, which he continues in and through us. We carry it forward into paths where it has never gone before.

We are called to become, in the words of our ancestors, "little Christs." The miracle of a Christ-ened life is that we who have been made from carbon dust and clay can take the name of Christ: Christian. Jesus said that we all are branches of the one vine. Today he might say we are all cells of the one body, which is Christ. We are called, not to imitate Christ, but to become Christians—a Christ presence and power—to allow Christ so to live in us that "for to me, to live is Christ and to die is gain."[48] The French translation of 1 John uses, for *word,* the term *verb.* If Jesus is the verb of God, the action of God in the cosmos, then disciples of Christ are little verbs. And little verbs don't have to worry so much about subjects and objects.[49]

The Word of God was made flesh not to deliver some fresh insights, or to recite a new law code, or to enunciate some new teachings. The Word of God was made flesh to deliver us from sin and death through the mysterious power of a love bred by a beaten human hanging on a cross. "God abides in those who confess that Jesus is the Son of God, and they abide in God."[50] Christ died for us. Christ lives in us. You and I personify the gospel.

If we are to get the hang of Christian faith, we must not stop at Christ's hanging. What makes Jesus ultimately different is not his message but his Resurrection. The gospel is a power let loose in the world. The very energy of God's Spirit that was at work in Paul is at work in you! As Paul put it, "God made you alive with Christ."[51] Your life and Christ's are indistinguishable.

In her classic text on mysticism, Evelyn Underhill defined a mystic as someone who is "in love with the Absolute."[52] But not if that Absolute is reduced to an abstract principle. Only if that Absolute is honored and taken up as a relationship. The Christian kind of mysticism doesn't pull one away from the world, but draws one deeper into the world. A mystic is not someone who hears voices others don't. A mystic is someone who is awake to the voices that everyone hears.

The Life of Mystery

God does not come to us offering rules; God comes offering relationship. Truth is not found in the solving of difficult theological riddles. Truth is found as we get lost in the mystery of faith. You can maintain your bearings while getting lost…if Jesus is leading the way.

As you inhabit the Mystery that is God in you, you experience the GodLife relationship, which brings truth and hope to the world. Jesus never commanded us to learn the right things about him, but rather to follow him. We find the truth and help reveal the hiddenness and mystery of God in Christ as we lose ourselves in the GodLife relationship. There is a time to leave words behind for a walkabout with Jesus of listening and seeing and adoring a world rimmed with sunsets but brimming with sunrises.

> Thee will I cherish
> Thee will I honor
> Thou my soul's glory,
> Joy, and crown.
>
> —SEVENTEENTH-CENTURY HYMN
> "FAIREST LORD JESUS"[53]

A man was standing over his baby's crib, intently staring. His wife entered the room and watched in silence. She saw in her husband's face a wide range of emotions: wonder, doubt, admiration.

Deeply touched, she put her arm around him and, with eyes glistening and voice trembling, said, "A penny for your thoughts." Unhesitatingly, he blurted out: "For the life of me, I can't see how anybody can make a crib like that for $89.95."

Agog over the manger, amiss to the baby in the manger.

It's time to trust the Mystery in the manger. As Henry Ward Beecher, one of the great preachers of the nineteenth century, drew his last breath, he uttered his final words: "Here comes the mystery…"

QUESTIONS FOR PERSONAL CONTEMPLATION AND SHARED CONVERSATION

The life of faith is not a process of rote learning or the intellectual pursuit of the right beliefs. Instead, it is a "lived relationship"—with God, with God's Word, with other people, with creation, with objects that point us to God, and with the spiritual realm. This guide is designed to help you go deeper into the relationships that reveal God.

The questions and observations are grouped in three levels: Take a Look (testing the waters), Look Inside (what it means to your life), and Talk About It (exploring in conversation with others). Contemplating the answers to the questions will help you look at God, and the relationships that reveal God, in new ways. Don't feel that you have to read through the guide sequentially. Explore the topics that interest you most or that speak most immediately to your own pursuit of the mystery of God. (An expanded discussion guide, with additional questions designed for both individual and group use, is available at www.waterbrookpress.com.)

Introduction: Where Did We Miss the Person and Get the Point Instead?

Faith is not a one-time decision or a once-in-a-life commitment. Rather, faith is a new life that we practice in the context of relationships. The Bible teaches that God is love, and love can't exist in isolation. There must be a Lover and also those who are recipients of God's love.

The life of faith is a deepening, expanding set of connections and relationships. These are the "practices" of the Christian life. Faith is the daily pursuit of God through a relationship with God's Son. As the first Christians obeyed Jesus's command to go into all the world, they invited others into a new relationship with God made possible by Jesus's death and resurrection.

Take a Look

1. God desires both our love and our obedience. But what produces right thoughts and actions? Is it a matter of believing the right

things, or a function of pursuing the right relationships—beginning with a relationship with God?

2. The author states that the number one problem in the world is people's living disconnected lives: detached from God, from others, from creation, and from themselves. Do you agree? If so, think of current examples that demonstrate the problems that result from people's being disconnected.

Look Inside

3. The author argues that a misguided allegiance to rules leaves a Christian with casual doctrinal assent that can exist independent of a changed life. Have you had the experience of studying doctrine and biblical facts but afterward feeling spiritually shallow? If so, what did you do about it?

Talk About It

If you are using these Interactives with another person or in a small group, the questions under the "Talk About It" heading are designed to spur a deeper level of conversation.

4. The author suggests that getting the life of faith back on a relational track requires that we seek answers to the following questions. Answer these questions in conversation with others:
    a. Why did God create you?
    b. What does the Lord require of you?
    c. What is the true, biblical essence of "faith in God"?

Part I: Faith Is a Relationship

Jesus did not say, "Agree to this teaching"; he said, "Follow me!" The essential destination of Christianity isn't *what* but *who*. The good news of the gospel is about a Person: Jesus (see 2 Corinthians 5:18; Colossians 1:20). Sadly, Christians in the West have largely missed the beauty and power of this central truth: The death and resurrection of Jesus make possible a relationship with God.

Take a Look

1. Someone has said, "If God so loved the world, why can't the church?" How do you respond to this question?

2. Jesus described himself as the Way, the Truth, and the Life, adding that a person can approach the Father only through Jesus (see John 14:6-7). What deeper truths do you find in Jesus's use of the words *Way, Truth,* and *Life?*

Look Inside

3. Consider this assertion by author and thinker Calvin Miller: "To desire only what Christ gives and not to desire Christ Himself is to be bought off by little trinkets, never to own the greater treasure of His indwelling presence."[1] Can you identify times when you were happier with spiritual trinkets than you were with Jesus's presence in your life? What were those times like?

4. One scholar contends that "many who remain in the church have faith in a God who only remotely resembles the God revealed by Jesus."[2] Do you agree or disagree? Why? What does your heart tell you?

Talk About It

5. Why do you think Christianity has been described as having "undescended spiritual testicles."[3] Are you comfortable with this metaphor? What are its positives as well as its negatives?

6. Discuss this admonition from emerging-church leader Todd Hunter to his parishioners: "I do not want things *from* you; I want things *for* you." How do you respond to his statement? Consider this as well: How many of us think of God as more wanting things *from* us than *for* us?

PART II: OUR RELATIONSHIP WITH GOD

A more astounding claim has never been made: The God of the universe wants to have a relationship with you and me. And as if to prove that God is serious about this, God gives us example after example of God's choice to pursue relationships with stubborn, rebellious people. One of the most vivid biblical accounts of God's pursuit of a deepening relationship with a human is the story of God and Abraham.

Take a Look

1. Prior to God's commanding Abraham to sacrifice his son, Abraham had the boldness to negotiate with God over the fate of Sodom and Gomorrah, which were filled with strangers. In contrast, when Abraham was commanded to sacrifice Isaac, Abraham obeyed without a word of objection. Why do you think Abraham was so willing to follow a command that contradicted everything he knew about God's character and God's promise to him?

2. In chapter 4, the author points out that after the angel prevented Abraham from slaying Isaac, God never again spoke personally to Abraham. The author further points out that there was no longer a relationship between Abraham and Sarah, Abraham and Isaac, or Abraham and Ishmael. What conclusions do you draw from this observation?

Look Inside

3. How does your soul respond when it hears these words: "Ephraim is joined to idols; leave him alone!" (Hosea 4:17)? What would it mean to you if these words were spoken about you? When God lets us alone, isn't that when we need to worry? On the other hand, when God wrestles with us, when we engage with God and argue with God, isn't this a sign of hope and true relationship?

4. The Bible says Enoch "walked with God; then he was no more, because God took him" (Genesis 5:24, NRSV). What would it mean for you to truly "walk with God"?

Talk About It

5. Share stories about what it feels like to be "sacrificed" by well-meaning people who were just trying to follow what they perceived to be God's leading. Examples might include a dictatorial pastor, a guilt-

inducing Bible teacher, an insecure committee chair. Without revealing identities or all the miserable details, talk about whether these
"sacrifices" were some of the worst experiences or some of the best
experiences of your life? What did you learn from them?

Part III: Our Relationship with God's Story

The Christian message is a story of love come down from heaven to earth. The
Bible is our family history, which gives us a rich and inspiring identity, as well
as a set of case studies from which we learn how to deal with situations in life.
The church is a community of people who live connected lives—in relationship with God's story and in connection with one another's stories.

Take a Look

1. The author makes this statement: "As we live in relationship with
    God, and as we tell stories of God's truth, we begin to become
    what we tell. When we tell the story of Jesus forgiving his enemies,
    for instance, we begin to become people who forgive our enemies."
    Think about a time when, in telling God stories, you experienced
    greater devotion and obedience in your own life.
2. In Jesus we get the best and truest experience of God. It is not a
    distant, objective, analytical look. It's a bone-deep experience. How
    would you describe the difference between a true *look* at God and
    a true *experience* of God?
3. It's possible that God never intended the Bible to be strip-mined for
    propositions or dissected and analyzed. It's plausible that God never
    wanted the Bible to be turned into a stringent code of conduct.
    What if, instead, God means for all of Scripture to be God's love
    story to us? If you were able to experience the full impact of God's
    love story, how do you think it would change the way you live?

Look Inside

4. Garry Wills wrote a book answering the question, "Why am I
    a Catholic?" This is his answer: "I am a Catholic because of the
    creed."[4] Why are you a Presbyterian or a Lutheran, a Methodist

or a Pentecostal? The author gives his own answer: "I am a Christian not because of dogma or doctrine or theology, but because of Jesus." What's your answer?

Talk About It

5. Biblical scholar Leslie Houlden has a thesis: Christian doctrine is problematic from the start because it cannot be based on the Scriptures.[5] Why? Because our foundation documents are either narratives, history, poetry, letters, or occasional writings. None of these is conducive to doctrine building or systematic thought. How would you respond to Houlden's thesis?

6. Discuss the following: We treat the Bible "as if it were a giant fortune cookie. Crack it open anywhere and you'll find wise and useful sayings, pithy insights to better your life, marriage, business, or finances. But whenever we give principles for life without threading them through what it means to lay down our lives and deny ourselves and follow Christ, we distort Christianity. We flip it around, and suddenly the self is at the center."[6]

Part IV: Our Relationship with Other People of Faith

When Jesus pointed out how we should love, he put it in the context of "one another" living—never in a vacuum. We don't love in isolation, we love in relationship. In fact, we have no identity in isolation; we are truly ourselves only when we operate within a network of relationships. Without faithful one-another living, there is no Christian discipleship. Spiritual life is dead without relationship with other Christians.

Take a Look

1. If someone asked if you were a "real Christian," how would you answer? Would you explain that you believe certain things? Or would you invite the person to follow you around for a day, or to become a part of your church for a month, so you could show the person what lived-out relationships look like?

2. Read Isaiah 58:6, Micah 6:8, James 1:27. How do these verses define obedience and faithful living? Do the standards of measure in these verses pertain more to doctrine and belief, or to how we conduct our relationships?

Look Inside

3. Fellow Christians are not useful to us simply for encouragement or help in times of need. They actually reveal God to us. God indwells us both individually and collectively. How have you experienced the presence and the ministry of God in God's people collectively? How has this differed from the way that you, as an individual, have experienced God?

4. Jesus invites us to become disciples, literally "learners." Jesus invites us to take his yoke and "learn from me" (Matthew 11:29). He even promises lifelong learning with a divine mentor, the Holy Spirit (see John 14:26). Where are you in the lifelong journey of learning from Jesus? Where would you like to be?

Talk About It

5. British theologian and master preacher Austin Farrer suggested that relationships are so critical in shaping who we are that "Jesus would have been a different Jesus if he had had different associates."[7] Do you agree or disagree with this statement? Why? Would you be a different person if you had different parents, siblings, or friends?

6. Read Matthew 21:23-32, where Jesus is asked, "By what authority are you doing these things?" and he responds by telling a story about two sons. One son refuses to go to the vineyard but ends up going. The other son obediently says he'll go but ends up not going. Which son was in relationship with his father, but neglectful of rules? Which son was rules-aware, but deficient in relationship? Which son did Jesus endorse?

7. Some people grow, Winston Churchill once said. Others just swell. Discuss together: Where are you growing? Where are you swelling?

Part V: Our Relationship with Those Outside the Faith and with Those Who Are Different

The Bible reminds us regularly of God's love and concern for those on the fringes. Certainly, we have a responsibility to care for those in the household of faith. But Jesus also modeled a life that gave priority to the marginalized. If a follower of Jesus fails to do likewise, then that person's life of faith is incomplete.

Take a Look

1. Jesus's favorite dinner companions included sinners. God, the relational Creator of the universe, commands us to be in fruitful relationship with those who are outside God's family—even those who oppose us, hate us, misuse us. How do you respond when you consider these truths?

2. There are two ways of describing each of us at this moment. We are either away from God but drawing near or near to God but drawing away. Which is the closest description of you right now? Why?

Look Inside

3. Pastor and author Tommy Barnett says disciples of Jesus do not understand the depth of God's love until they can, like Jesus, love those who have betrayed them.[8] Who has betrayed you? Do you still talk to this person(s)? Can you share a meal with him or her? Can you worship with this person?

4. Thomas Ralph Morton, Presbyterian Church in Ireland missionary to Manchuria, China, has said: "It is not in the church that we know Jesus, but in the world. We know him in the life of love, suffering, and hope that he shares with all men. But without the church few of us would be in the position to recognize him in the world."[9] What do you think Morton is getting at? How does it apply to your life?

Talk About It

5. John Bunyan, author of *Pilgrim's Progress,* said he was glad that John 3:16 said "whosoever." If it had said "John," he remarked, "I would

have thought it was some other John: but since it said 'whosoever,' that let me in."[10] Share together the words and images that have "let you in"—including what has invited you into the love of God and the message of the gospel.

6. Søren Kierkegaard liked to say that if you want to recognize your neighbor, you must first close your eyes.[11] Was he proposing an approach to circumvent biases that are aroused and justified by another person's outward appearance? Or do you think he meant something entirely different by his statement?

PART VI: OUR RELATIONSHIP WITH GOD'S CREATION

If God cared enough to create it, we should care enough to take care of it. Scripture tells us that Jesus died and rose from the dead to redeem not just humankind, but to reconcile *all* of God's creation. As followers of Jesus, we are partners in Jesus's reconciliation of the world to himself (see 2 Corinthians 15:14-21).

Take a Look

1. Paul pointed out the danger of being so enthralled with God's creation that we can be tempted to worship "created things rather than the Creator" (Romans 1:25). Some Christians have used this as an argument against environmentalism. How can Christians care for the earth, as Scripture instructs, while reserving their worship exclusively for God?

2. The church has been accused of using Genesis 1:28 as justification for exploiting the earth's resources, as if God's command to "fill the earth and subdue it" included the instructions to abuse the planet that God created. Is this a valid criticism of the conventional Christian approach to the earth? Why or why not?

Look Inside

3. Do you believe that God cares just for species as a whole (as Noah's ark seems to suggest)? Or does God care for individuals in each species (as Jesus intimated in his remark about sparrows falling to

the ground)? What does this mean to you as an individual member of a species?

4. For Augustine, all things pointed to God. Creation served as testimony to the Creator. For Ignatius of Loyola, God was present in all things. Thus, all things have value and deserve honor. What difference does this make, if any, in how you live the life of faith?

Talk About It

5. My mother's mantra was one we all were forced to memorize: "Eat it up, wear it out, make it do, or do without." Is this folk wisdom something we have lost at our peril? Or are one or more of the four parts of the folk wisdom part of our problem?

6. There is a movement in the legal profession toward "restorative justice" in which crime is redefined as a breakdown of relationships. Justice then becomes a reconciling of the offender and victim. How do you feel about this more relational understanding of justice. How do you think it would affect offenders and victims if it became a widespread practice?

PART VII: OUR RELATIONSHIP WITH SYMBOLS, ARTS, ARTIFACTS, AND "THINGS"

Christians are correct in maintaining a clear distinction between the Creator and the created. Perhaps that's why we may grow uncomfortable when asked to consider our relationship with artifacts—human-made objects that can serve as symbols that draw us to God. Artifacts possess no special power of their own. They simply have the ability to point us to God in special ways, and then we find the power of the Almighty.

Take a Look

1. Those who were raised in the Protestant tradition might have been taught that statues, icons, crucifixes, relics, and so forth actually distract us from God, who is Spirit not object. How do you feel about the ability (or inability) of certain artifacts to direct our gaze toward God?

2. While God hates idolatry of all sorts, God honors the arts and artists, craftsmanship and creativity, that bring glory to God. How can Christians draw a biblical distinction between idolatry and art that glorifies God?

Look Inside

3. To test your tendency to devalue the physical while elevating the spiritual, ask yourself if you feel it's appropriate to pray for courage in a time of crisis, but inappropriate to seek God's assistance in finding a lost wedding ring. What does your answer tell you about the way you practice the life of faith?

4. America Online founder Steve Case claimed almost from day one that while "content was king," much of that content would come from the sense of community that AOL subscribers were encouraged to share. How do you use the Internet—primarily to gather information (function and pragmatism) or mostly to keep in touch with others (relationship and community)?

Talk About It

5. Try this exercise together: Venture some of the most far-out things you can imagine about life in the future. Let your imagination run wild. After everyone has had a chance to paint the future, analyze the discussion you just had. How much of it focused on issues of science and technology? How much of it centered on issues of truth, trust, values, God, consciousness, community?

6. What machines are you in a relationship with—your laptop, cell phone, automobile, motorcycle, hair dryer? How reluctant are you to share these machines with others?

PART VIII: OUR RELATIONSHIP WITH THE SPIRITUAL WORLD

As Christians, we are physical beings residing in the realm of the Spirit. Put another way, we are spiritual beings residing in physical bodies, until we complete this life and are ushered into God's presence. In the meantime, we live with one foot in the physical world and one foot in the spiritual.

Take a Look

1. Jesus taught, "God is spirit, and his worshipers must worship in spirit and in truth" (John 4:24). In light of chapter 13, has this verse taken on new meaning for you? If so, how?

2. In the modern era, people wanted to know more about God. It was as if God could be fully comprehended if only we could analyze God enough. But in the postmodern era, people suspect that God is much harder to pin down, more "out there" than we can imagine. How would you describe your sense of God right now?

Look Inside

3. Relationships stay alive only by remaining a mystery. Relationships need strangeness, mystery, unpredictability. It's the same in our relationship with God. Remember God's self-chosen name: I will be what I will be (see Exodus 3:14-15). What intrigues you the most about the Mystery that is God? What concerns you the most about the Divine Mystery?

Talk About It

4. A professional masseur at Drew Health Services in New Jersey tells of her various techniques and the benefits of a massage. But she ends her litany with: "What I really offer students is a relationship." When have relationships—personal, professional, familial, or otherwise—been sources of healing in your life?

5. Here is a prayer Søren Kierkegaard liked to pray. Conclude your time together by reciting this prayer in unison: "Father in heaven, when the thought of thee wakes in our hearts, let it not awaken like a frightened bird that flies about in dismay, but like a child waking from its sleep with a heavenly smile."[12]

Acknowledgments

1. For Anthony of Egypt, see Arm. 12, 1B; II, 148.
2. For Origen, see Hom, 2-3.
3. "Not All the Blood of Beasts," first published in *Hymns and Spiritual Songs,* 2nd edition (London, 1709).

Introduction

1. See the ads from Chase Bank. The problem is, when the corporate world steals the church's lines, it twists the meaning of those words into something it's not.
2. Consider that the nature of capitalism is changing from buying things to interacting with people. Think Starbucks, shopping as recreation, and so forth. See Harry Beckwith, *Selling the Invisible* (New York: Warner, 1997).
3. For a meditation on the metaphor of the church as a boat, see my *AquaChurch* (Loveland, Colo.: Group, 2000). For a biblical introduction to the Jesus trimtab, see James 3:4.
4. See Adrian Hastings, ed., *A World History of Christianity* (Grand Rapids: Eerdmans, 1999). Here is a book in which Jesus the Christ is largely absent.
5. As suggested by A. E. Harvey, "The Full Umwelt," *TLS: Times Literary Supplement* (4 October 2002): 13.
6. David Hamlyn, "Newman In, Hume Out," a review of Anthony Kenny, *A Brief History of Western Philosophy.* The review was published in *TLS: Times Literary Supplement* (19 March 1999): 30.
7. Michael Martin, *Atheism, Morality, and Meaning* (Amherst, N.Y.: Prometheus, 2002), 166.
8. The statistics are those of Laurie Register, a consultant with the Southern Carolina Woman's Missionary Union, quoted in *Louisiana Baptist Message* (1 July 1999): 10. According to Register, "43 percent of the members of a typical conservative church youth group are sexually active." As reported by Tony Imms, "Understanding Culture, Language Called Necessary for Youth Ministry," *BP News,* 14 June 1999, www.bpnews.net/bpnews.asp?ID=765.
9. "The Millennium of the West," *The Economist* (31 December 1999): 9.
10. David Bruce, founder of HollywoodJesus.com, a Web site geared to exploring pop culture from a spiritual point of view. Quoted in Donald F. G. Hailson,

"The Sanctified Soak: Cultural Engagement Evangelism," *Journal of the Academy for Evangelism* 17 (2001–2002): 70.

11. With thanks for this metaphor to John Baker-Batsel, United Methodist minister and former theological librarian.

12. Joan Chittister, *In Search of Belief* (Liguori, Mo.: Liguori/Triumph, 1999), 11.

13. Jack Nelson-Pallmeyer, *Jesus Against Christianity: Reclaiming the Missing Jesus* (Harrisburg, Pa.: Trinity, 2001), 329.

14. "What sustained many Christians, even more than belief, were stories—above all, shared stories of Jesus's birth and baptism, and his teachings, his death, and his resurrection." Elaine Pagels, *Beyond Belief: The Secret Gospel of Thomas* (New York: Random House, 2003), 28.

15. Michael E. Williams, "The Midwives' Story: An Image of the Faithful Friend," *Weavings* 7 (June–July 1992): 23.

16. "The recovery of relationality in Christian teaching and preaching is not a concession to modernity or to postmodernity; it is a recovery of the original Hebraic and early Christian ontology, and in the end it may be as critical of contemporary views of human nature and destiny as it should always have been in the tradition of Athens." Douglas John Hall, *The Cross in Our Context: Jesus and the Suffering World* (Minneapolis: Fortress, 2003), 105.

17. Micah 6:8, NRSV.

18. John 3:16.

19. Christian A. Schwarz calls the First Reformation a reform of theology, the Second Reformation a reform of spirituality, and the Third Reformation a reform of structure. See his *Paradigm Shift in the Church: How Natural Church Development Can Transform Theological Thinking* (Saint Charles, Ill.: ChurchSmart Resources, 1999), 86-8, 90-1, 93-4, respectively.

20. Richard Conniff, *The Natural History of the Rich: A Field Guide* (New York: Norton, 2002), 135.

21. The early Christian group known as the Ebionites always prayed facing Jerusalem as an expression of their desire to continue Judaism.

22. Herbert McCabe, "A Sermon for Easter," in *God Still Matters,* ed. Brian Davies (New York: Continuum, 2002), 227.

23. See my *Postmodern Pilgrims: First Century Passion for the 21st Century World* (Nashville: Broadman & Holman, 2000).

24. Matthew 16:15.

Chapter 1

1. John 14:6 and John 1:43.

2. See Louis Nowra's "Letter to the Editor" in *TLS: Times Literary Supplement* (3 May 2002): 17.

3. "Faith is the medium of the saving relationship between the human subject as believing sinner and the divine subject incarnate in Jesus Christ." Kathryn A. Kleinhans, "Why Now? The Relevance of Luther in a Post-Modern Age," *Currents in Theology and Mission* 24 (December 1997): 488-95 (quote on 495).

4. Romans 6:4, RSV; see also Colossians 2:12-13; 3:1-3.

5. David Martin, "On Faith and Being Made Whole," *Christian Language in the Secular City* (Burlington, Vt.: Ashgate, 2002), 103.

6. "That God invites our friendship, our participation in God's own peaceable life, is the most astounding, extravagant, but wonderfully remarkable fact of salvation." Jim Fodor, "Christian Discipleship as Participative Imitation: Theological Reflections on Girardian Themes," in *Violence Renounced: René Girard, Biblical Studies and Peacemaking,* Studies in Peace and Scripture 4, ed. Willard M. Swartley (Telford, Pa.: Pandora, 2000), 257.

7. Eugene H. Peterson, *Living the Message: Daily Reflections* (San Francisco: HarperSanFrancisco, 1996), 9.

8. 2 Corinthians 5:19, RSV; see also Colossians 1:20.

9. John 1:14.

10. Michael Rie, "What Is Christian About Christian Bioethics?" *Christian Bioethics* 5, no. 3, (1999): 263-6 (quote on 263).

11. Rie, "What Is Christian?" 263-4.

12. C. K. Barrett, *The Signs of an Apostle: The Cato Lecture, 1969* (Philadelphia: Fortress, 1972), 88.

13. Joseph Sittler, "Ecological Commitment as Theological Responsibility," *Zygon* 5 (1970): 174.

14. Anne Foerst, "Birthing the BOT," *Forbes ASAP* (4 October 1999): 73, www.forbes.com/asap/99/1004/073.htm.

15. According to the U.S. Census Bureau and the National Center for Health Statistics.

16. With thanks to Craig Oldenburg for this observation.

17. This observation was first made by Neil A. Gershenfeld in *When Things Start to Think* (New York: Henry Holt, 1999), 101-2.

18. Umberto Eco, quoted in Andy Clark, *Natural-Born Cyborgs: Minds, Technologies, and the Future of Human Intelligence* (New York: Oxford University Press, 2003), 177.

19. Amy A. Kass, "A Case for Courtship," keynote address, Institute for American Values Annual Symposium, 22 September 1999, www.americanvalues.org/Wp73.pdf. For the second quote, see Anjula Razdan, "What's Love God to Do with It," *Utne* (May–June 2003): 71.

20. I do not agree with John L. Locke's thesis in *The De-Voicing of Society: Why We Don't Talk to Each Other Anymore* (New York: Simon & Shuster, 1998),

138-50. I argue that digital technology is reinventing our social relationships, not robbing us of them. For more on this idea, see my *Carpe Mañana: Is Your Church Ready to Seize Tomorrow?* (Grand Rapids: Zondervan, 2001).

21. For the ways in which teenagers in evangelical churches are dropping their allegiance to traditional Christian truths, see "Teenagers and Their Relationships," 22 January 2000, Barna Research Online, http://207.198.84.9/cgi-bin/PagePressRelease.asp?PressReleaseID=21 (no longer active). See also "Teenagers Embrace Religion But Are Not Excited about Christianity," *Barna Updates,* 10 January 2000, www.barna.org/cgi-bin/PagePressRelease.asp?PressReleaseID=45&Reference=B.

22. Harry James Cargas, "After Auschwitz: 'A Certain Script,' an interview with Elie Wiesel," *Christian Century* (17 September 1975): 791.

23. John 13:35.

Chapter 2

1. John 15:16.
2. Psalm 19:7.
3. Dave Barry, introduction to "Dear Gangster…," Gangster of Love, *Advice for the Lonelyhearted from The Gangster of Love* (New York: Penguin, 1996), viii.
4. See Romans 3:22-23; Ephesians 2:4-5; Titus 3:4-7.
5. 1 Corinthians 1:23.
6. John 15:16.
7. Matthew 9:9; Mark 2:14; Luke 5:27.
8. *Austin Farrer: The Essential Sermons,* ed. Leslie Houlden (Cambridge, Mass.: Cowley, 1991), 15.
9. Mark 4:11, NRSV.
10. Evagrius of Pontus, *The Praktikos: Chapters on Prayer,* trans. John Eudes Bamberger, Cistercian Studies series 4 (Spencer, Mass.: Cistercian, 1970), 65.
11. See the dedication in my *SoulSalsa: 17 Surprising Steps for Godly Living in the 21st Century* (Grand Rapids: Zondervan, 2000), v.
12. Acts 17:28, NRSV.
13. L. Robert Keck, *Sacred Quest: The Evolution and Future of the Human Soul* (West Chester, Pa.: Chrysalis, 2000), 183.
14. See Ephesians 4:19-20.
15. See Matthew 10:32; Luke 12:8.
16. See Mark 9:37; Luke 9:48.
17. James Wood, *The Book Against God* (New York: Farrar, Straus & Giroux, 2003), 112-3.
18. Rodney Needham, *Belief, Language, and Experience* (Chicago: University of Chicago Press, 1972).

19. For more on "believe" as better described as "be live," see "Be Is for Be-Living," in Leonard Sweet, Brian D. McLaren, and Jerry Haselmayer, *A is for Abductive: The Language of the Emerging Church* (Grand Rapids: Zondervan, 2003), 42-4.

20. Wilfred Cantwell Smith, *Faith and Belief: The Difference Between Them* (Boston: Oneworld, 1998), 105-6. Smith also warns that "in other parts of the world it may not have occurred to the religious that as evidence of his or her faith a person should believe something," 15.

21. See Rabbi Daniel Gordis, *God Was Not in the Fire: The Search for a Spiritual Judaism* (New York: Scribner, 1995), 55.

22. Gotthold Lessing, quoted in Søren Kierkegaard, *Kierkegaard's Concluding Unscientific Postscript,* trans. David F. Swenson and Walter Lowrie (Princeton, N.J.: Princeton University Press, 1941), 97.

23. Parts of this chapter were originally published in my "The Jesus Meme," *Youthworker* (March/April 2000), www.youthspecialties.com/articles/topics/theology/Jesus_meme.php.

24. 1 John 4:17, NRSV, and Galatians 4:19, NRSV.

25. 2 Corinthians 3:6.

26. Henri Nouwen, *In the Name of Jesus* (New York: Crossroad, 1993), 32.

27. Joseph Kerman, "A Few Canonic Variations," *Critical Inquiry* 10:1 (1983): 107.

28. Thanks to Bruce Larson for the influence of his writings here.

Chapter 3

1. Genesis 12:2.

2. Tertullian, *Adversus Marcionem,* ed. and trans. Ernest Evans (Oxford: Clarendon, 1972), 1:225.

3. My first dip into the waters of theology was Søren Kierkegaard's *Fear and Trembling,* where Abraham is a knight of faith because the very second he knew he could kill his son if God commanded it, he also knew that the command was not to be carried out. Somehow, Abraham was capable of radical obedience to God but also privy to significant insider information the rest of us don't have. And having the inside track on knowing the future would render his radical obedience unnecessary. Such double-speak failed to satisfy my struggles with this central father-son story of Scripture. I never could be persuaded that God played a "you bet your son, I'll bet my son" game of chicken.

4. Recorded in William S. Burroughs, *Dead City Radio,* compact disc (New York: Island Records, 1990) and quoted in Andy Clark, *Natural-Born Cyborgs: Minds, Technologies, and the Future of Human Intelligence* (New York: Oxford University Press, 2003), 197.

5. See Genesis 22:1-19.

6. "The *Akedah* [the binding of Isaac] has remained one of the most difficult texts in Tanakh to understand, justify and transmit to new generations." Lippman Bodoff, "The Real Test of the Akedah: Blind Obedience Versus Moral Choice," *Judaism* 42 (Winter 1993): 71-2. The word *Akedah* comes from the root *'aqd*, which means "to bind." On Abraham's ten tests, the Mishnah refers to "ten trials," but commentators disagree about what the ten are, and some think there are more than ten. For more, see Yehuda Nachshoni, "The Influence of Akedah on Our People's Life," *Studies in the Weekly Parashah: The Classical Interpretations of Major Topics and Themes in the Torah*, trans. Shmuel Himelstein (Jerusalem: Mesorah, 1988), 1:99-100.

7. Qur'an 37:99-113.

8. Paul refers to the story in Romans 8:32, and he clearly has it in mind in Romans 3:25.

9. We are tipped off to the significance of this story by the "third day" reference in Genesis 22:4. On the "the third day" Abraham prepared to sacrifice Isaac. "The third day" refers to threshold moments and movements, dramatically and dynamically nonlinear crossovers in time beyond which nothing is the same again. "On 'the third day,' for instance, God seals the covenant with Moses. On 'the third day' Esther goes to the King to beg for the safety of the Jews." See Joan Chittister, *In Search of Belief* (Liguori, Mo.: Liguori/Triumph, 1999), 135.

10. John 8:58, NRSV.

11. John 8:40.

12. John 8:56.

13. John 8:59.

14. French philosopher Jacques Derrida summarizes his own struggle with the text: "The story is no doubt monstrous, outrageous, barely conceivable: a father is ready to put to death his beloved son, his irreplaceable loved one, and that because the Other, the great Other asks him or orders him without giving the slightest explanation. An infanticide father who hides what he is going to do from his son and from his family without knowing why, what could be more abominable, what mystery could be more frightful—vis-à-vis love, humanity, the family, or morality?" See chapter 3, "Whom to Give to (Knowing Not to Know)," in Jacques Derrida, *The Gift of Death*, trans. David Wills (Chicago: University of Chicago Press, 1995), 53-81; quote on 67.

15. Adapted from Carol Delaney, *Abraham on Trial: The Social Legacy of Biblical Myth* (Princeton, N.J.: Princeton University Press, 1998), 35, 41.

16. Rabbi Moshe Weissman, *The Midrash Says: The Narrative of the Weekly Torah-Portion in the Perspective of Our Sages. Selected from the Talmud and Midrash* (Brooklyn, N.Y.: Benei Yakov, 1980), 192.

17. See Genesis 42:15.

18. See 1 Kings 10:1.

19. See for example Matthew 4:7 (Satan), Matthew 19:3 (Pharisees), Matthew 22:23 (Sadducees), Matthew 22:35, KJV (lawyers).

20. See Mark 4:35-40.

21. See John 6:1-21.

22. Genesis 18:19.

23. See Genesis 12:2,7; 13:14-17; 15:4-5,13-16,18; 17:2-8; 18:18-19; 22:16-18, as documented by David Lee Miller, *Dreams of the Burning Child: Sacrificial Sons and the Father's Witness* (Ithaca, N.Y.: Cornell University Press, 2003), 21.

24. Hebrews 11:17-19.

25. Anyone writing about the Akedah is almost forced into a litany of questions. Here's one from Harold M. Schulweis: "Why did he not protest? How could God make such immoral demands of Abraham? How did Abraham decide which voice to listen to, that of God or that of God's angel? Is God's word to be obeyed even when obedience can lead to the death of innocence?" Harold M. Schulweis, *For Those Who Can't Believe: Overcoming the Obstacles to Faith* (New York: HarperCollins, 1994), 78.

26. Golda Meir, quoted in Cynthia Ozick, "In the Land of Sharon," *TLS: Times Literary Supplement* (2 March 2001): 5.

27. This silence also has troubled scholars as diverse as Søren Kierkegaard and Jacques Derrida. For Kierkegaard, see *Fear and Trembling; Repetition,* "problem III," ed. and trans. Howard V. Hong and Edna H. Hong (Princeton, N.J.: Princeton University Press, 1983), 82-120. For Derrida, see "Whom to Give" in *The Gift of Death,* 59.

28. This distinction is found in Howard Moltz, "God and Abraham in the Binding of Isaac," *Journal for the Study of the Old Testament* 96 (2001): 59-69 (quote on 64).

29. See Genesis 22:19.

30. In Genesis 24, Abraham engages in a ritual ceremony with his servant to prevent Isaac from marrying among the Canaanites. Abraham can't go to his son himself.

31. See Genesis 24:67.

32. As suggested by Karen Armstrong, *In the Beginning: A New Interpretation of Genesis* (New York: Knopf, 1996), 71.

33. See Genesis 32:28. See also "Israel," in Bible Resource Center, *Bible Dictionary,* www.bibleresourcecenter.org/index/search.dsp.

34. Genesis 22:5.

35. W. Dow Edgerton, "The Binding of Isaac," *Theology Today* 44 (July 1987): 217.

36. Brown University professor Jung H. Lee has challenged scholars to look at the whole "pattern of attachment" between Abraham and God in his essay, "Abraham in a Different Voice: Rereading Fear and Trembling with Care" in *Religious Studies* 36 (2000): 377-400.

37. Harvard's James L. Kugel writes: "No one would seek to be in their company for any length of time or have a relationship with a god—that was too frightening, too dangerous." *The God of Old: Inside the Lost World of the Bible* (New York: Free Press, 2003), 82.

38. See Genesis 9:1-17.

39. See Genesis 9:5-6.

40. See Genesis 15:6.

41. Alan M. Dershowitz, *The Genesis of Justice: Ten Stories of Biblical Injustice That Led to the Ten Commandments and Modern Law* (New York: Warner, 2000), 6.

Chapter 4

1. W. Dow Edgerton, "The Binding of Isaac," *Theology Today* 44 (July 1987): 216-7.

2. Elie Wiesel, *Messengers of God: Biblical Portraits and Legends,* trans. Marion Wiesel (New York: Random House, 1976), 95.

3. Immanuel Kant, *The Conflict of the Faculties: Der Streit der Facultäten,* trans. Mary J. Gregor (New York: Abaris Books, 1979; orig. pub. 1798), 115 footnote.

4. One of the greatest sermons ever preached on this Abraham/Isaac text is David Buttrick's sermon on Genesis 22:1-19, as found reproduced in his *Homiletic: Moves and Structures* (Philadelphia: Fortress, 1987), 357-60. The greatest literary introduction to the narrative structure of Genesis 22 is Erich Auerbach's *Mimesis: The Representation of Reality in Western Literature* (Princeton, N.J.: Princeton University Press, 1953), especially 11-2.

5. See Genesis 21:12.

6. Or in Kierkegaard's words, in faith "the single individual as single individual is higher than the universal" because "the single individual as the single individual stands in an absolute relation to the absolute." Søren Kierkegaard, *Fear and Trembling: Repetition,* ed. and trans. Howard V. Hong and Edna H. Hong (Princeton, N.J.: Princeton University Press, 1983), 54-6.

7. See Jon D. Levenson on this idea in "Abusing Abraham: Traditions, Religious Histories, and Modern Misinterpretations," *Judaism* 47 (Summer 1998): 270.

8. "That Abraham is required to choose his fear of God over his love of Isaac may seem unfair or unnecessary, but it is precisely the agony of the choice that makes the act a 'sacrifice' in the larger sense of the word." Levenson, "Abusing Abraham," 270.

9. The most talked about philosopher of our day, Jacques Derrida, loves the Abraham and Isaac story. For Abraham, the temptation is to do the ethical, and he must resist the moral. In fact, Derrida uses Abraham to prove that the ethical is what makes us unethical, and we are most ethical when we act most unethically. "Whom to Give to (Knowing Not to Know)," in his *The Gift of Death,* trans. David Wills (Chicago: University of Chicago Press, 1995), 67.

10. See Joel Wolowelsky, "Testing God—A Midrash on the *Akedah,*" *Dor le Dor,* VIII (Winter 1979–80): 98. See also Rabbi Shlomo Riskin, *Baltimore Jewish Times* (3 November 1990): 52; and Neil Gillman, "A Sabbath Week," *Jewish Week* (25-31 October, 1991).

11. Genesis 22:2, NRSV.

12. So argues Joseph Albo in his *Sefer Ha-'Ikkarim: Book of Principles,* ed. Isaac Husik (Philadelphia: Jewish Publication Society of America, 1946), 4:127-9.

13. Nehama Leibowitz, *Studies in Bereshit (Genesis): In the Context of Ancient and Modern Jewish Bible Commentary,* trans. Aryeh Newman, 4th rev. ed. (Jerusalem: World Zionist Organization Department for Torah Education and Culture, 1981), 188-93 (quote on 191).

14. Genesis 18:19, NRSV.

15. See Genesis 12:1.

16. For the "test" of the Akedah as "also a test of growth in Abraham's moral character," see Robert Eisen, "The Education of Abraham: The Encounter Between Abraham and God Over the Fate of Sodom and Gomorrah," *Jewish Bible Quarterly* 28, no. 2 (2000): 80-6.

17. See 2 Chronicles 20:7.

18. In the Christian tradition, the Rule of Saint Benedict opens with these words: "Listen carefully, my son, to the master's instructions, and attend to them with the ear of your heart." As cited by Bonnie Thurston, "Rules of Life," *Spirituality* 9 (March–April 2003): 73-6 (quote on 73).

19. See Daniel 3:4-6,12-18 and 6:7-23, as examples from Scripture.

20. Erich Fromm, "Disobedience as a Psychological and Moral Problem," in *On Disobedience and Other Essays* (New York: Seabury, 1981), 16.

21. This quote, near the beginning of this Steven Spielberg movie (2000), is by the convener of a company planning session for the creation of an advanced prototype robot child programmed to show unconditional love, in response to a staff member's question about whether humans could love a mechanical being back.

22. For the insistence that what Jacob fought with was not merely an "angel" but God, see James L. Kugel, *The God of Old: Inside the Lost World of the Bible* (New York: Free Press, 2003), 30-31.

23. Old Testament Professor at Brite Divinity School, John Stewart, used to say this. With thanks to Clifford E. McLain for this reference.

24. Hence the divine promise of Deuteronomy 24:16 (NRSV): "Parents shall not be put to death for their children, nor shall children be put to death for their parents."

25. All three instances are discussed in chapter 19:33 in *Midrash Rabba: Numbers,* trans. Judah J. Slotki (London: Soncino, 1983), 782-5.

26. See Exodus 32:7-14; Deuteronomy 9:14.

27. Conrad Gempf, *Jesus Asked: What He Wanted to Know* (Grand Rapids: Zondervan, 2003), 109.

28. See Genesis 18:25.

29. See Romans 12:1-2ff.

30. Genesis 21:14-16. In a classic exegesis of verse 11 in chapter 22, Robert Alter notes the similarity between the Isaac and Ishmael stories. "This is nearly identical with the calling-out to Hagar in 21:17. In fact, a whole configuration of parallels between the two stories is invoked. Each of Abraham's sons is threatened with death in the wilderness, one in the presence of his mother, the other in the presence (and by the hand) of his father. In each case the angel intervenes at the critical moment, referring to the son fondly as *na'ar,* 'lad.' At the center of the story, Abraham's hand holds the knife, Hagar is enjoined to 'hold her hand' (the literal meaning of the Hebrew) on the lad. In the end, each of the sons is promised to become progenitor of a great people, the threat to Abraham's continuity having been averted." Robert Alter, *Genesis: Translation and Commentary* (New York: W. W. Norton, 1996), 106.

31. Karen Armstrong, *In the Beginning: A New Interpretation of Genesis* (New York: Knopf, 1996), 64.

32. Of course, some *madrassas* are no different from orthodox Jewish schools.

33. "Palestinians Get Saddam Funds," *BBC News: World Report,* 13 March 2003, http://news.bbc.co.uk/2/hi/middle_east/2846365.stm.

34. Nicholas Peter Harvey, *Morals and Meaning of Jesus: Reflections on the Hard Sayings* (Cleveland, Ohio: Pilgrim, 1993), 84-5. Harvey writes: "This essentially non-coercive obedience has to be learned, and can only be learned in the testing exercise of the freedom of authentic personhood," 85.

35. Quoted in Greg Cook, "The Jesus Prayer," *Parabola* 26 (November 2001): 72.

36. I have lost the source of this quote. Can any reader help me?

37. For an interpretation of the Sodom and Gomorrah text (Genesis18:17-33) as less an "argument" and more a lesson in "moral education," see Robert Eisen, "The Education of Abraham: The Encounter between Abraham and God

Over the Fate of Sodom and Gomorrah," *Jewish Bible Quarterly* 28, no. 2 (2000): 80-6.

38. With thanks to Thomas G. Biatek for this "double failure."

Chapter 5

1. G. K. Chesterton, "The Priest of Spring," in *A Miscellany of Men* (New York: Dodd, Mead, 1912), 112.

2. See John 8:32.

3. John 1:14.

4. See Wilfred Cantwell Smith, *Faith and Belief* (Princeton, N.J.: Princeton University Press, 1979), 118, 105, 113.

5. This is the argument of Richard Firth Green's important study *A Crisis of Truth: Literature and Law in Ricardian England* (Philadelphia: Pennsylvania University Press, 1999), xiv and chap. 1, "From Troth to Truth," 1-40.

6. D. A. Carson, *The Gagging of God: Christianity Confronts Pluralism* (Grand Rapids: Zondervan, 1996), 257.

7. John 14:6, NRSV.

8. John 8:32, NRSV.

9. See Colossians 1:26.

10. Colossians 1:27, NRSV.

11. "Christ himself is 'the mystery of God'; not just a clue or a key to it," writes N. T. Wright, "as though it were something other than himself, a proposition which, however, true, remained abstract." N. T. Wright, *The Epistles of Paul to the Colossians and Philemon: An Introduction and Commentary* (Grand Rapids: Eerdmans, 1986), 95.

12. In *Truth and Progress* (New York: Cambridge University Press, 1998), 3, Richard Rorty states: "Granted that the criterion of truth is justification, and that justification is relative, the nature of truth is not." For a discussion of Rorty's revised thought, see Matthew Halteman and Andrew Chegnell, "Agent Provocateur," *Books & Culture* 6 (July/August 2000): 10.

13. Irenaeus, "Against Heresies" in *The Ante-Nicene Fathers, Translations of the Writings of the Fathers Down to A.D. 325,* ed. Alexander Roberts and James Donaldson (New York: Scribner, 1905), 1:448, www.ccel.org/fathers/ANF-01/iren/iren3.html#Section19.

14. Michel Henry, *I Am the Truth: Toward a Philosophy of Christianity,* trans. Susan Emanuel (Stanford, Calif.: Stanford University Press, 2003), 20.

15. Henry, *I Am the Truth,* 11.

16. See John 10:10.

17. Philippians 1:21.

18. Jesus is Life in all of life's dimensions. He is the Water of Life (see John 4:14), the Bread of Life (see John 6:48), the Words of Life (see Acts 5:20), the Tree of Life (see Revelation 22:2).

19. Leslie Houlden says it this way: "Jesus was not only one whom Christians had beliefs *about,* he was the one they believed *in.*" *What Did the First Christians Believe?* (Guildford, Surrey: Lutterworth, 1982), 19.

20. Henry puts it like this: "The truth of Christianity is that the One who called himself the Messiah was truly that Messiah, the Christ, the Son of God, born before Abraham and before time, the bearer in himself of Eternal Life, which he communicated to whomever he wanted, making that which is be no longer, or else that which is dead come alive." Henry, *I Am the Truth,* 6.

21. Galatians 4:4, KJV, and Isaiah 9:6, KJV.

22. As recorded in Fyodor Dostoyevsky, "To Natalya Fonvizina, End of January-Third Week of February 1854. Omsk," in his *Complete Letters,* ed. and trans. David Lowe and Ronald Meyer (Ann Arbor: Ardis, 1988), 1:195.

23. Psalm 34:8, NRSV.

24. See Romans 2:28-29.

25. 1 Corinthians 2:2, NRSV.

26. John 5:39-40, NRSV.

27. Matthew 7:23.

28. Matthew 5:20.

29. Chuck Smith jr., *Epiphany: Discover the Delight of God's Word* (Colorado Springs, Colo.: WaterBrook, 2003), 11.

30. John 5:39-40.

31. Robert E. Webber, *Ancient-Future Faith: Rethinking Evangelicalism for a Postmodern World* (Grand Rapids: Baker, 1999), 45.

32. I am indebted to James Logan, a Presbyterian pastor in Charlotte, North Carolina, for this metaphorical use of the Prego commercial.

33. For more on the power of the words *in there,* see my *Jesus Drives Me Crazy: Lose Your Mind, Find Your Soul* (Grand Rapids: Zondervan, 2003), 35-9, 94-6.

34. For this metaphor I thank Howard G. Hendricks and William D. Hendricks, *Living by the Book* (Chicago: Moody, 1991). Also see the metaphor appearing again in John Eldredge, *The Journey of Desire* (Nashville: Nelson, 2000), 130.

35. Eldredge, *Journey of Desire,* 203-4.

36. For the reality-structuring function of stories, see the pioneering work of Misia Landau, "Human Evolution as Narrative," *American Scientist* 72 (May/June 1984): 262-8.

37. With thanks to Leon Seaman for focusing my attention on the character of God. 17 August 2000 e-mail.

Chapter 6

1. James 1:21, MSG.

2. N. T. Wright, *The Epistles of Paul to the Colossians and Philemon: An Introduction and Commentary* (Grand Rapids: Eerdmans, 1986), 124.

3. Psalm 1:2, MSG.

4. Stanley Kunitz, "The Round," in his *Passing Through: The Later Poems New and Selected* (New York: Norton, 1995), 129.

5. "A Conversation with Brett Lott," *Image: A Journal of the Arts and Religion* 37 (Winter 2002–2003): 52.

6. The story of Alexander the Great taking the *Iliad* to bed with him I learned from Mark Galli and Craig Brian Larson, *Preaching That Connects: Using the Techniques of Journalists to Add Impact to Your Sermons* (Grand Rapids: Zondervan, 1994), 81.

7. Quoted in Charles Osborne, "Obiter Dicta," in his *W. H. Auden: The Life of a Poet* (New York: Harcourt Brace Jovanovich, 1979), 332.

8. For this interpretation of James 1:21, see Howard G. Hendricks and William D. Hendricks, *Living by the Book* (Chicago: Moody, 1991), 289.

9. Psalm 1:2, MSG.

10. Letter 22. Or in another translation, "Let sleep steal upon you with a book in your hand, and let the sacred page catch your drooping head." *Select Letters of Saint Jerome,* trans. F. A. Wright (Cambridge: Harvard University Press, 1933), 87.

11. Harry D. Clarke, "Come into My Heart, Lord Jesus," Hope Publishing, 1924.

12. Brennan Manning, *Abba's Child: The Cry of the Heart for Intimate Belonging* (Colorado Springs, Colo.: NavPress, 1994), 99.

13. Perry G. Downs, *Teaching for Spiritual Growth* (Grand Rapids: Zondervan, 1994), 65.

14. Luke 15:31.

15. 1 Corinthians 2:10.

16. See 2 Peter 3:15-16.

17. *Westminster Confession of Faith: A New Edition,* ed. Douglas Kelly, Hugh McClure, and Philip B. Rollinson (Greenwood, S.C.: Attic Press, 1979), 5.

18. Walter Wink, *The Bible in Human Transformation: Toward a New Paradigm for Biblical Study* (Philadelphia: Fortress, 1973), 10.

19. See 2 Timothy 2:15.

20. For more on the third testament, see my *Quantum Spirituality: A Postmodern Apologetic* (Dayton, Ohio: Whaleprints, 1991), 249-61.

21. Galatians 2:20, NRSV.

22. See 1 Corinthians 7:10; 11:23-25.

23. See Galatians 3:16-18.

24. Ezekiel 36:26, NRSV.

25. Colossians 3:16, NRSV.

26. See Martin Buber, in the preface to his *Tales of the Hasidim: The Early Masters,* trans. Olga Marx (New York: Schocken Books, 1947), v-vi.

27. "What kind of biblical teaching is this!" is the point of Michael Frost and Alan Hirsch, *The Shaping of Things to Come: Mission and Innovation for the 21st-Century Church* (Peabody, Mass.: Hendrickson, 2003), 111-33.

28. Psalm 66:10.

29. Proverbs 17:3, NRSV.

30. Zechariah 13:9.

Chapter 7

1. John 13:34, MSG.

2. This was first published in my "Being Right or Being in Relationship," *REV.* magazine, September–October 2003, www.revmagazine.com.

3. See Mark 2:27. Also, Mark 3:1-6; John 7:23-24.

4. See John 17:6-12, 15-20.

5. In 2000, the research company Taylor Nelson Sofres Intersearch surveyed 2,298 adults and asked them to rate on a scale of one to ten the quality of the following five aspects of their lives: relationships, health, personal fulfillment (personal growth and job satisfaction), financial status, and leisure activity. The results showing the percent that chose the category as most important: relationships (28%); health (22%); personal fulfillment (22%); financial status (16%); leisure activities (13%). For more see David J. Lipke, "Life Is Beautiful," *American Demographics* 22 (August 2000): 18.

6. Aristotle, *Nicomachean Ethics,* trans. and ed. Roger Crisp (New York: Cambridge University Press, 2000), 143.

7. Stanley J. Grenz, "Belonging to God: The Quest for a Communal Spirituality in the Postmodern World," *Asbury Theological Journal* 54 (Fall 1999): 41-52.

8. Brother Roger, *Parable of Community: The Rule and Other Basic Texts of Taizé,* trans. Emily Chisolm and the Brothers (New York: Seabury, 1981), 11-2.

9. David Steindl-Rast, *Music of Silence: A Sacred Journey Through the Hours of the Days* (Berkeley, Calif.: Seastone, 1998), 6.

10. In the development of the five relationship rules for growing in grace in one-another living, I am drawing heavily on the arguments of psychoanalyst-philosopher James Hillman and his case for preserving the language of growth. For more on these ideas, see James Hillman, *Kinds of Power: A Guide to Its Intelligent Uses* (New York: Doubleday, 1995).

11. See Richard Douthwaite, *The Growth Illusion: How Economic Growth Has Enriched the Few, Impoverished the Many, and Endangered the Planet* (Tulsa, Okla.: Council Oak, 1993), 284-8.
12. Hillman, *Kinds of Power,* 47.
13. Hillman, *Kinds of Power,* 50. I am indebted to Hillman for his five redefinitions of "growth" discussed more carefully in the next chapter.
14. See 1 Corinthians 11:23-26; 12:28; Ephesians 2:21-22.
15. See Galatians 5:22-25.
16. James 1:21.
17. For more on leaders as "consummate relationship builders," see Michael Fullan, *Leading in a Culture of Change* (San Francisco: Josey-Bass, 2001), 5.
18. See 1 Corinthians 14:14-19.

Chapter 8

1. Annie Dillard, *Holy the Firm* (New York: Harper & Row, 1977), 59.
2. Catherine Marshall, *Meeting God at Every Turn: A Personal Family Story* (Carmel, N.Y.: Guideposts, 1980), 26-7. This story is used in Graham Johnston, *Preaching to a Postmodern World: A Guide to Reaching Twenty-First-Century Listeners* (Grand Rapids: Baker, 2001), 70.
3. James Hillman, *Kinds of Power: A Guide to Its Intelligent Uses* (New York: Doubleday, 1995), 52.
4. Richard Crashaw, "In the Holy Trinity of Our Lord God: A Hymn Sung as by the Shepherds" (1546), *Seventeenth-Century Verse and Prose,* ed. Helen C. White et al. (New York: Macmillan, 1951), 1:411.
5. See Philippians 2.
6. Ephesians 4:10. For more on Christianity as a "down-to-earth" religion, see my *Eleven Genetic Gateways to Spiritual Awakening* (Nashville: Abingdon, 1998), 100-11.
7. Luke 12:37, NRSV.
8. Sobonfu Somé, *The Spirit of Intimacy: Ancient African Teachings in the Ways of Relationships* (New York: Morrow, 1999), 32-3.
9. In the arts, the mark of good intensification is not efficiency, but quality. See Hillman, *Kinds of Power,* 54.
10. See Louis-Ferdinand Céline, *Mea Culpa and The Life and Work of Semmelweis,* trans. Robert Allerton Parker (New York: Fertig, 1979), 37-175.
11. This story has been told by many people. I first heard it told by Dr. Larry Dossey.
12. The Catholic Church did not reverse its condemnation of Galileo's theories about a heliocentric solar system until 1992.

13. So argues Joseph Sittler, "The View from Mount Nebo" in *The Care of the Earth, and Other University Sermons* (Minneapolis: Fortress, 1964), 75-87.

14. See Isaac Bickerstaff's discourse from White's Chocolate House, *Tatler* 21 (26 May 1709): 1.

15. Brian McLaren, *More Ready Than You Realize* (Grand Rapids: Zondervan, 2003), 15.

16. Roger Lancelyn Green and Walter Hooper, *C. S. Lewis: A Biography* (New York: Harcourt, Brace, Jovanovich, 1974), 116. Magnification was the precise metaphor that C. S. Lewis used to describe the "how" of his conversion. He could date the "when:" He was on a motorcycle heading to the zoo.

17. Fanny Hurst, quoted in John Ardoin, "Aïda's Brothers and Sisters: Black Voices in Opera: A Look at the Work: Remembering Marian Anderson," Great Performances, www.pbs.org/wnet/gperf/aidas/look.html.

18. Matthew 28:19.

19. As a noun, the word is found 269 times in the New Testament. The verb form, *matheteuo,* occurs four times in the gospels and once in Acts.

20. Xavier Léon-Dufour, *Dictionary of the New Testament* (San Francisco: Harper & Row, 1980), 165-6.

21. John 14:26, NRSV.

22. See Proverbs 9:10. It's interesting to note that early Christians called themselves a People of the Way—the church was seen as a community of pilgrims.

23. The apostle Paul himself was still learning near the end of his life, admitting that he still did not comprehend it all: "I do not reckon myself to have got hold of it yet" (Philippians 3:13, NEB).

24. 2 Corinthians 11:3, NASB.

25. One of Bettelheim's favorite sayings, as referenced in Theron Raines, *Rising to the Light: A Portrait of Bruno Bettelheim* (New York: Knopf, 2002), 321.

26. 1 John 2:21.

27. Yushi Nomura, *Desert Wisdom* (Maryknoll, N.Y.: Orbis, 1982), 17.

28. With thanks to Lutheran pastor Peter Balaban for this story.

29. Ludwig Wittgenstein, *Cambridge Letters: Correspondence with Russell, Keynes, Moore, Ramsey and Sraffa,* ed. Brian McGuinnes and G. H. von Wright (Cambridge, Mass.: Blackwell, 1995), 74, 79-80.

30. Stephen Ambrose, quoted in "Pure Ambrosia," *Fast Company,* May 2001, 172.

31. So says Joe Tucci, chief executive of EMC, one of the world's leading data storage companies. *Trend Letter* 21 (12 August 2002): 1.

32. Quoted in Steven Johnson, "Mind Share: BLOG Space: Public Storage for Wisdom, Ignorance, and Everything in Between," *Wired* (June 2003): 258.

33. Nicholas of Cusa, *Of Learned Ignorance,* trans. Germain Heron, introduction by D. J. B. Hawkins (London: Routledge and Kegan Paul, 1954), 9.

34. Hillman, *Kinds of Power,* 59.

35. See Matthew 6.

36. Romans 8:26, NRSV.

37. See John 19:34.

38. This insight comes from Austin Farrer, "The Legacy," in *Austin Farrer: The Essential Sermons,* ed. Leslie Houlden (Cambridge, Mass.: Cowley 1991), 72.

39. See Genesis 1:2,6-9 and Revelation 22:1-2.

40. See John 4:10,14.

41. John 7:37-38, NRSV.

42. Perhaps Jesus is quoting forward not backward, from Revelation 22 where the Bible ends with "the river of the water of life."

43. See Romans 6:3-4.

44. The image of Christ as water table is drawn from Ronald Blythe, *The Circling Year* (Norwich, Conn.: Canterbury, 2001), 61.

45. According to Eastern Orthodox tradition, the three angels enjoying Abraham's hospitality at Mamre represent the Father, the Son, and the Holy Spirit, and their meal anticipates the Eucharist (see Genesis 18:1-15).

46. John 13:15.

47. Philippians 1:29.

48. See Psalm 150.

49. Luke 19:46; John 2:16.

50. The accumulation of pollutants from copiers, hair spray, paint, adhesives, particle board, and so forth create "sick building syndrome."

51. For more on the church as a Community of the Kiss, see my *Postmodern Pilgrims* (Nashville: Broadman & Holman, 2000), 3-19.

52. Jan Winebrenner, *Intimate Faith* (New York: Warner Books, 2003), 191.

53. Philippians 2:6-7, NRSV.

54. See Romans 5:8.

55. John Updike, "The Cold," in his *More Matter: Essays and Criticism* (New York: Knopf, 1999), 135.

56. John 16:7.

57. Madeleine L'Engle, quoted in the theme issue on "Chaos and Order" in *Parabola* 28 (August 2003): 53.

58. Frederick Buechner, *The Return of Ansel Gibbs* (New York: Knopf, 1958), 303-4.

59. I owe this story to Michele Weiner-Davis, *Divorce Busting: A Revolutionary and Rapid Program for Staying Together* (New York: Fireside, 1992), 145-46.

60. Douglas Dunn, "If Only," *The Year's Afternoon* (London: Faber, 2000), 47.

61. Matthew 26:38, NRSV.

62. Rowan Williams, quoted in Anna Marie Aagaard, "The Church, the Churches, the Orthodox Churches, and the World Council: Notes on 'Ecclesiology and

Ethics' in Conciliar Debate" in *For All People: Global Theologies in Context: Essays in Honor of Viggo Mortensen,* ed. Else Marie Wiberg Pedersen, Holger Lam, and Peter Lodberg (Grand Rapids: Eerdmans, 2002), 172.

63. See, for example, Colossians 3:15.

64. One Archbishop of York kicked over the Archbishop of Canterbury's chair because it was higher than his. (As relayed in Robert Bartlett, "Norman Fathers of Monks," *TLS: Times Literary Supplement* (25 July 2003): 24.

65. Peter J. Prime, "Evangelism: Doctrine of Love or Love of Doctrine?" *Ministry* 73 (May 2000): 4.

66. See John 13:35; 17:20-21.

67. Matthew 5:21-22.

68. Matthew 11:29.

69. Ephesians 5:21.

70. 2 Corinthians 5:14, KJV.

71. *Vancouver Sun,* cited in "The Best and the Worst," *Parade* (29 December 1996): 6.

72. Romans 3:23.

Chapter 9

1. Greg Brown, "So Hard," *Dream Café,* compact disc (St. Paul, Minn.: Red House Records, 1992).

2. Erin Curry, "June Carter Cash's Christian Faith, Devotion to Family Remembered," *Reporter Interactive* 4.2 (27 June 2003), www.reporterinteractive.org/news/052803/Cash.htm.

3. Emmanuel Lévinas loved to quote Aloyosha Karamazov in *The Brothers Karamazov:* "We are all responsible for everyone else—but I am more responsible than all the others." From *The Lévinas Reader,* ed. Seán Hand (Cambridge, Mass.: Blackwell, 1989), 1.

4. Margaret J. Wheatley, *Turning to One Another: Simple Conversations to Restore Hope to the Future* (San Francisco: Berrett-Koehler, 2002), 3.

5. See Jonathan Sacks's *The Dignity of Difference* (New York: Continuum, 2002), 5. The exact quote is, "Can we make space for difference?"

6. Michael Green, *Acts for Today: First-Century Christianity for Twentieth-Century Christians* (London: Hodder & Stoughton, 1993), 38.

7. See Jan Phillips, *God Is at Eye Level: Photography as a Healing Art* (Wheaton, Ill.: Quest, 2000), 113.

8. Phillips, *God Is at Eye Level,* 36-7.

9. Midrash on Deuteronomy 5:4. Rabbi Phinehas, *Pesikta Rabbati: Discourses for Feasts, Fasts and Special Sabbaths,* trans. William G. Braude (New Haven: Yale University Press, 1968), 1:421 [Piska 21:6].

10. Matthew 22:36-37,39-40.

11. Philosopher Jacques Derrida, in his book *Deconstruction in a Nutshell: A Conversation with Jacques Derrida,* ed. John D. Caputo (New York: Fordham University Press, 1997), 110-2, points out that the etymology of the word *hospitality* is oxymoronic. From the Latin *hospes* we get the concept of "stranger," and from the Latin *potentia* we get the concept of empowerment. Hospitality is empowering (inviting, welcoming) the stranger—we extend this to you as long as you follow our rules and live within these boundaries. Absolute hospitality is empowering the strange—we accept you and respect you as you are, without conditions.

12. See Genesis 18:1-15.

13. Hebrews 13:2.

14. The metaphor of "conversation" is that of Evagrius of Pontus, quoted in Olivier Clément, *The Roots of Christian Mysticism: Text and Commentary* (New York: New City Press, 2000), 181.

15. This is a reworking of a Robert Benson phrasing.

16. Before entering the Carmelite order, Edith Stein made this confession: "I believe that the deeper one is draw into God, the more one must 'go out of oneself'; that is, one must go to the world in order to carry the divine life into it." From Edith Stein, "Letter to Sr. Calista Kopf, OP," in her *Self Portrait in Letters 1916–1942, The Collected Works of Edith Stein 5,* trans. Josephine Koeppel (Washington, D.C.: ICS, 1993). See also www.catholic-forum.com/from_parishes/from_parishes_981011.html.

17. Romans 12:13, NRSV.

18. As in Romans 1:13.

19. Matthew 11:19.

20. See John 21:12.

21. The recipe can be found on a 3,800-year-old clay tablet as part of a hymn to Ninkasi, the Sumerian goddess of brewing. It is hotly debated whether the motivation for domesticating cereal crops (which morphed our ancestors from a nomadic to a settled lifestyle) was the desire to make beer rather than bread. See "Uncorking the Past," *The Economist* (22 December 2001): 29-32.

22. As cited by Joseph A. Califano Jr., chairman and president of the National Center on Addiction and Substance Abuse at Columbia University. See Cheryl Wetzstein, "Project Invites Families to Dinner," *The Washington Times,* 4 September 2003. The original research was conducted by Dr. Kathleen Mullin Harris, researcher from the University of North Carolina, and presented to the American Psychological Association Annual Convention, 2003.

23. See Luke 14:16-24.

24. See John 4:34.

25. Augustine, *Confessions,* trans. Henry Chadwick (New York: Oxford University Press, 1991), 124.

26. Louise Witt, "Why We're Losing the War Against Obesity," *American Demographics* (January 2004): 27.

27. In 2003, USAmericans got slightly thinner for the first time in recorded history.

28. As cited in "Letters to the Editor," *TLS: Times Literary Supplement* (14 November 2003): 17.

29. For more on the phenomenon of simultaneity, see my *Carpe Mañana: Is Your Church Ready to Seize Tomorrow?* (Grand Rapids: Zondervan, 2001), 125-36.

30. According to a survey conducted by eNation, a service of the Schaumburg, Illinois–based research firm Market Facts, as referenced in John Fetto, "Love Stinks," *American Demographics* 25 (February 2003): 10.

31. John Fetto, "One Is the Loneliest Number," *American Demographics* 25 (February 2003): 12.

32. That's an 87 percent increase in the number of people who lived alone in the last two decades. Only 25 percent of those who live alone are divorced.

33. "According to the latest U.S. census, as of the year 2000 there were approximately 27.2 million single-person households versus about 16.6 million three-person family households. And the percentage of single-person households in the U.S.—now at 26 percent—has been steadily marching upward for at least three decades." James Morrow, "A Place for One," *American Demographics* (November 2003): 25.

34. *World of Quotes.com: Historic Quotes and Proverbs Archive,* www.worldofquotes .com/author/Lil-Tomlin/1/index.html.

35. Claire Booth Luce, "The 'Love Goddess' Who Never Found Any Love," *All the Available Light: A Marilyn Monroe Reader,* ed. Yona Zeldis McDonough (New York: Simon & Schuster, 2002), 83-102.

36. Joseph R. Myers, *The Search to Belong: Rethinking Intimacy, Community and Small Groups* (Grand Rapids: Zondervan, 2003), 7, 36.

37. Chris Clarke and Isabelle Clarke, "The Primacy of Connectivity," *Network: The Scientific and Medical Network Review* 76 (August 2001): 4, www.scispirit.com/connectivity.htm.

38. Andrew Boyd, *The Agony of Being Connected to Everything in the Universe* (New York: Norton, 2002), 39.

39. *The Chronicle of Richard of Devizes of the Time of King Richard the First,* ed. John T. Appleby (New York: Nelson, 1963), 65.

40. J. H. Jowett, *The Friend on the Road and Other Studies in the Gospels* (New York: Doran, 1922), 116-8.

41. Ezekiel 34:16.

42. J. R. R. Tolkien, *The Hobbit: or There and Back Again* (Boston: Houghton Mifflin, 1940), 62.

43. See 2 Corinthians 5:19.

44. Matthew 14:20.

Chapter 10

1. Matthew 25:40, MSG.

2. See Luke 14:13.

3. Matthew 25:40. Compare also Matthew 25:45.

4. See *Low-Wage America: How Employers Are Reshaping Opportunity in the Workplace,* ed. Eileen Appelbaum et al. (New York: Russell Sage Foundation, 2003).

5. See Job 29:15-16.

6. Quoted in Dolores Greeley, "Saint John Chrysostom: Prophet of Social Justice," *Studia Patristica,* vol. 17:3, ed. Elizabeth Livingstone (New York: Pergamon, 1982), 1164.

7. David Martin, "Signs of New Creation," *Christian Language in the Secular City* (Burlington, Vt.: Ashgate, 2002), 158.

8. Tommy Barnett shares Ayers's conclusion in *Multiplication: Unlock the Biblical Factor to Multiply Your Effectiveness in Leadership and Ministry* (Lake Mary, Fla.: Creation House, 1997), 145. Barnett writes, "Isn't it interesting that Jesus's circle of intimate friends included Judas?"

9. Quoted in Chrys McVey, "Befriending: The Heart of Mission," *Spirituality* 9 (May–June 2003): 188, www.sedos.org/english/mcvey_3.htm.

10. See Matthew 5:43-45.

11. McVey, "Befriending, 188.

12. Romans 3:3-4, NRSV.

13. Romans 5:10.

14. Michael L. Lindvall, *The Christian Life: A Geography of God* (Louisville, Ky.: Geneva Press, 2001), 126. Thanks to a sermon by John Buchanan in Rockefeller Chapel for pointing me to this book.

15. Gangster of Love, *"Dear Gangster...": Advice for the Lonelyhearted from the Gangster of Love* (New York: Penguin, 1996), 148.

16. Ecclesiastes 7:20, NRSV.

17. John A. Huffman Jr., "Lenten Lessons from Peter," Saint Andrew's Presbyterian Church, Newport Beach, California, 16 March 2003, www.standrews pres.org/sermons/SERM031603.htm.

18. These figures are those of Robert S. McNamara and James G. Blight, *Wilson's Ghost: Reducing the Risk of Conflict, Killing, and Catastrophe in the 21st Century* (New York: Public Affairs, 2001), 22.

19. Denise Levertov, *The Mass for the Day of St. Thomas Didymus* (Concord, N.H.: Ewert, 1981), 109.

20. Austin Farrer, "A Christian's Dilemmas," in *Austin Farrer: The Essential Sermons,* ed. Leslie Houlden (Cambridge, Mass.: Cowley, 1991), 125.

21. Cornelius Plantinga, "Not the Way It's S'pposed to Be: A Breviary of Sin," *Theology Today* 50 (1993): 179-92 (quote on 184).

22. Douglas John Hall, *The Cross in Our Context: Jesus and the Suffering World* (Minneapolis: Fortress, 2003), 104.

23. "It is this relational understanding of sin that has to be grasped in the churches today, and that can be grasped if there is any serious attention on the part of the teaching ministry to the theology of the cross." Hall, *The Cross in Our Context,* 104.

24. Herbert McCabe, "The Prodigal Son," in *God Still Matters,* ed. Brian Davies (New York: Continuum, 2002), 239.

25. Philippians 3:6, NRSV.

26. Gerald W. Hughes, *God of Surprises* (London: Darton, Longman and Todd, 1985), 68-9.

27. Hughes, *God of Surprises,* 73.

28. See Luke 15:11-32.

29. John J. Shepherd, "The Essence of Christian Belief," *Religious Studies* 12 (June 1976): 231-7, especially 234-6.

30. McCabe, "The Prodigal Son," in *God Still Matters,* 239.

31. See John 15:15-16.

32. To the extent that the parable doesn't convey sufficiently the sense of God's prevenient action in the world to bring us that salvation, the Prodigal Son needs to be supplemented by the other two parables of Luke 15 that extend the metaphor of "lostness": Lost Coin and Lost Sheep.

33. James Richardson, *Vectors* (Keene, N.Y.: Ausable Press, 2001), 63.

34. Matthew 8:11.

35. Donald Miller's *Blue Like Jazz: Nonreligious Thoughts on Christian Spirituality* (Nashville: Nelson, 2003).

Chapter 11

1. William Temple, quoted in R. V. C. Bodley, *In Search of Serenity* (Boston: Little Brown, 1955), 149.

2. See Genesis 15:18.

3. Genesis 9:16, NRSV.

4. Exodus 10:26, NRSV.

5. See Colossians 1:18-20.

6. James B. Jordan calls trees "arboreal theophanies" in his classic *Through New Eyes: Developing a Biblical View of the World* (Eugene, Oreg.: Wipf and Stock, 1999), 84.

7. Saint Bonaventure, "Commentarius in Distinctionem," sent. xvi, 1.1, in his *Opera Omnia Commentaria in Quatuor Libros* (Quaracchi: Collegii S. Bonaventurae, 1885), 2:395.

8. For Treebeard's description of Saruman, see J. R. R. Tolkien, *The Two Towers, Being the Second Part of The Lord of the Rings* (Boston: Houghton Mifflin, 1965), 76.

9. The Pentagon study, "An Abrupt Climate Change Scenario and Its Implications for United States National Security," by Peter Schwartz and Doug Randall, October 2003, is available at www.environmentaldefense.org/documents/ 3566_AbruptClimateChange.pdf. A 2004 movie about the security threat of global warming is *The Day After Tomorrow.*

10. Fish is now like beef and vegetables—farm raised, not wild. More than 90 percent of salmon is already farmed.

11. The phrase was that of Alexandre Dumas in 1873, referenced in Anthony Browne, "Cod Almighty," *Observer,* 13 May 2001, http://observer.guardian .co.uk/foodmonthly/story/0,9950,488334,00.html.

12. Michael Greenberg, "Freelance," *TLS: Times Literary Supplement* (26 September 2003): 16.

13. Evelyn Underhill, *Mysticism: A Study of the Nature and Development of Man's Spiritual Consciousness* (New York: E. P. Dutton, 1930), 262.

14. A famous seminar paper, written by Daniel H. Janzen and Paul W. Martin, "Neotropical Anachronisms: The Fruits the Gomphotheses Ate," *Science* 215 (1982): 19-27, proposed this answer to the enigma. Referenced in Connie Barlow, *The Ghosts of Evolution: Nonsensical Fruit, Missing Partners and Other Ecological Anachronisms* (New York: Basic, 2001), 6-7.

15. Brian McLaren, *The Church on the Other Side: Doing Ministry in the Postmodern Matrix* (Grand Rapids: Zondervan, 2000), 41.

16. "Animal Doctors," *The Economist* (20 April 2002): 77. For more on the self-medicating behavior of animals in the wild, see Cindy Engel, *Wild Health* (London: Weidenfeld and Nicolson, 2002), especially 12, 62-70, and her demonstrations that animals know how to both get well and stay well.

17. "Animal Doctors," *Economist,* 78.

18. See Engle, *Wild Health,* 122.

19. "Animal Doctors," *Economist,* 78.

20. See the research of William Karesh of the Wildlife Conservation Society, as reported in "Animal Doctors," *Economist,* 77-8.

21. Abraham Joshua Heschel, *I Asked for Wonder: A Spiritual Anthology* (New York: Crossroads, 1984), 3-5.

22. Charlene Spretnak, *The Resurgence of the Real: Body, Nature, and Place in a Hypermodern World* (New York: Routledge, 1999), 129.

23. Johann Wolfgang von Goethe, *The Sorrows of Young Werther,* trans. Michael Hulse (New York: Viking, 1989; orig. pub. 1774).

24. Psalm 19:1.

25. Fara Warner, "Qwest Finds Itself a Head," *Fast Company* (August 2003): 32, interview with Qwest Chair and CEO Richard Notebaert.

26. Psalm 121, KJV.

27. The nature video research was done by Texas A&M scientist Roger Ulrich. See Roger S. Ulrich, "Biophilia, Biophobia, and Natural Landscapes," *The Biophilia Hypothesis,* ed. Stephen R. Kellert and Edward O. Wilson, (Washington, D.C.: Island Press, 1993), 73-137. See also Richard Conniff, "The Natural History of Art: Beauty is not Just in the Eye of the Beholder: It's Embedded in Our Genes," *Discover* 20 (November 1999): 97.

28. The study "ruled out the possibilities that older people give less and are more likely to die, that females give more and are less likely to die, and that people who are depressed or in poor health are both less likely to be able to help others and more likely to die." See comments by Stephanie Brown, Minnesota Board on Aging, January 2003, reported in "Mortal Lessons: Givers Live Longer Than Receivers," *Spirituality & Health* (November/December 2003): 23, www.spiritualityhealth.com/newsh/items/article/item_6896.html.

29. See Harold Koenig's study, cited in Gregg Easterbrook, "Faith Healers: Is Religion Good for Your Health," *New Republic* (19 and 26 July 1999): 20, and discussed in Robert Pollack, *The Faith of Biology and The Biology of Faith: Order, Meaning, and Free Will in Modern Science* (New York: Columbia University Press, 2000), 54-5.

30. *The Home Planet,* ed. Kevin W. Kelley (Reading, Mass.: Addison-Wesley, 1988), 76.

31. The figures are those for 1996, reported in Robert Hughes, *A Jerk on One End: Reflections of a Mediocre Fisherman* (New York: Ballantine, 1999) 110-1.

32. The metaphor is that of Scott Weidensaul, *The Ghost With Trembling Wings: Science, Wishful Thinking, and the Search for Lost Species* (New York: North Point, 2003), 34: "We are witness to the gathering pace of what ecologists have labeled the Sixth Extinction, and this time we are the asteroid, blistering the world with our appetites, our habitat destruction and climate change, all driven by the crushing weight of our population."

33. J. R. McNeill, *Something New Under the Sun: An Environmental History of the Twentieth-Century World* (New York: Norton, 2000), 111-3, quote on 111.

Midgley contracted polio in 1940 and four years later died suspended above his bed, entangled in a network of ropes he had designed to pull himself in and out of bed.

34. Richard H. Roberts, *Religion, Theology, and the Human Sciences* (New York: Cambridge University Press, 2002), 15.

35. Martin J. Rees, *Our Final Hour: A Scientist's Warning: How Terror, Error, and Environmental Disaster Threaten Humankind's Future in this Century on Earth and Beyond* (New York: Basic, 2003), 8, 74.

36. See Revelation 11:18.

37. Luke 12:24,27, KJV.

38. Ralph A. Lewin, "Accommodation," *The Biology of Algae and Diverse Other Verses* (Pacific Grove, Calif.: Boxwood, 1987), 130.

39. See also Hebrews 2:1-4.

40. Ephesians 4:6.

41. Mark 16:15, REB. The Greek word here is *ktisis* or "creation."

42. See John 12:32. The Greek word here *pantas* or *pas* means "all things."

43. See 2 Corinthians 5:14-21.

44. See Philippians 3:10 and Romans 8:17.

45. See Philippians 4:8.

46. John Updike, "The Cold," in his *More Matter: Essays and Criticism* (New York: Knopf, 1999), 135.

47. Robert Hughes, *A Jerk on One End: Reflections of a Mediocre Fisherman* (New York: Ballantine, 1999).

48. The word *tentmaker* was a euphemism for *leather worker*, since that is what most tents were made of.

49. Gertrude Stein, "Identity a Poem," *What are Masterpieces* (New York: Pitman, 1970), 71.

50. See Revelation 22.

51. This was first published in my "Being Right or Being in Relationship," *REV.* magazine, September–October 2003, 17.

52. See Ephesians 2:14-15.

Chapter 12

1. Joan Miro, quoted in Loren Niemi and Elizabeth Ellis, *Inviting the Wolf In: Thinking About Difficult Stories* (Little Rock, Ark.: August House, 2001), 157.

2. See *Lived Religion in America: Toward a History of Practice,* ed. David D. Hall (Princeton, N.J.: Princeton University Press, 1997).

3. Meredith B. McGuire, "Why Bodies Matter: A Sociological Reflection on Spirituality and Materiality," *Spiritus* 3 (Spring 2003): 15.

4. The words are those of John Perry Barlow, "The Next Economy of Ideas: Will Copyright Survive the Napster Bomb? Nope, but Creativity Will," *Wired* (October 2000): 242.

5. See Exodus 31:2-6; 35:30,34.

6. Psalm 27:4, NRSV.

7. Patrick Sherry, *Spirit and Beauty: An Introduction to Theological Aesthetics* (Oxford: Clarendon, 1992), v.

8. See Daniel Taylor, "Soul Friends," *Image* 38 (Spring 2003): 33.

9. I did a whole book on this cross called *Strong in the Broken Places* (Akron, Ohio: University of Akron Press, 1995).

10. Thomas R. Hawkins, *Faithful Leadership: Learning to Lead with Power* (Nashville: Discipleship Resources, 1999), 100-1.

11. Sherry, *Spirit and Beauty*, 181.

12. *Notebooks of Simone Weil*, trans. Arthur Wills (New York: Putnam, 1956), 1:206.

13. Simone Weil, *Gravity and Grace* (London: Routledge and Kegan Paul, 1952), 136-7.

14. Acts 2:46-47.

15. Isaiah 25:6, NRSV.

16. Eutychius of Constantinople, Serm.Pasch. iii, PG 86, 2392.

17. Dennis E. Smith, *From Symposium to Eucharist* (Minneapolis: Fortress, 2003), 276.

18. Gijs van Hensbergen, *Gaudí: The Biography* (San Francisco: HarperCollins, 2001).

19. Magen Broshi, "Bread, Wine, Walls and Scrolls," *Journal for the Study of the Pseudopigrapha* (London: Sheffield, 2001), 130.

20. See Numbers 11:5.

21. Magen Broshi, "Bread, Wine, Walls, and Scrolls," 130.

22. Samuel Johnson, *A Dictionary of the English Language* (Beirut: Librairie du Liban, 1978; London: Strahan, 1773), 2:1325.

23. John Wesley, "Minutes of Several Conversations Between the Rev. Mr. Wesley and Others from the Year 1744 to the Year 1789," *The Works of John Wesley*, 5th ed. (London: John Mason, 1860), 8:315.

24. David McCullough, *John Adams* (New York: Simon & Schuster, 2001), 618.

25. Stephen Dobyns, "Bead Curtain," in his *Common Carnage* (Newcastle upon Tyne: Bloodaxe, 1998), 29.

26. Review of Nicholas Murray, *Aldous Huxley: An English Intellectual* (London: Time Warner, 2002), in Stefan Collini, "The Blind Magpie," *TLS: Times Literary Supplement* (10 May 2002): 3.

27. Stephanie Russo, "ICA Promotes Automotive Affection," *Professional Car-washing and Detailing Magazine* (March 2003), www.carwash.com/article .asp?IndexID=6633456.

28. Mike Godwin, "Cybergreeb: Bruce Sterling on Media, Design, Fiction and the Future," *Reason* 35 (January 2004): 46, www.reason.com/0401/fe.mg .cybergreen.shtml.

29. "Theologians of a Kind," interview of Anne Foerst by Douglas Hardy, *Research News & Opportunities in Science and Theology,* 2 (November 2001): 25. Foerst distinguishes between "human" and "person" based on her research in robotics.

30. For more on this idea, see my *Jesus Drives Me Crazy: Lose Your Mind, Find Your Soul* (Grand Rapids: Zondervan, 2003), 101-21.

31. Andy Clark, *Natural-Born Cyborgs: Minds, Technologies, and the Future of Human Intelligence* (New York: Oxford University Press, 2003), 5. Clark has argued that this development is actually nothing new. "We were always hybrid beings, joint products of our biological nature and multilayered linguistic, cultural, and technological webs." See also Clark, *Natural-Born Cyborgs,* 195.

32. See Clark, *Natural-Born Cyborgs,* 190.

33. T. S. Eliot, *Four Quartets: Little Gidding* (London: Faber and Faber, 1943), 32.

34. Avishai Margalit, *The Ethics of Memory* (Cambridge, Mass.: Harvard University Press, 2002), 111-7.

35. W. Gordon Lawrence, *Tongued with Fire: Groups in Experience* (New York: Karnac, 2000).

36. Alas, Zwicker (1612–1678) eventually became a Socinian.

37. Hebrews 11:33-34, NRSV.

38. Hebrews 11:35-38, NRSV.

39. One remembrance ritual is the involuntary human behavior of breathing. We breathe in and out about ten million times a year. The Harvard astronomer Harlow Shapley calculated that, with each breath, we take in about 30,000,000,000,000,000,000 atoms of argon, an inert gas. "Your next breath will contain more than 400,000 of the argon atoms that Gandhi breathed in his long life," Shapley writes. "Argon atoms are here from the conversations at the Last Supper, from the arguments of diplomats at Yalta, and from the recitations of the classic poets." Harlow Shapley, *Beyond the Observatory* (New York: Scribner, 1967), 45, 48. For more on breathing rituals as anamnesis, see my *Quantum Spirituality: A Postmodern Apologetic* (Dayton, Ohio: Whaleprints, 1991), 299-301.

40. See Matthew 19:30; 20:16.

41. Charles H. Spurgeon, "Commenting and Commentaries," *Lectures Addressed to the Students of the Pastors' College, Metropolitan Tabernacle* (New York: Sheldon, 1876), 11

42. See Matthew 25:37-40.

43. Sheldon B. Kopp, *If You Meet the Buddha on the Road, Kill Him: The Pilgrimage of Psychotherapy Patients* (New York: Bantam, 1976), 22.

44. *Out of the Kitchen* (Succasunna, N.J.: Temple Shalom, 2001), 34, with thanks to Sherri Van Houten for this reference.

45. John Howard Yoder, *Body Politics: Five Practices of the Christian Community Before the Watching World* (Nashville: Discipleship Resources, 1992), 78.

46. See Exodus 20:1-17.

47. Quoted in Austin Farrer, *Austin Farrer: The Essential Sermons,* ed. Leslie Houlden (Cambridge, Mass.: Cowley, 1991), 154.

48. H. Tristram Engelhardt Jr., "Can Philosophy Save Christianity? Are the Roots of the Foundations of Christian Bioethics Ecumenical? Reflections on the Nature of a Christian Bioethics" in *Christian Bioethics* 5, no. 3 (1999): 203-12 (quote on 207).

49. University of Edinburgh missiologist André Walls, the successor to Kenneth Scott Latourette, maintains: "Christians must read their tradition not over against but through the encounter with the religious other" (unpublished lecture delivered at 2002 Foundation for Evangelism conference, Candler School of Theology, Atlanta, Georgia). In his writings, Walls has made a superb case for an enlarged understanding of Christ through cross-cultural contact.

50. George M. Marsden, *Jonathan Edwards: A Life* (New Haven, Conn.: Yale University Press, 2003).

51. Geneen Roth, *When You Eat at the Refrigerator, Pull Up a Chair* (New York: Hyperion, 1998), 128-31.

Chapter 13

1. 21 May 1738. Probably sung the next day by John Wesley upon his conversion. First published in John and Charles Wesley, *Hymns and Sacred Poems* (1739). See *The United Methodist Hymnal: Book of United Methodist Worship* (Nashville: United Methodist Publishing, 1989), 342.

2. Quoted in Peter Weiss, "Getting Warped," *Science News* (21 December 2002). The Einstein exhibit ran through 10 August 2003 in New York.

3. For an excellent children's book that tells this story, see Shulamith Levey Oppenheim and George Juhasz (illustrator), *Rescuing Einstein's Compass* (Northampton, Mass.: Interlink, 2003).

4. For more along these lines, see my *Jesus Drives Me Crazy: Lose Your Mind, Find Your Soul* (Grand Rapids: Zondervan, 2003).

5. John A. Wheeler, quoted in Malcolm W. Browne, "Where Does the Time Go? Forward, Physics Shows," *New York Times,* 22 December 1998, www.jlab.org/news/internet/1998/time_physics.html.

6. For more, see Charles Seife, *Alpha and Omega: The Search for the Beginning and End of the Universe* (New York: Viking Press, 2003).

7. J. B. S. Haldane, quoted in opening preface of Amir D. Aczel, *Entanglement: The Greatest Mystery in Physics* (New York: Four Walls Eight Windows, 2002), ix.

8. "Think God's thoughts after him" is a phrase used by Cornelius Van Til, *The Defense of the Faith* (Philadelphia: Presbyterian and Reformed, 1955), 64-5.

9. John Shelby Spong, *Here I Stand: My Struggle for a Christianity of Integrity, Love, and Equality* (San Francisco: HarperSanFrancisco, 2000), 387.

10. Gregory Wolfe, "Editorial Statement: Shaggy Dog Stories," *Image: A Journal of the Arts & Religion* 38 (Spring 2003): 4.

11. See Bruce Ellis Benson, *Graven Ideologies: Nietzsche, Derrida, and Marion on Idolatry* (Downer's Grove, Ill.: InterVarsity, 2002).

12. As told by L. Robert Keck, *Sacred Quest: The Evolution and Future of the Human Soul* (West Chester, Pa.: Chrysalis Books, 2000), 128.

13. See John 3:8.

14. See Luke 7:1-10.

15. See John 11:1-44.

16. Emily Dickinson, quoted in Jan Phillips, *God Is at Eye Level: Photography as a Healing Art* (Wheaton, Ill.: Quest, 2000), 59.

17. David Martin, "Resurrection: Singing and the Kingdom," in his *Christian Language in the Secular City* (Burlington, Vt.: Ashgate, 2002), 58.

18. I owe this word to Richard A. Shweder, *Why Do Men Barbecue?* (Cambridge, Mass.: Harvard University Press, 2003), where he argues that the knowable world is "incomplete if seen from any one point of view, incoherent if seen from all points of view at once, and empty if seen from 'nowhere in particular.'" Hence he recommends: "the view from manywheres."

19. Jeremiah 1:5, NRSV.

20. James L. Kugel, *The God of Old: Inside the Lost World of the Bible* (New York: Free Press, 2003), 36.

21. A single African Adam who lived around sixty thousand years ago. For more on the science of genetics, see Spencer Wells, *The Journey of Man: A Genetic Odyssey* (Princeton, N.J.: Princeton University Press, 2003).

22. Radiologist Sister Rosalie Bertell shows how they are present in our bodies, in our ovaries and gonads, in our DNA. As referenced by Joanna Macy in "All the Time in the World," *EarthLight* 12 (Winter 2002): 25.

23. So estimates Lyall Watson, *Lifetide: A Biology of the Unconscious* (London: Hodder and Stoughton, 1979), 30.

24. "In the QM world, physical objects have not well-defined properties but *probabilities of having properties.* Take the location of any given particle—QM is stubbornly unwilling to tell you where each electron in your body's roughly billion billion billion (10 to the 27th) atoms *is* right now. Chances are, they're all pretty much where you think they are, but there is a real (though extraordinarily small) chance that right now, at least one of your electrons 'is' outside of your personal space." "Quantum Mechanics & the Creator: Physics Points to a World in Which Relationships Matter Most," *The Lutheran* (August 2002): 12-5, adapted from "The Strangely Relational World of Quantum Mechanics," *Re:Generation Quarterly* 6 (Spring 2000): 25.

25. See Dan Zahavi, "Michel Henry and the Phenomenology of the Invisible," *Continental Philosophy Review* 32 (1999): 223-40.

26. Exodus 3:14-15, footnote.

27. Exodus 33:11, NRSV.

28. See Exodus 33:18-23.

29. For more on this idea, see my *Carpe Mañana: Is Your Church Ready to Seize Tomorrow?* (Grand Rapids: Zondervan, 2001).

30. Nicholas Wolterstorff, *Reason Within the Bound of Religion* (Grand Rapids: Eerdmans, 1976), 95. I want to thank C. Stephen Evans for pointing me to this reference.

31. 1 Timothy 3:16, NRSV.

32. Quoted in Cardinal Basil Hume, *The Mystery of the Incarnation* (Brewster, Mass.: Paraclete, 1999), 66.

33. See Gary L. Thomas, *Seeking the Face of God* (Eugene, Ore: Harvest House, 1994), 67.

34. Colossians 2:3, NRSV.

35. Ephesians 1:9-10, NRSV.

36. See "Mystery," my sermon on open secrets, 4 January 2004, www.preaching plus.com.

37. Gerard W. Hughes, *God of Surprises* (London: Darton, Longman and Todd, 1985), 150.

38. See Matthew 11:25.

39. Colossians 4:3, NRSV.

40. Colossians 1:26-27, NRSV.

41. Romans 8:11. See also Galatians 2:20, as paraphrased by Don Stone: "I live, but I don't live; Christ lives in me. And I want you to know that Christ lives in you."

42. See Luke 17:21.

43. John 12:50.

44. 1 John 4:4, KJV.

45. See John 14:12.

46. John 14:9.

47. John 20:21, NRSV.

48. Philippians 1:21.

49. With thanks to Lutheran chaplain Donna King for the French translation.

50. 1 John 4:15, NRSV.

51. Colossians 2:13.

52. Evelyn Underhill, *The Mystic Way: A Psychological Study in Christian Origins* (London: Dent, 1913), 10.

53. Phrase at the end of the first verse of "Fairest Lord Jesus." The words were written by German Jesuits as *Schönster Herr Jesu* in the seventeenth century and first published in the *Münster Gesangbuch,* 1677, and translated from German to English by Joseph A. Seiss in 1873.

Interactives

1. Calvin Miller, *Into the Depths of God* (Minneapolis: Bethany, 2000), 83.

2. Jack Nelson-Pallmeyer, *Jesus Against Christianity: Reclaiming the Missing Jesus* (Harrisburg, Pa.: Trinity, 2001), vii, 336.

3. So Rupert Brooke said of the Strachey brothers, quoted in Elizabeth Lowry, "Unreliable Man of Grantchester," *TLS: Times Literary Supplement* (10 December 1999): 11.

4. Garry Wills, *Why I Am a Catholic* (Boston: Houghton Mifflin, 2002), 6. Wills adds, "The real object of my belief [is] the creed. That, after all, is why I am a Catholic," 7.

5. Leslie Houlden, *The Strange Story of The Gospels: Finding Doctrine Through Narrative* (London: SPCK, 2002), 7.

6. David W. Henderson, *Culture Shift: Communicating God's Truth to Our Changing World* (Grand Rapids: Baker, 1998), 26-7.

7. Austin Farrer, "A Share in the Family," in *Austin Farrer: The Essential Sermons,* ed. Leslie Houlden (London: SPCK, 1991), 175. The first part of the sentence: "Jesus could only be Jesus, by having Peter, James and John to be himself with," 174.

8. Tommy Barnett, *Multiplication: Unlock the Biblical Factor to Multiply Your Effectiveness in Leadership and Ministry* (Lake Mary, Fla.: Creation House, 1997), 145.

9. T. Ralph Morton, *Knowing Jesus* (Philadelphia: Westminster, 1974), 129-30.

10. Quoted in Jim McGuiggan, "Pretend You Know Me," *Heartlight* (Internet magazine), www.heartlight.org/articles/200001/20000118_pretend.html.

11. Søren Kierkegaard, *Works of Love,* trans. Howard V. Hong and Edna H. Hong (Princeton, N.J.: Princeton University Press, 1995), 68.

12. Søren Kierkegaard, "The Thought of Thee," *The Prayers of Kierkegaard,* ed. Perry D. LeFebre (Chicago: University of Chicago Press, 1956), 38.